Photography, like every form of art, becomes a form of therapy – for those behind the lens as well as those who view the result. Like a visual ethnographer, Abele Navin immerses himself in another reality and documents it through images: we see the streets of Tokyo with their chaos, night-time interiors of bars and arcades, architecture silhouetted against pale or purplish skies. And then, again, the night lights, the metro, the glowing billboards. Navin's detours, as the title suggests, lead us toward an unfamiliar, suspended vision, where even natural elements like whether cherry blossoms, bare winter branches, and gardens, appear alien, as if observed for the very first time.

Navin positions himself by blending into the context and returns it to us as if we were the ones looking through the lens. This is not just a portfolio, but the visual story of an expat. The camera becomes a kind of talisman in his hands, a device endowed with meaning and capable of generating it, even when the chemistry of his brain seems to erase every possibility.

Here is his arrival in Japan and the onset of illness, fatherhood, solitude as a salvific defense mechanism. As Susan Sontag writes in her seminal essay 'On Photography', photography is "one of the chief means for experiencing something, for giving an appearance of participation." And so it was for Navin in his initiation during high school, and again in this journey, where, as an adult, he is called to face depression.

Perhaps we must let ourselves be crossed by the detours that appear before us, simply accepting that they exist without struggling against the current. Whether it be a lonely overpass or a football team in training, reality reveals itself to our eyes – and all we can do is capture it.

Fuani Marino

This is a peculiar project. It is not a photographic portfolio, and it does not aim to be the fictionalised autobiography of an expat in Japan. The common thread connecting the images to the text is the illness of depression. The goal is to show how photography has been an integral part of my antidepressant therapeutic journey. Here, photography becomes a ritual, a mechanism not only useful but fundamental for facing panic attacks and depression.

When it comes to depression, 'coming out' is not simple. The stigma of mental illness exists, and it's brutal. Prejudices come easy, as does the self-blame that arises within those who suffer from the condition. The book starts from this point: the need to 'come out' and show a part of my life that I kept hidden for a long time. The way I have chosen to do this is through photography, something that forms part of my antidepressant therapy, alongside medication and the support of family members.

This essay is based on real events. However, the names of individuals and some places have been changed to preserve the anonymity of those involved.

PART ONE: THE ILLNESS AND ARRIVAL IN JAPAN

I am woken up by the cry of my daughter. The three-hour truce has passed, and she demands, rightly so, her feeding. I let my wife rest and go to give her the bottle of milk. It's four in the morning, but as usual my sleep is restless; not because of Suzu, but due to my dreams. The sleeping pill has run its course. I take it every night, and the doses vary depending on my mental state, from half a pill to four. The sleep induced by the pill is never normal; the following day I'm always tired and weak. It only works to make me fall asleep, but cannot bring me rest. I wake up in the morning as if I had lain down for only five minutes, despite having slept for a good eight hours. Nine hours would be my ideal sleep, but that's a luxury considering childcare and work commitments.

My sleep, as always, is very light. I manage to wake up at the slightest noise despite the medication.

Beyond how I sleep, it's a good time in the course of my antidepressant therapy. This period, which should be stressful due to the few hours of sleep brought on by our newborn Suzu, is turning out to be the best in a long time. The worsening of my illness, coinciding with the birth of Ryo (our firstborn), may not be related to postpartum stress, which can affect father's too. Perhaps Ryo's birth was a contributing factor, but not the main reason.

I have lived with the symptoms of depression for several years now – thirteen in total. However, five years ago, the illness manifested with a certain abruptness, worsening significantly. There were numerous coincidences that made a diagnosis difficult: a bad bike accident and the birth of my son Ryo. I spent a considerable amount of time exploring why I suddenly felt this way. There had been no family bereavement, yet I felt a heavy sense of loss. At the time of the collapse, I hadn't had any particularly important work assignments, but I was constantly exhausted. Although I hit my head hard in the bike accident, the tests indicated that everything was fine, with no traces of permanent trauma. I had, and still have, a wonderful family, made even more so by Suzu's arrival. But their affection and support wasn't sufficient for my happiness. I had my dream job: an architect in a renowned international studio. However, a constant sense of melancholy and inadequacy seemed to overshadow my days. I could boast a circle of splendid friends, but I felt alone and misunderstood. I couldn't come to terms with my state of mind.

Why me? Why now?

I knew I had given too much to my career in the recent years, and pushed myself too hard in university. During my studies, as in the office, sleepless nights were common but seemed routine, merely minor concerns. I was convinced I could handle extreme hours easily – I was young after all. One sleepless night leads easily to another, until sleeplessness becomes routine.

The passion for architecture made overtime less burdensome. I was doing the thing I was most interested in, and if this occupied more time than necessary, it should be seen as time well spent. I couldn't comprehend that excess is excess, regardless of context – not so different from addiction to alcohol or drugs. I had become addicted to work – I couldn't do without it. Workaholics rarely consider too much work a problem, and in the common view of people, an individual who works a lot is well-regarded. How can working be negative? Well, consider this: my promotions and raises were rewarding the very behaviour feeding my dependency.

I was aware that the previous year's stress had accumulated until it led to nervous exhaustion. I found it absurd that this had happened when I was no longer under stress. The easing of office pressure was like a rope that breaks once weight is released. It's as if my body had been held together by this tension generated by compulsive work and, once relaxed, it collapsed.

My psychiatrist said my search for answers was futile. Without years of psychoanalysis, I would never know the exact nature of my ailment. The psychiatrist only provided me with pharmacological treatment, which lacks the care provided by a psychologist Also, my ailment could be genetic. Though not simply inherited, I am part of the 5% genetically predisposed to depression. My body's chemistry makes me more vulnerable to this disease, alongside the environmental and behavioural factors that led to my collapse. Apparently, I'm more fragile than I thought I was. At some point, my body had to put on the handbrake – a handbrake I'm no longer able to remove. Like a cautious old man, the autopilot took over. When the pilot persists on a wrong course, safety systems activate, forcing a slowdown, and then detour – a necessary divergence. Through illness, the body speaks.

The doctor told me that one in four women and one in eight men experience depression at least once in their lifetime, and the average age of onset is approximately thirty. I'm not exactly sure where he was going with this data and statistics, but they certainly made me reflect. The next day, entering the office, I thought that among these three hundred people surrounding me, there were at least twenty people who felt a little like I do. It's encouraging not to be alone!

I had dealt with episodes of depression in Italy, my home country, many years before this crisis, right after graduation. On that occasion, I could easily spot the origin of my depression: the end of a relationship that had lasted six years. I began a psychoanalysis which proved to be unproductive, and I emerged from the episode consumed by work, neglecting all other aspects of life, from the sentimental to the social. It's the notion of reverse causality: the work that would later cause my deterioration was, ironically, 'curing' me then. Well, consider this: my promotions and raises were rewarding the very behaviour feeding my dependency. Feeling engaged and productive at work to address emotional problems seemed to be the remedy I undertook at that time.

I couldn't understand having free time or idle moments. I wanted to minimise extracurricular activities as much as possible and replace them with work. While I meticulously scheduled work, everything else in life happened by chance. My family's approval of this work-first mindset only fuelled my determination, leading me to pursue an internship abroad.

I had only one destination in mind: Tokyo. I wanted to work in the most important studio in Japan at the time, an office we'll call Studio A. There was another in Tokyo that I was interested in too, which we'll call Studio B. The two offices represented almost opposite visions of architecture, and both intrigued me. I was also drawn to Denmark, but I wanted somewhere exotic, as far away from home as possible. My goal was to ensure that once I left, there would be no turning back. Going to the opposite side of the world made me more vulnerable and exposed. I wouldn't have easy visits from friends or relatives, and there was no simple escape route home if things didn't go as I hoped. It was a leap into the unknown. Tokyo represented a challenge, and I wanted to overcome it.

I wrote to both A and B studios. The first positive response came from A in the summer of 2010. I remember reading the email several times. I couldn't believe it: a commitment to take me on as an intern.

There was no turning back now. I was thrilled, and celebrated with my friends as if I was already an employee of the studio. It's like a fashion designer joining Prada or Gucci, or a mechanic landing a role at Ferrari. Studio A represented that same level of prestige. A little later, I also received an email from B consenting to the start of my internship with them, but my mind was set on A.

I arrived in Japan in mid-November of the same year. I decided to come to Tokyo a couple of weeks before starting my three-month internship to get accustomed to the surroundings. I knew that once I started working, I would have very few opportunities to explore the city. Little did I know how my life would change from that moment onwards. Everything would turn upside down in less than two months. A friend handed me the contact details of a person in Tokyo in case I had any problems. They proved useful, especially during my initial excursions to the supermarket. I learned not to confuse bleach with regular liquid laundry soap, and how to identify unsalted butter. I soon began to distinguish between the various types of tofu, and eventually started experimenting with Japanese food, even trying the traditional fermented soybeans, *natto*.

The excitement stemming from this Japanese adventure was overwhelming. For a while, it was enough to bury the demon that gnawed at me inside and kept me from sleeping at night.

At that time, my problems were mostly related to sleep and a poor appetite. I was also self-loathing following the breakup with my previous girlfriend. I couldn't seem to commit to a new relationship. I had the opportunity to go out with girls, but despite their good intentions, I retreated into my shell and severed the newly formed bonds shortly after. This happened both in Italy and Japan.

I ended up hurting some people who meant a lot to me, and now they barely talk to me, some cutting off communication altogether. I was still in love with my ex. I couldn't forget her. Even two years later, she haunted my dreams and I compared her to any other girl I dated. It took me a few years to emerge from this torpor. I suppose time resolved the problems; or, as I like to imagine, I simply managed to fall in love again with another woman: my wife Sumire.

The impact Tokyo and Studio A had on me was devastating. It dismantled my certainties as a young Italian architect. Everything seemed new and unfamiliar. 'I know nothing,' I would say to myself. In Europe, we revere context: our cities grow around historic cores, and we build houses to last centuries. But Tokyo defied all this. Here, houses live just 26 years on average, and there's often just 50cm between each dwelling. There's no historic centre, no permanent architecture – the city seems to whisper 'forget what you know.' The dialogue between buildings that Western architecture schools teach us to prize simply doesn't exist here. Even the city's heart defies Western logic: where we expect grand public squares, Tokyo offers the Imperial Palace park – a vast, inaccessible void at its centre.

Tokyo is polycentric. Its different centres correspond to the main metro stations, especially those along the Yamanote Line: Shinjuku, Yoyogi, Ebisu, Meguro, Ikebukuro, Shibuya, Shinagawa, Ueno, and Tokyo. These are all urban centres. There are many others, but the Yamanote line forms a ring that defines what can be called Tokyo's 'metropolitan centre'. During severe moments of depression, I found myself sitting on the Yamanote line for one or two full rounds (it takes about an hour for it to complete a loop). Despite my confusion, watching the ebb and flow of people entering and leaving the metro reassured me. Seeing the world rotate and continuing its course through the succession of individuals occupying or leaving the train carriages brought me peace.

I live in Shinjuku, the heart of the city. Living downtown has many advantages, but living in Shinjuku has even more. It is the busiest metro and railway station in the world and has connections to the rest of Tokyo and Japan. I can easily reach the two airports – Haneda and Narita – from Shinjuku's train or bus terminals, and I can hire a car without a problem. We have a parking space in the condominium, but considering the efficiency of transportation in Tokyo, owning a car is unnecessary. My wife doesn't even have a driver's license.

The apartment where we live with our two children has become tight, and we have often considered moving to a larger, more remote house. But then we realise that it will be impossible to find the same level of comfort that Shinjuku offers, so we postpone the decision or abandon it altogether. Another convenience that makes Shinjuku special is the number of hospitals and the relative ease of finding a nursery for children. There was a time when we were seriously considering a move and had already found a buyer for the apartment. Then the problem arose of finding a nursery for the children, which was not guaranteed in the municipality of the new residence, and everything fell apart. Now I consider myself fortunate to have stayed. I can go to the office by bike or on foot, and freely go on my photographic outings and explore the urban centre of Shinjuku.

Tokyo is chaotic. Its structure and growth seems to happen spontaneously. Everything appears metabolic. Streets crisscross each other at three or four levels, and rivers are invaded by cars, with overpasses compressing them into tight spaces. The initial image I had of Tokyo, based on numerous images I had seen of Shinjuku before arriving, was almost immediately demolished when I saw that the urban fabric is predominantly made up of small houses placed next to each other. Each house is approximately eighty-square-metres, and they have become a measurement unit for the city. Once you turn the corner from a central area, you enter these extensive residential areas, packed with labyrinthine streets that stretch as far as the eye can see. These dense low-rise developments are a result of increasing land costs over the years, leading to its subdivision into smaller parts, transforming single houses with a garden into denser typologies. In the same lot, instead of one house with a garden, there are three or four, with only a 50cm gap between each residence.

I made my first mistake by living too far from the office – in Wakoshi, the last stop on the dark brown Fukutoshin Line, one of Tokyo's thirteen metro lines. I had no transfers, it still took me almost an hour to get to work door-to-door. The room was part of a shared house and was tiny, but the price was reasonable because it was far from the metro station. The house was three stories tall, with a pitched roof and horizontal pale-pink wooden slats covering its exterior. It was called Sakura House, a decidedly unoriginal name.

There was a small staircase at *the genkan* (entrance), which was spacious and, as usual, consisted of the traditional step where you remove your shoes, and the locker where you leave your footwear. My room was on the ground floor. I saw the second floor's common area only a couple of times, and my memory of it is vague. There was a long, narrow kitchen and a modest living room with a worn-out sofa and a coffee table. The main wall of the living room was occupied by a large bookshelf stocked with all kinds of manga and *Lonely Planet* travel guides.

I called my room the 'Shoe Box' because of its size. I could barely open the door because it hit the bed. The bed was high from the ground so I could use the space underneath as additional storage. That's where my suitcase would go. The rest of the room consisted of a petite desk with a chair and an Ikea wardrobe. The entire room was covered with awful beige wallpaper. The only window with a grille opened onto a cultivated backyard, which constituted my morning view. The house also had a laundry room with coin-operated washers and dryers. My room and my flatmate's room were located in front of it, which caused some noise issues. The problem was particularly felt by my flatmate, who couldn't understand why I had to do laundry at 3am. It was the only time I had free. I was yet to comprehend the rhythm of office life.

I often missed the last train home and found myself having to sleep in the Cyber Manga Café in Shibuya. I think I still have the membership card somewhere at home. The structure of the manga café was equipped with 'cubicles', which contained either mattresses or a foldable chair and a computer. The fee included access to manga – which did not interest me – a cubicle where I could access the internet or sleep, and a large bathroom with showers, as well as a variety of beverages. I slept for a few hours, took a quick shower, and then returned to the office.

I moved apartments five times in six years. In most cases, I found myself sharing a house with young men who were in Japan for one of two reasons: studying Japanese or teaching English. I tolerated English teachers the least. They worked few hours and spent most of the day throwing parties in the common area. At one house in Yoyogi Hachiman, there were parties practically every night. The house was isolated enough and surrounded by shops that were closed at night, so there were no neighbours to disturb. But for someone like me who had to work a lot, a few hours of sleep were vital, and the noises coming from the ground floor annoyed me. I didn't want to argue, so instead of addressing the issue with the other tenants, I moved out. I didn't have many things with me, so moving to a new place was simple.

In one house, I ended up sharing living space with just one other tenant, Shai, an eccentric but friendly guy I'm still friends with. Itai had lived alone in that apartment for a long time and initially saw my arrival as an intrusion into his space. The entire house had been furnished and decorated according to his taste. Itai was an English teacher who also owned an art gallery and collected art. The problem was that the art he collected always related to sex or homosexuality, which meant having phalluses scattered around the house and hanging on the wall. Since I didn't spend much of my day at home, I paid little attention and let him decorate the house as he pleased. With each apartment I lived in, I got closer and closer to the office, until I found one all to myself, a five-minute walk to work. At the entrance of the building, a large sign in English and Japanese read: NO DOGS, NO CHILDREN. It meant silence, and that's what I was looking for. I stayed there for two years. After marrying Sumire, I took a leap: buying a flat in Shinjuku, though it meant moving farther from work again.

The first two years in Tokyo were fuelled on pure adrenaline. I combined sleepless nights in the office with nighttime outings with friends across the city, attending parties and nightclubs with other interns. My flatmates never saw me. I was the ghost flatmate who came and went at night. Friendships with other interns were peculiar; the internships were short, about three months on average, but during that brief period, strong friendships were formed. I am still in contact with those who worked alongside me at Studio A despite them choosing different paths. We communicate regularly on Facebook or via email. Some of them have even started their own businesses as CG designers or local architects, and Studio A has become one of their partners. While everyone worked hard, some interns prioritised having fun. There were a couple of French interns who always seemed to know where the coolest parties in the city were. Just follow them, and you were sure to have a fun evening.

The language spoken in the office is English. Mine was not the best at first, and I had to refine it in an environment with people from all over the world, and in a country where a different, complicated language is spoken. However, I quickly improved thanks to the help of my intern friends.

The office's workaholic culture led me to smoking. I also drank a lot, mainly beer, which was unusual for me as I only occasionally drank wine in Italy. I had never smoked before Japan, but I started going through almost a pack a day. It was as if the cigarette break justified my interruption from work. As if the break from work couldn't be considered unless I had a cigarette between my fingers. The only place to smoke was, and still is, a small terrace on the third floor of the office called Qubo, overlooking the courtyard of a kindergarten. The office consisted of that structure plus four other annexes scattered across neighbouring blocks. I worked in the main block, the Qubo on the third floor, and later on the second floor.

I had lost fourteen kilograms. I ate sporadically and very little. The internship wasn't well paid, and I couldn't afford restaurant lunches and dinners. The contract stipulated working six days a week, but I worked seven.

Still, I was satisfied with the pay; my two internships in Italy had never paid me for the two years of work I had completed. Also, many other renowned Japanese studios didn't pay interns at all. Even preparing food at home was not an option. I always ended up buying my meal at the *konbini* (a kind of convenience store) or the supermarket near the office. The food was inexpensive, but it wasn't the best, and the Japanese portions were not comparable to those in Italy. I told my family I was watching my diet and staying active.

Working late at the office didn't faze me – I'd grown used to long nights during university. This resilience made me feel invincible. I was convinced I had no limits and could push my work regime without compromising my mental or physical health. I had no idea how wrong I was. In a way, work dependence had cured me of my previous episode of depression, and I didn't want to fall back into that. So, it was crucial for me to focus as much as possible on work. My mother and my entire family knew that I worked crazy hours (often twenty or more hours a day), but they were not aware of the details. Still, they sensed what was happening and kept urging me to slow down. For a long time I didn't listen to them, and I now regret that decision.

One day, during a project delivery, I worked for seventy-two hours straight. I woke up in the hospital after fainting on the subway. I didn't want to stay in the hospital for the various checks, so as soon as I came to, I decided to leave. The doctors agreed to release me, only advising me to sleep more and work less. I nodded without paying too much attention and left the facility in a hurry.

Every time you entered the office, you would find someone sleeping on the floor or table, sometimes just crouched in some corner. Now, thinking about it makes me shudder, and I can't imagine what it would be like to go back to a life like that. I used to just smile and accept it. It seemed normal to endure a certain workload for the sake of the office and for the love of architecture. What nonsense!

There were other things that put pressure on me in addition to the work. For one, I didn't have a mobile phone. Instead, I used public phones to communicate with others. To navigate around the city, I had a Moleskin with a map of Tokyo, the subway and railway line networks, and, most importantly, addresses. This is how I got around.

The Japanese language was another obvious issue. Although English is spoken in the office, in daily life, one must grapple with one of the world's most difficult languages. I began to study it on several occasions, but work didn't leave me much time. I have never been good at multitasking. Even during university, I always admired those who could study and work. I must do one or the other and put a hundred percent into it; otherwise, I don't accomplish anything.

But I tried. I started taking lessons during lunch breaks. An elderly retired teacher came to Harajuku, the metro station near the office, to teach me Japanese. I never completed the assignments she gave me, and I never read the short notes she gave me at each meeting. Soon, I decided to suspend the lessons and accept the fact that I would never learn Japanese. Later, after the birth of Ryo, I took a break from work to be with the family and decided to enrol again in a Japanese school. I learned a lot in a very short time because I had no work to do. Sumire was very surprised at my progress. However, once back in the office, I forgot the little I had learned. That was the last time I tried to learn Japanese. It should also be mentioned that my wife speaks excellent English and some Italian, which makes me lazier. All our friends speak perfect English too. The fact that I don't have to speak Japanese at work makes me less motivated to learn the language.

The language barrier, however, means you are always a stranger. I will never be able to integrate into society and feel a part of it, despite now having a permanent visa, acquired after fourteen years of work and almost ten years of marriage. Being a stranger in this way makes you even more lonely.

Fourteen years ago, Studio A's office was different to what it is now. In just a few years, we went from fifty employees to about 350 architects in Tokyo alone, not counting the other studios in China (Beijing and Shanghai) and London. Now the office functions more like a large corporation where no one knows anyone, but this means more normal hours are kept. They decided to move from the annexes to a multistorey tower near Qubo. It now occupies five floors of a tower. Things are different from those days of familiar faces and shared all-nighters – a time I remember fondly. The work was hard, but it was what I was looking for, and I learned a lot in a short time. Rather than focus on one solution, I learned to explore six different options before presenting them to my superior and A-san, our founder and CEO.

I immediately established a good bond with my then supervisor. He is a person with a splendid mind, speaking six languages, including Italian, something that facilitated my entry into the office. Together we won two big competitions, one of them in Italy, and collaborated on many other projects. Spending Christmas and New Year working in the office became normal. In early December 2010, after an intense delivery, my supervisor advised me to take three days off to visit

Kyoto. I went to Kansai, took an overnight bus and reached the city in eight hours. It was the least expensive solution, but also the most stressful. Despite being provided with a tiny bunk bed on the bus, I couldn't get any sleep. I stayed in the city for two nights and returned on another overnight bus. Apart from the intense cold, I liked Kyoto a lot and decided to go back in the future. I've been there three times, and I plan to return with my family.

At the end of January 2011, my visa was due to expire, and I was mentally preparing to go home. It was my boss who asked me to stay longer and extend my internship for another three months. For this to happen, however, I had to resolve the issue of my visa, and the simplest way to do this was to leave Japan and then re-enter, obtaining a second visa. You could only do this once to avoid problems with border police.

I went to Seoul, South Korea. It was the beginning of February, and the cold in Seoul was biting, penetrating your bones. I have beautiful memories of the city, its food, and its people. Despite the cold, I got around by bicycle in order to save on transportation costs. At that time, I was taking photos with the camera I had received for my graduation – an old Canon EOS 400D with a standard 18-55 lens. It wasn't the best, but I could take decent photos with it.

Not long after I returned to Japan, on 11 March, 2011, the Tohoku earthquake hit. The tremors seemed endless, and the fear was palpable. I was on the third floor of the office. It wasn't the first tremor I had experienced in Japan – there had been numerous mild ones. But on 11 March it was devastating, even in Tokyo. Our building swayed, and many models fell from the shelves. A colleague fell down the stairs, but other than that, there were no injuries. I remember how, initially, everyone continued to work as if nothing had happened, but within minutes, images from near Fukushima arrived, and news of the tsunami circulated around the office. It shook me deeply.

Two policemen came and evacuated the building, escorting us to the park in front of the elementary school. I recall someone shouting at us to save work files before leaving. We sat in the schoolyard, watching the surrounding skyscrapers oscillating like huge puddings. People on the higher floors were still crouched under the tables. There didn't seem to be any damage to the buildings – not even a cracked window.

Some stayed overnight in the school, but I decided to go home. I immediately informed my family that I was safe. My mother called me in tears, having seen the images on TV in Italy. I tried to reassure her, telling her that our area was not hit too hard, but for her, all of Japan was Tohoku or Fukushima. My family's concern was understandable, although I felt safe given how the buildings had reacted. The affected areas were mostly made up of vulnerable wooden constructions, not like the earthquake-resistant concrete towers in central Tokyo. Saying that, if a similar tremor had occurred in the centre of Tokyo, I can't imagine how the city would have reacted. For years they have been talking about a possible seismic event in Tokyo, and I really hope that the apartment where I live is strong enough.

After that day, many foreign colleagues decided to leave Japan due to the news coming from Fukushima. The fear was related to radiation. I didn't want to leave; I knew that if I went back to Italy, I might not be able to return to Japan. My parents would have opposed it, and rightly so. I stayed for a few more days until the embassy advised me to at least move further south. I headed to Osaka, but only stayed for four days. The embassy continued to provide unsettling news about the Fukushima nuclear plant. Convinced that going to Italy would cost me my career, I decided to accept an invitation from my friend Ratna in Bali. We'd met in Kyoto when I mistook her for a local while searching for a temple. She was, in fact, Indonesian and a tourist like me – though not in quite the same way. I later learned she was among Bali's wealthiest and most influential figures. While she stayed in an exclusive *ryokan*, I slept in a capsule hotel, tucked into a cubicle resembling a giant washing machine for a few hours' rest. Despite our different circumstances, we formed a lasting friendship.

When Ratna heard about the earthquake, she called me in concern and offered a ticket to Bali. My arrival in Indonesia seemed absurd both to me and to my family. Suddenly, I found myself in paradise, far from earthquakes and tsunamis. I reassured the office of my intention to return as soon as possible, but this ended up being delayed.

A bereavement drew me back to Italy – the mother of one of my best friends had passed away. After two weeks, I had to convince my worried family to let me return to Japan. The Fukushima news remained unsettling, but my office kept sending reassuring updates about Tokyo's air quality. Certain my future hinged on returning, I persuaded my mother – though my parents would still need to fund the flight, as my intern's salary couldn't cover it. But change was coming: passing the office exam would secure me an office position.

Back in Tokyo, I took the test. It involved designing a modest building in twelve hours, from 10am to 10pm. The project required presentation to the principal with drawings and physical models. I presented three solutions to A-san and one of the partners. They were impressed with my work, and I got the job.

My official role at Studio A started in August 2011. I had the opportunity to return home before starting to work. This would be my last carefree holiday in Italy as a single person.

Looking back from my current state, I barely recognise myself. Where is that Abele who juggled multiple architecture competitions while maintaining an intense social life in Tokyo – all with a smile? My depression now makes it impossible to imagine myself without illness. I can't remember my last moment of excitement walking into the office. Memories of my younger, healthier self seem like distant dreams.

Depression clouds everything in uncertainty. Thoughts race, focus scatters. When I asked my doctor if I'd ever return to my former self, his response was pointed: 'Before what? Before the illness, you had another illness: workaholism. That's not a life to aspire to. Focus instead on who you want to become now, what kind of life you want to build, and how this experience might reshape you.'

Part of me still yearns to work at 500% capacity, while another part grapples with my new identity as a forty-year-old father. I must accept that I can never be who I was before – nor should I want to be.

My psychiatrist also serves as my psychotherapist. Though our main objectives wrap up in ten minutes – checking my emotional state and medications – sessions often stretch to thirty. We meet weekly or biweekly on Saturdays to accommodate work, though he'll suggest skipping sessions when I'm stable. Yet despite his care, I miss the deeper work only a psychologist can provide.

In fourteen years at Studio A, I've climbed to chief project manager. While becoming a partner feels unlikely now, especially given my condition, I'm content with my achievements. My job demands frequent travel: in 2019, before Covid-19, I flew monthly between London, Dubai and Moscow. Back in 2016, I was in Switzerland every two weeks. What once felt like an adventure now weighs heavily. Beyond the strain on family life, each trip requires a week's recovery toll. My doctor is always concerned when I travel – scrutinising details, checking medications, trying to minimise stays. As he reminds me: each hour of time difference demands a day to recover.

Around this time my depression was severe, but I was still able to manage office commitments and numerous trips, mainly because my wife Sumire, who has always supported me. She took on the significant workload at home while I was elsewhere.

I met Sumire at a party organised by friends at the office. She was a friend of a colleague's wife. When I first saw her, I joked to a friend that if she didn't speak English, I'd finally have to learn Japanese – she'd be worth it! Now she is my lighthouse in the storm, more pivotal to my recovery than even my children or family in Italy. She has the gift to look deep into people's hearts, and knows me better than anyone. She's the one who got me to quit smoking, who first noticed my symptoms changing, who insisted I see a psychiatrist. Now she urges me to see a psychotherapist, despite my psychiatrist's concerns about stress and time. Once again, I trust her judgement.

Sumire embraced me without knowing about my illness. I often think that if she had known what she was getting into, she might never have married me. Of course, she denies it, but the weight on her shoulders is undeniable, and my doubt remains.

I was ashamed about my mental illness. The idea that someone might suspect I had depression terrified me. I felt eyes on me, analysing every move that might reveal my true condition. I made a lot of effort to appear as a social being, in tune with the rest of the world. I feared the judgment people might pass on me if they knew I was depressed, especially at the office. I often imagined my migraines as the result of people I knew screaming in my head.

I finally heeded Sumire's advice and sought a psychiatrist after months of suffering: insomnia and apathy plagued me alongside sudden, uncontrollable crying and panic attacks. My hands and face trembled, concentration failed me, and overwhelming fatigue set in. Constant headaches and recurring suicidal nightmares compounded my deep, persistent melancholy, while crushing feelings of insignificance and guilt consumed me. Thanks to a long course of therapy, I accepted that depression is an illness and there is no reason to feel ashamed about it.

Fortunately, I found a clinic just ten minutes by bike from home. The psychiatrist – a stocky man in his mid-forties with a shaved head and gentle, round face – speaks perfect English from his time in the United States. The clinic serves mainly English, Spanish, and Portuguese-speaking expats like me. While health insurance coverage helps financially, it has its drawbacks: the waiting room often overflows, especially on Saturdays.

The clinic occupies the ground floor of a Yotsuya condominium, where the reception sits awkwardly next to the waiting area. Your reason for visiting becomes everyone's business – the fact that fellow patients share similar struggles offers little comfort. A massive column dominates the room, wrapped in wallpaper of white dolphins leaping across blue seas, contrasting with orange and pink walls. Mismatched sofas in various colours cluster around this centrepiece.

Though spotlessly clean with friendly staff, the space feels unsettling. Two corridors branch off toward consultation rooms with walls so thin – some not even reaching the ceiling – that conversations drift into the waiting area. On my first visit, this left me wondering: how could anyone speak freely when every word might carry to waiting ears?

My first visit took an unexpected turn. The intake form became a mirror of my symptoms: changes in appetite, decreased sex drive, difficulty concentrating, fatigue, insomnia, indecision, low self-esteem, guilt, suicidal thoughts, hallucinations, amnesia – I ticked almost every box, feeling each symptom intensify as I wrote. In the waiting room, I clutched a detailed account I'd prepared, fearing I'd forget something crucial. More than just a list of symptoms, it was an emotional chronicle, analysing the history of my condition. I'd described myself as a broken vase, desperately trying to reassemble itself with missing pieces. I was proud of this metaphor.

In the furthest consultation room, I began reading. Halfway through, without warning or reason, I dissolved into tears. Not desperate or cathartic crying – this felt as natural as breathing, a physiological response I couldn't control. The psychiatrist simply offered tissues and waited, taking notes as I continued. While I spoke, my mind kept straying to the thin walls, wondering who might hear. Sensing my discomfort, he had reception turn on music in the waiting room. As melody drifted down the corridor, I finally began to relax.

Physical fatigue consumed me most. An unrelenting exhaustion dragged at my body, paired with a drowsiness nothing could shake. My limbs felt leaden, every movement was like wading through water – even standing drained me. Sleep offered no refuge: insomnia plagued my nights, and on the rare occasions I slept, morning felt mere minutes later. The simplest tasks demanded monumental effort; even moving my eyes became a struggle. I found myself behaving like an elderly person, always seeking the elevator. How could I work, exercise, or be present as a father when even moving a computer mouse felt overwhelming?

Panic attacks were moments of extreme fear – ten minutes that seemed to last an eternity. They appeared without warning, reaching a crescendo, making my heart beat wildly and my body break out into cold sweats. Dizziness and vertigo followed, creating the sensation that the ground had vanished beneath my feet. Then came the bone pain and irregular heartbeat, lasting until everything gradually returned to normal. It was like a tsunami of the body.

The unpredictable nature of these attacks bred constant anxiety about when the next one might strike. I lived in continuous tension, which only intensified during vulnerable moments like important work meetings.

I once fainted when walking home from the office late at night. I was on a quiet street and had no chance to take medication to calm the attack, so I passed out and hit my head. I woke up after about ten minutes. I didn't tell Sumire anything as I didn't want to worry her more. It didn't happen again, it made me more cautious – and now I keep my medication more accessible at all times.

I've grown accustomed to the deep sadness, apathy, and self-disappointment. Depression breeds loneliness – my friendships have withered as I've retreated into having only occasional meetings. After enough declined invitations, people naturally drift away, especially when they don't understand your withdrawal. The Covid-19 isolation barely affected me; my illness had already turned me inward.

Among the things that distressed me the most was the way that depression wasn't understood by others. I described this in the notes I wrote to the doctor. Those who haven't experienced it can't truly understand – they oscillate between blame and pity, or worse, resort to gossip. I was afraid that the office would fail to grasp that I needed urgent help. To my surprise, HR proved to fully understand the situation. Apparently, I wasn't the first at the studio, and it later became clear that there had been numerous cases in the past.

Career fears and shame about my vulnerabilities haunted me. I believed leadership meant hiding such weakness, but I'd reached a breaking point. The doctor had already contacted the office – now I faced discussing my condition with HR.

I confided my fears to the doctor about reactions beyond my workplace and Italian family. Depression defies simple explanation – it's nothing like ordinary melancholy. Acquaintances, I feared, would either dismiss it as weakness or brand it as madness. Either response felt unbearable: being seen as feeble or, worse, receiving unwanted pity.

The last thing I needed were hollow attempts at cheer: 'Pull yourself together,' 'Everyone gets sad,' 'Just focus on the positives.' These well-meaning platitudes miss the fundamental truth: major depression bears no resemblance to common mood swings. There's a vast gulf between feeling 'down' and being engulfed by inexplicable apathy and sadness.

Really? You seem so cheerful!' they say, as if depression demands constant visible despair. If only their 'why?'

became genuine understanding – an offer to listen and help – everything would be simpler.

I've learned to be selective about sharing. While I want understanding, it needn't come from everyone. Those who truly care grasp my struggle; for the rest – well, patience. Close friends still ask how I am, but it's mostly ritual. They know that in my darkest moments, I retreat, so I simply answer: 'Fine, thank you.' Some seem to fear my condition, avoiding any mention of it, as if I'd never disclosed my illness. I often wonder how they see me now – whether I remain myself in their eyes, or if their view of me has shifted irrevocably.

I described to my psychiatrist the flip side: moments of uncontrollable euphoria when I feel almost divine. During these highs, I surge with energy at work and launch into new projects. I spend recklessly on frivolities, my mind racing with uninhibited – often unreasonable – expectations for both family and office. I become aggressive, especially with Sumire. She notices immediately and gives me space. While she may never fully understand the disease, she genuinely tries.

These periods last days, sometimes weeks, before I plunge back into depression's Mariana Trench. Now I recognize them as hypomanic episodes.

The psychiatrist's response was immediate after I finished: Bipolar disorder type 2. My pain crystallized in those few words. How could he be so certain, categorising me after just one session? Yet I learned to trust his judgment.

I realise my fortune. Many with depression cycle through treatments, medications, and doctors before finding their path to recovery. My body responded quickly to treatment – a blessing I don't take for granted.

The doctor illustrated my condition with a graph: mood on the vertical axis (ranging from positive to negative) and time on the horizontal. A 'normal' person's emotions follow a gentle, predictable sine wave – dipping with loss of loved ones or jobs, rising with marriages or births. But my bipolar curve looks different: a violent roller coaster plunging twice as deep as normal lows, shooting into brief, erratic peaks. Most unsettling is its randomness – these dramatic swings need no trigger. They simply happen.

The psychiatrist prioritized two things: sleep and eliminating suicidal thoughts. Everything else would follow. 'You've been defaulting on sleep payments to your body for too long,' he explained. 'Now comes the debt collection.' The suicidal thoughts concerned him most – red flags demanding immediate intervention with specific medications.

He prescribed three core medications: a mood stabilizer, anti-panic medication, and powerful sleeping pills – eight tablets in total. While dosages vary with my condition, these three remain constant. They've become my nightly ritual, the first items packed for any trip. My son Ryo watches this routine with curiosity. 'Dad, why do you always have a headache?' he asked one day. How to answer? Children perceive our vulnerabilities, no matter how we try to hide them.

At the height of my hypomanic episodes, lithium became part of my regimen, requiring constant blood monitoring. After a year, seeing my mental state improve, my analyst discontinued it.

In Japan, pills arrive counted and loose, not boxed. The panic medication was for attacks as they occurred; the others belonged to my nightly routine.

The doctor wrote my office a sealed letter in English – its exact contents still unknown to me – which I delivered to my boss and HR. The response was immediate: three months' mandatory leave and a change of supervisor. Three months without work seemed absurd, as if the world might stop turning in my absence. I couldn't imagine enduring such a break. Of course, the studio managed fine, easily finding my temporary replacement.

Bipolar disorder manifests uniquely in each person, defying any notion of an 'average patient.' Everyone's symptoms and responses differ, which is why treatment often proceeds by trial and error. The first approach isn't always the right one.

After my first appointment, scheduling the next, I asked about the total sessions needed. In my mind, this was just a brain cold requiring quick medication. I wanted to know the severity and timeline to recovery. The psychiatrist's smile told me everything – we weren't talking months, but years.

Though I've never needed hospitalization, there were times I begged for it, especially when the voices grew insistent. I wanted isolation – needed assurance I wouldn't take that fatal step. The doctor reassured me I was already under close observation – clearly meaning Sumire.

I wish I could say everything improved after those first meetings – that the medication cocktail worked instantly, that recovery came swiftly. Instead, my body resisted the treatment. I gained significant weight while new symptoms emerged: psychosis, hallucinations, amnesia. In some ways, I deteriorated. Convinced of a misdiagnosis, I rushed back to my psychiatrist. He assured me these were known bipolar symptoms, though they required treatment adjustments – tweaks that continue even now, responding to my emotional state.

The improvement came gradually. 'Your desire for a second child proves this,' my doctor noted. Anxious thoughts have grown rare, suicidal nightmares vanished. The psychotic episodes and hallucinations have long since faded and the panic attacks have diminished. Slowly, I'm rediscovering my confidence.

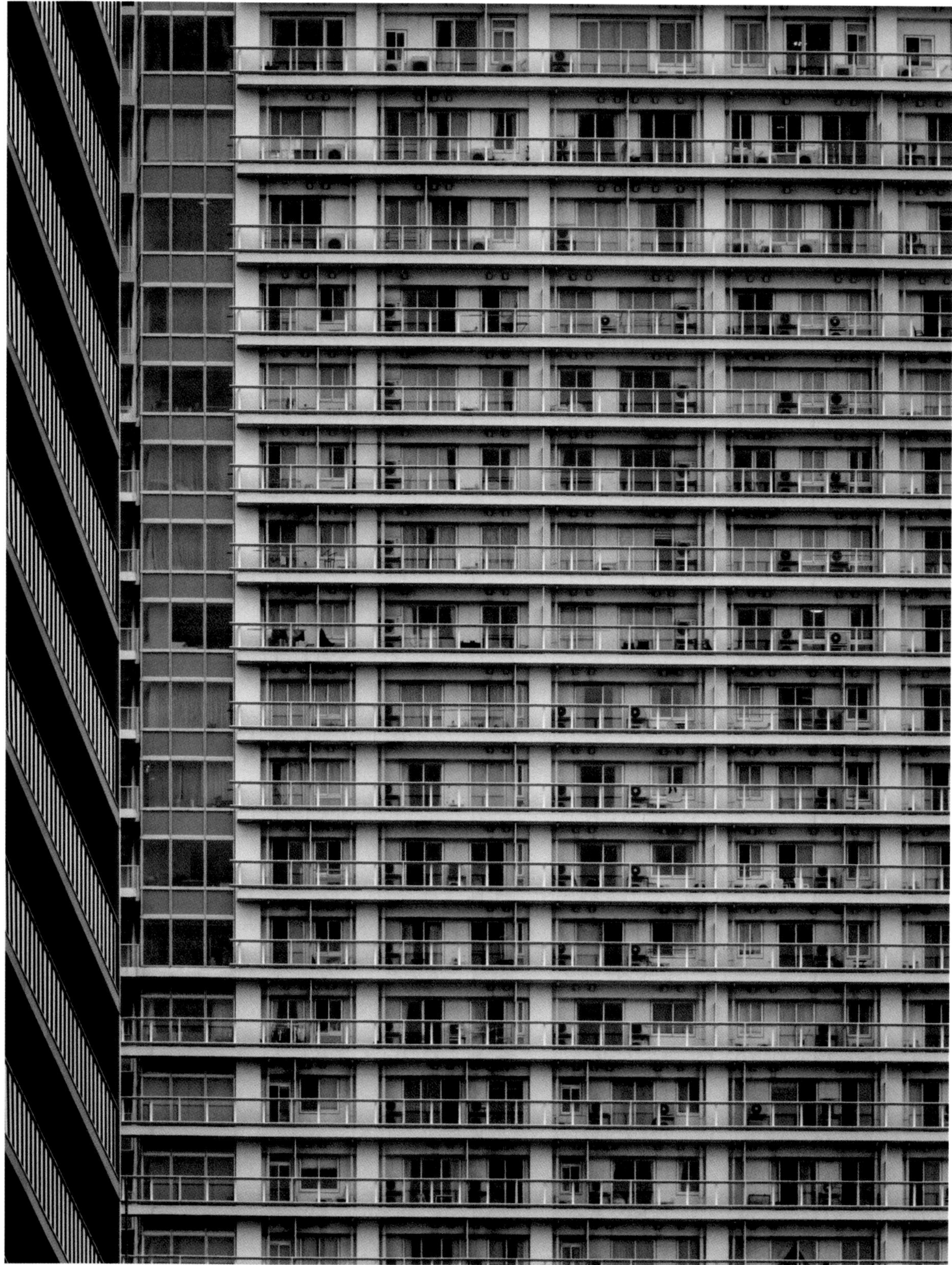

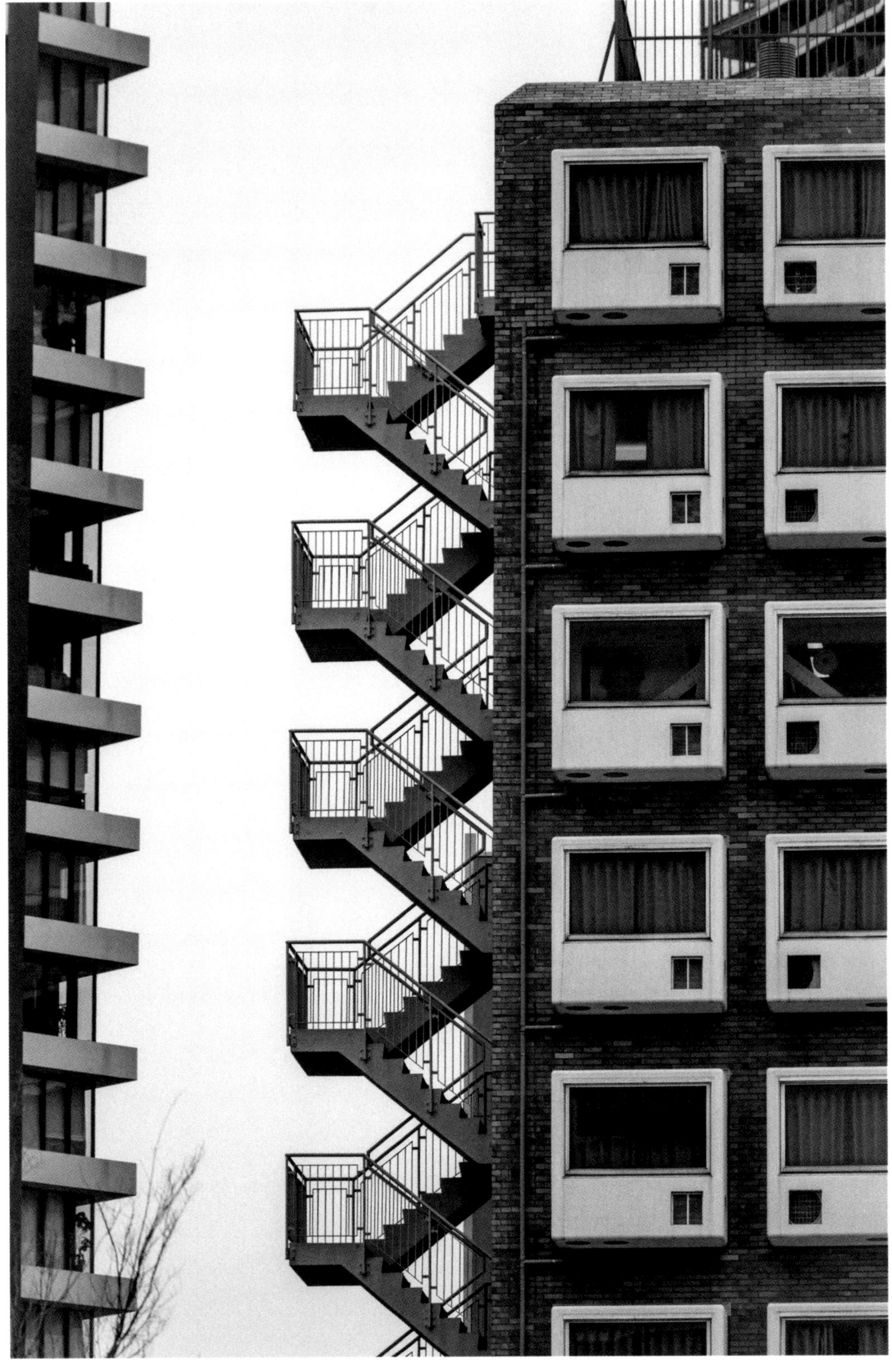

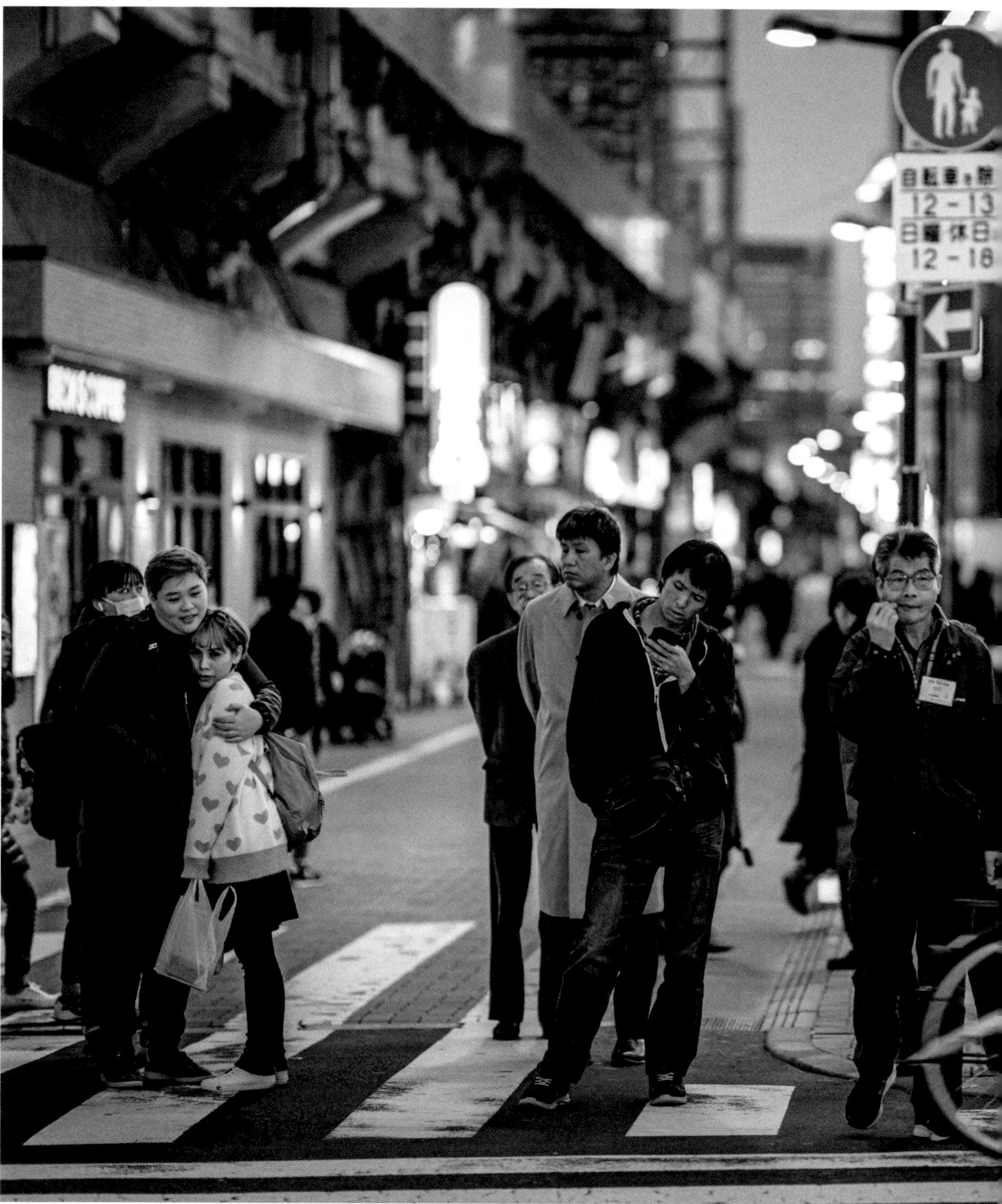

自転車を除く
12 - 13
日曜 休日
12 - 18

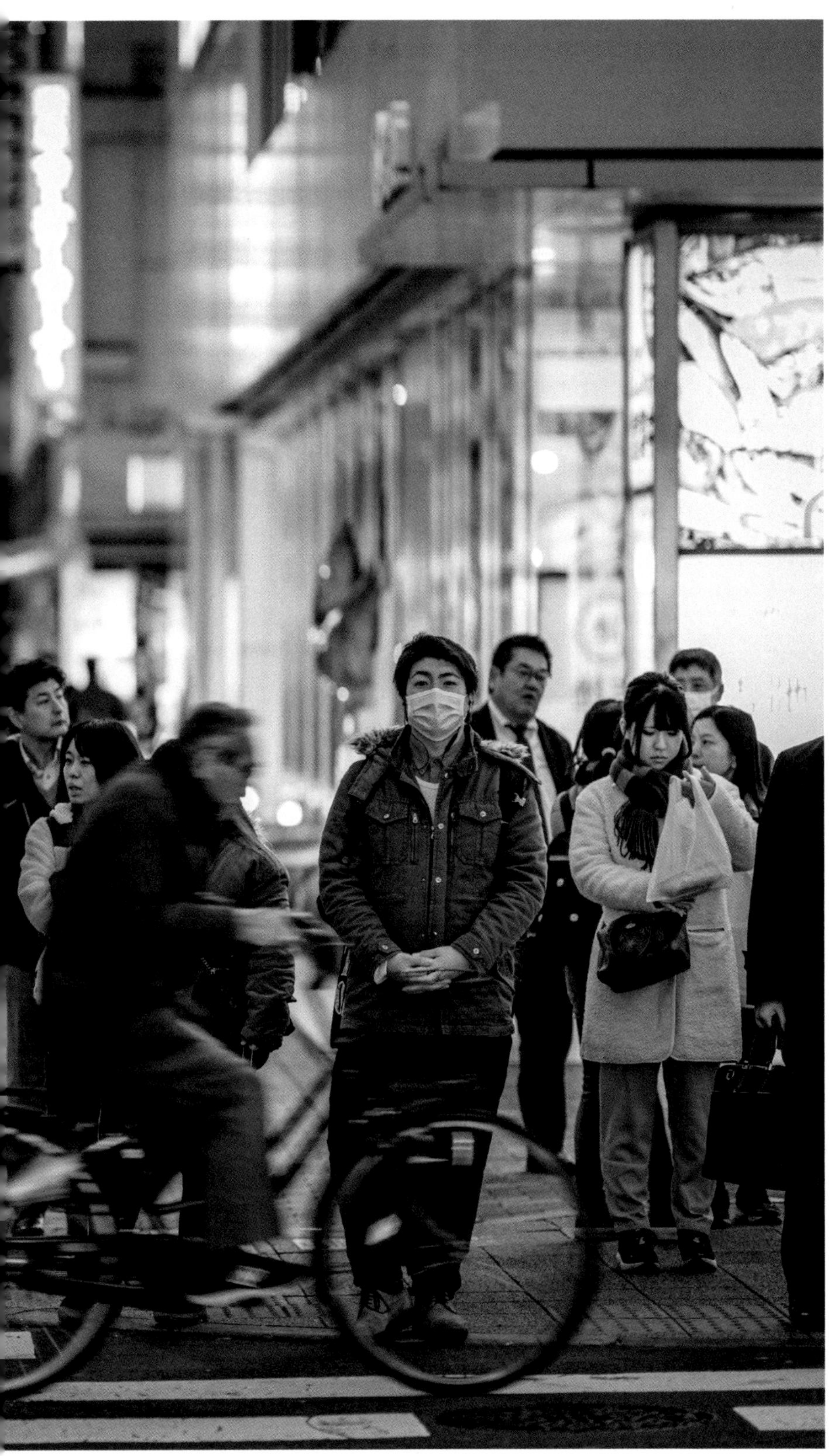

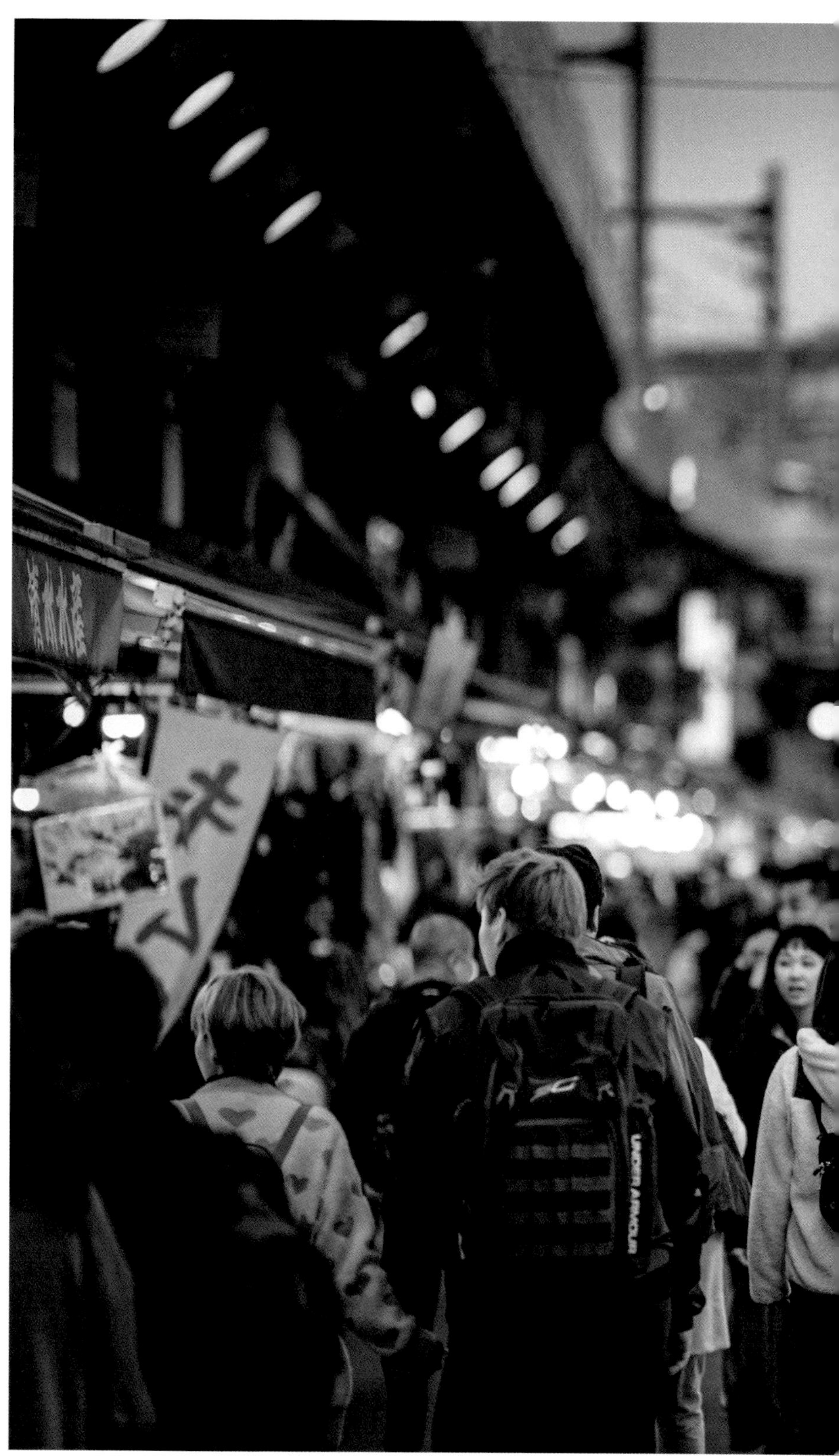

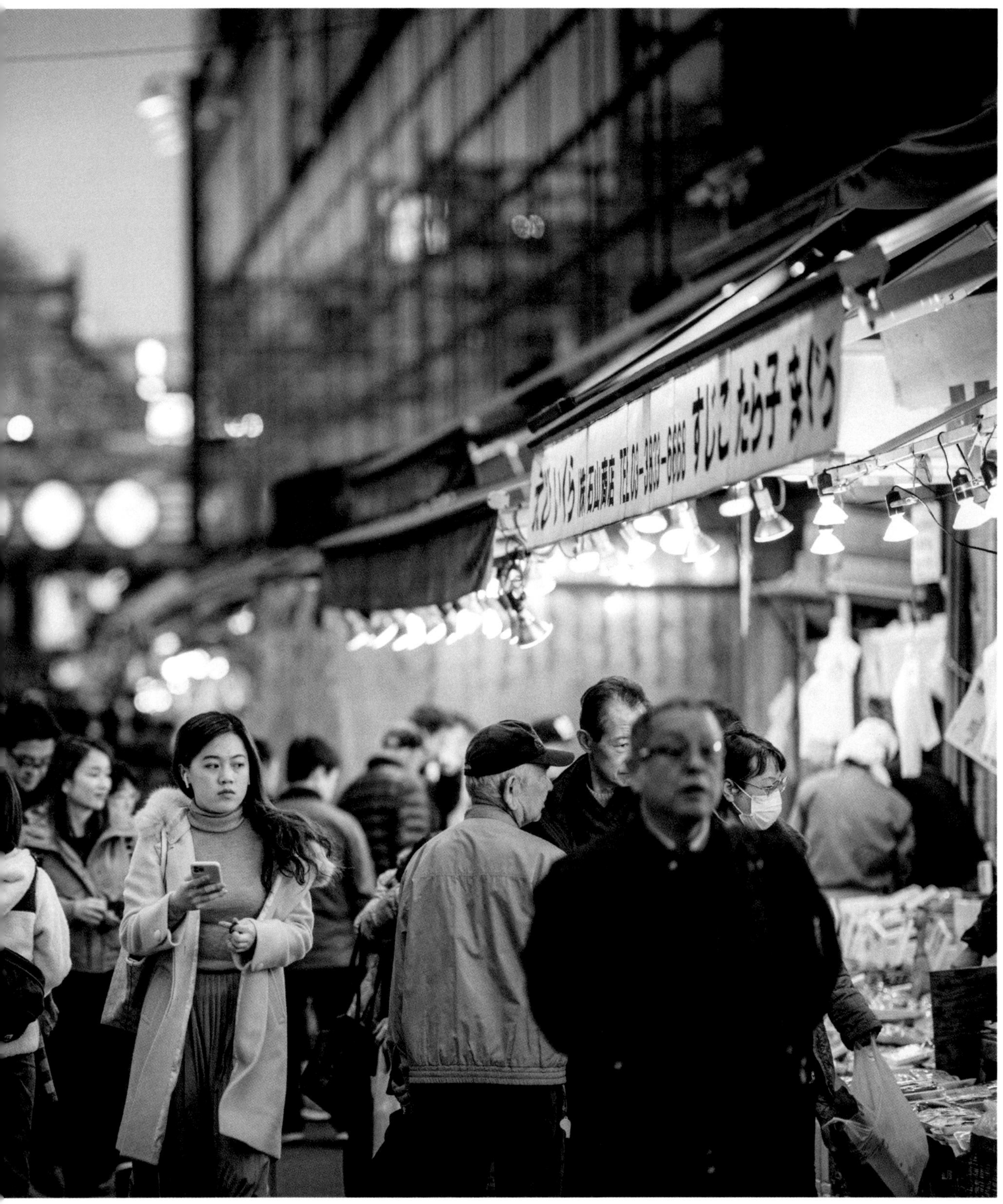
すじこ たらこ まぐろ
うにといくら 魚石山商店 TEL 03-3832-6558

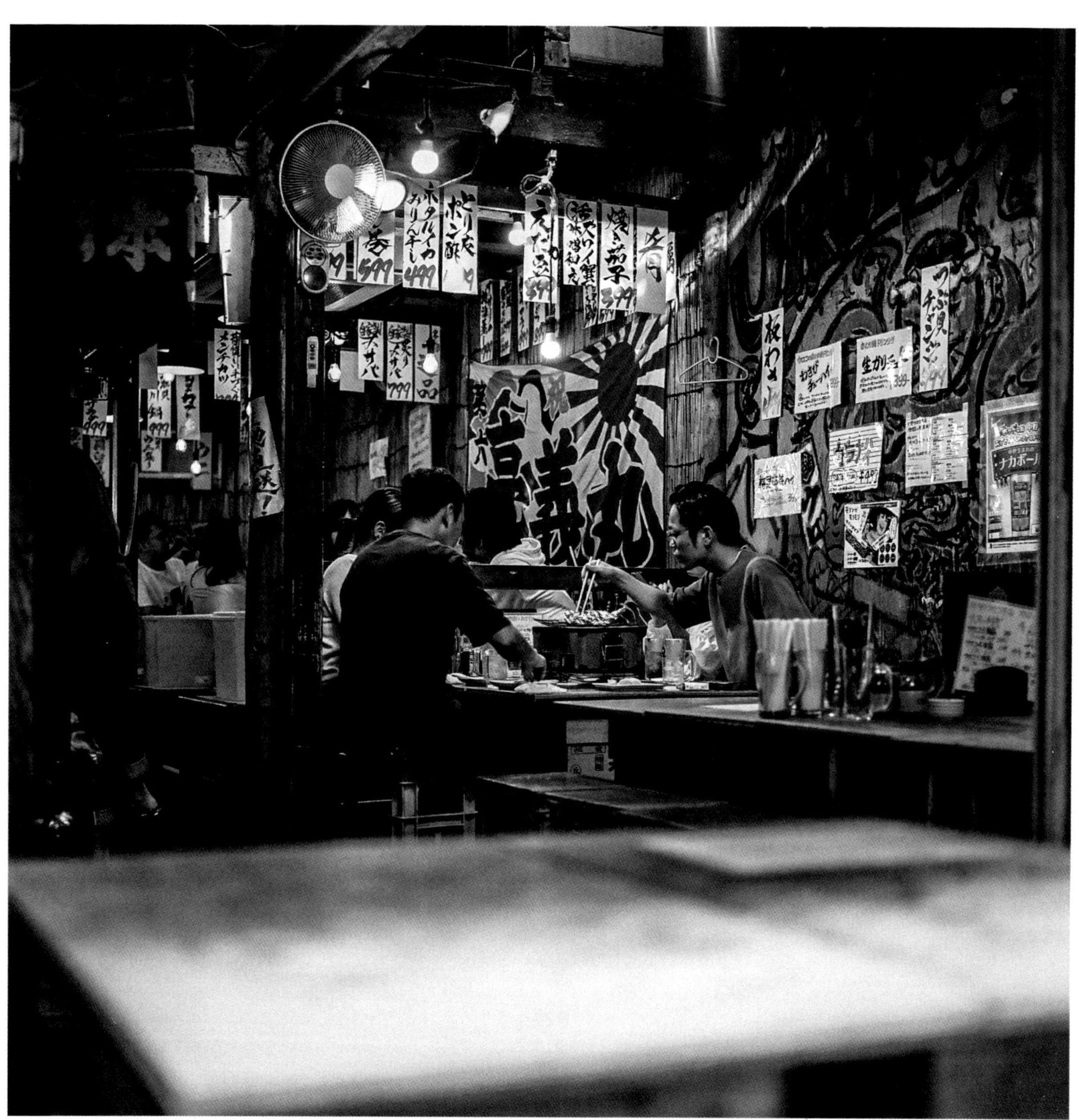

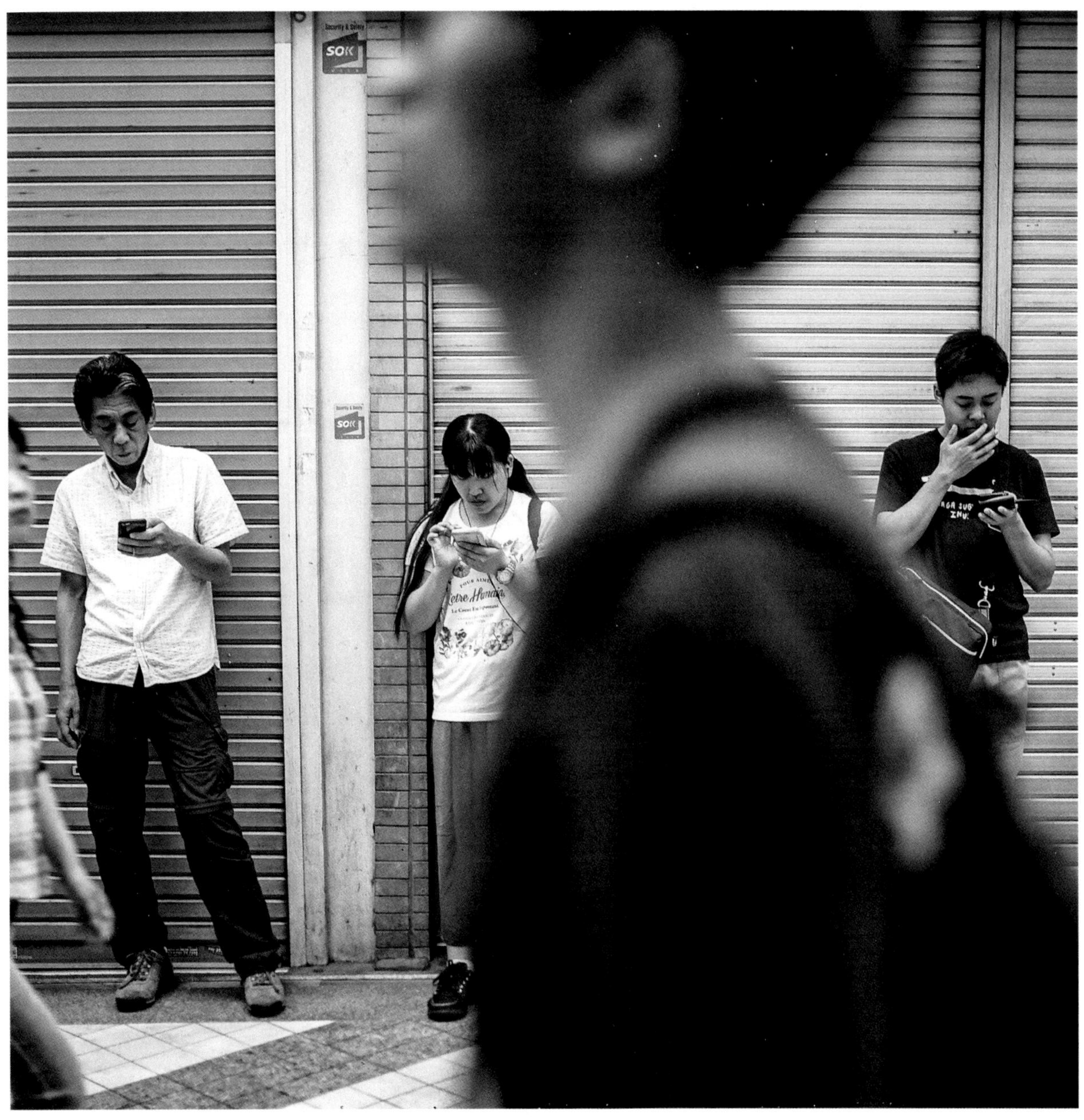

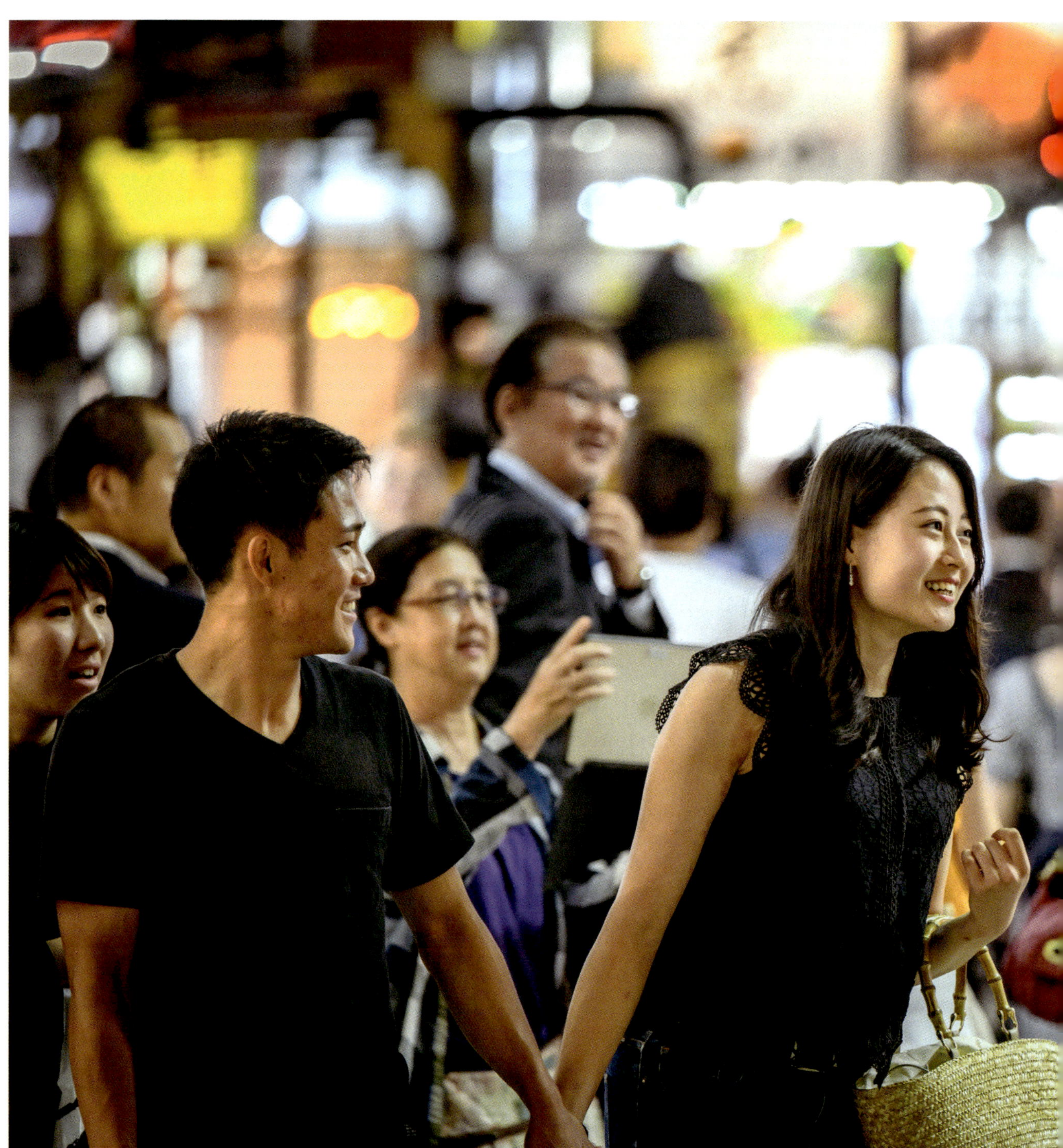

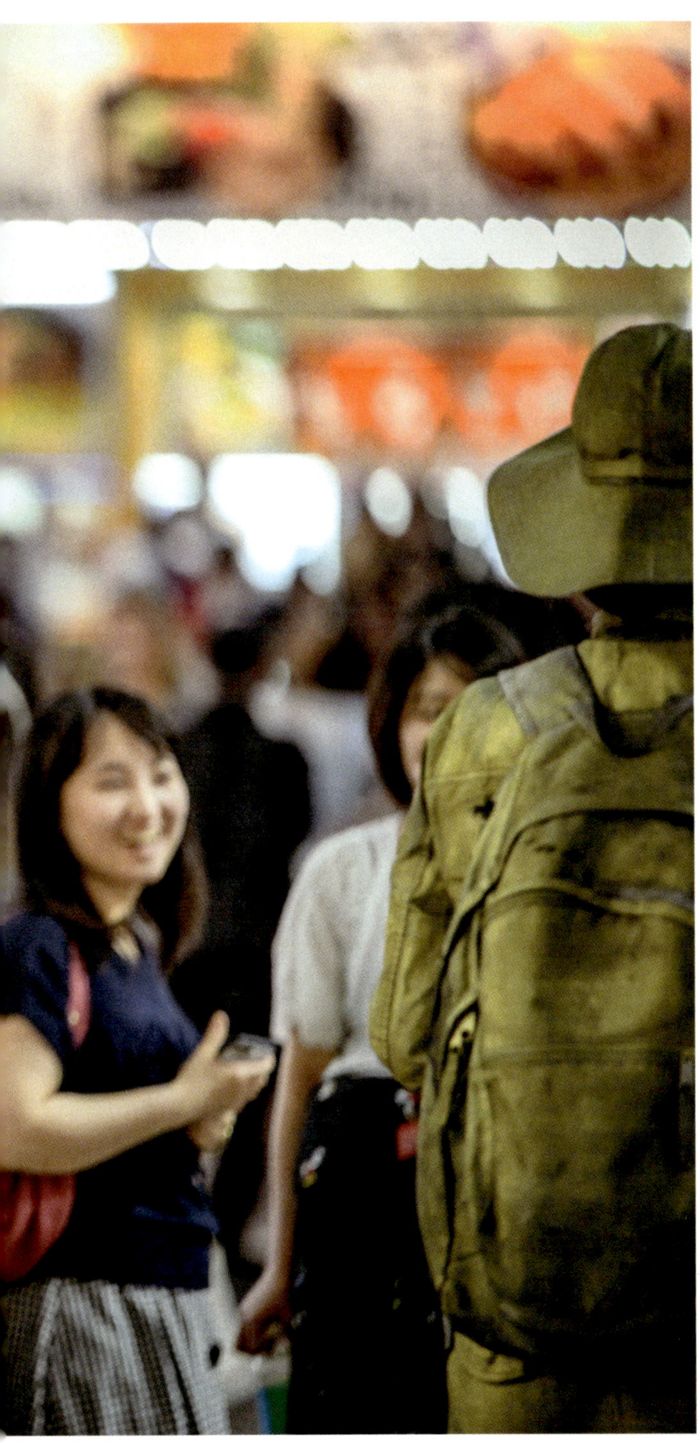

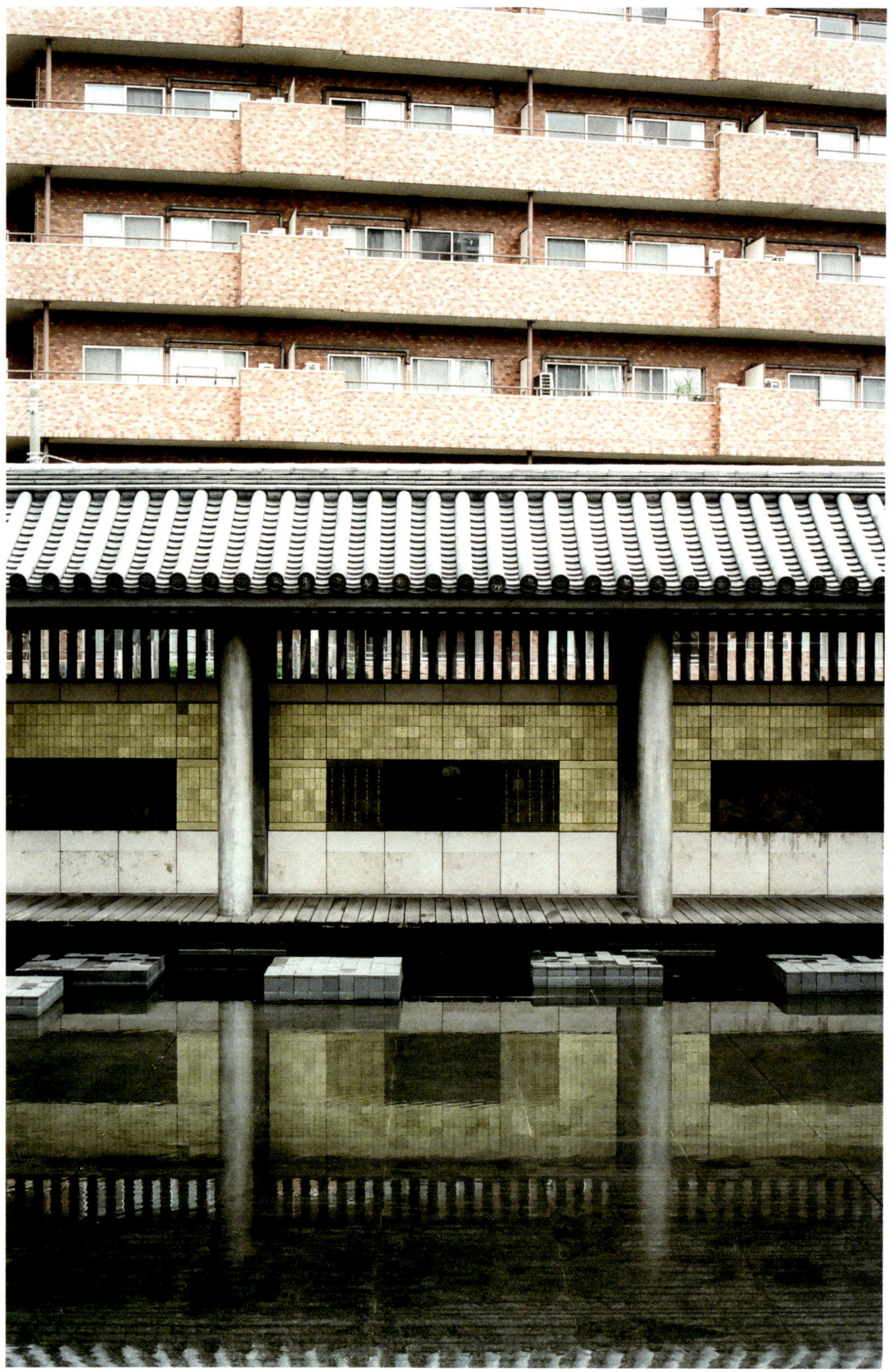

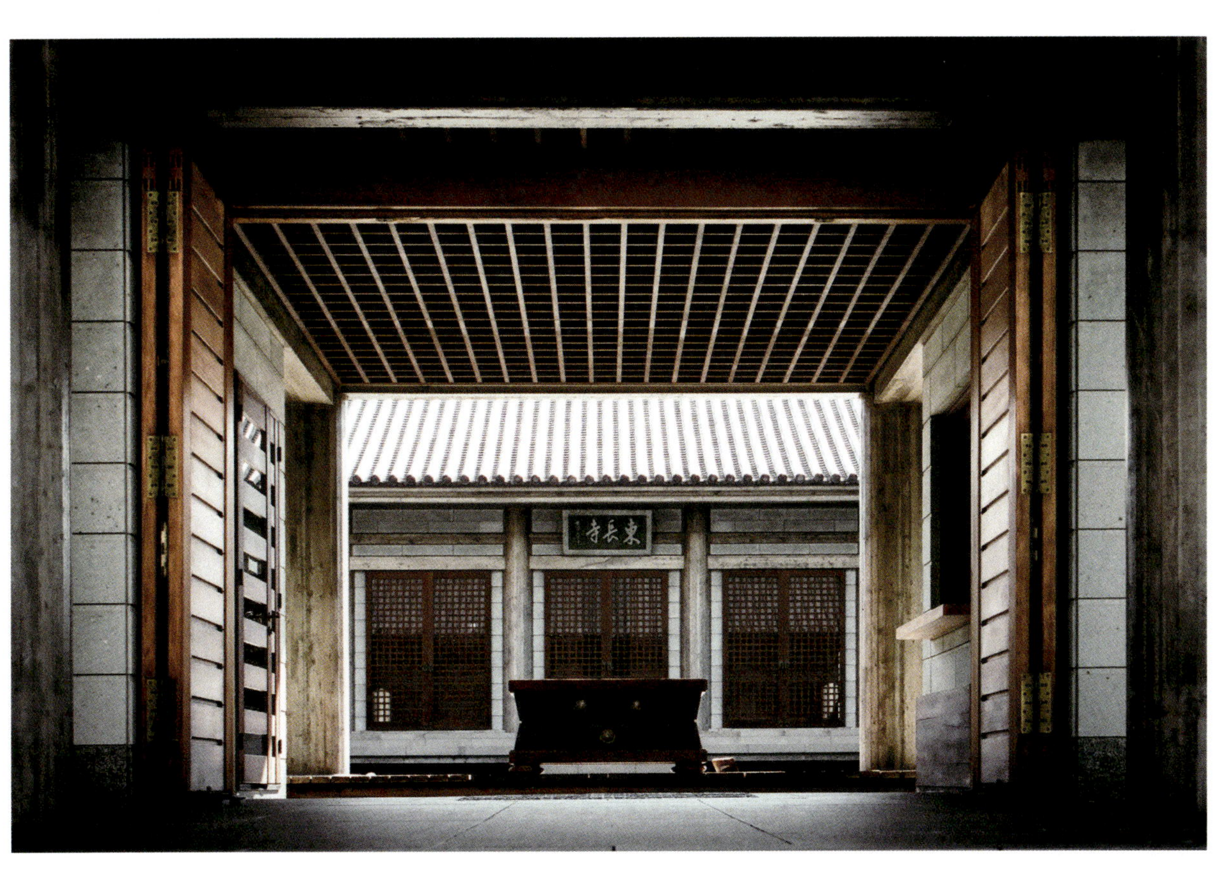

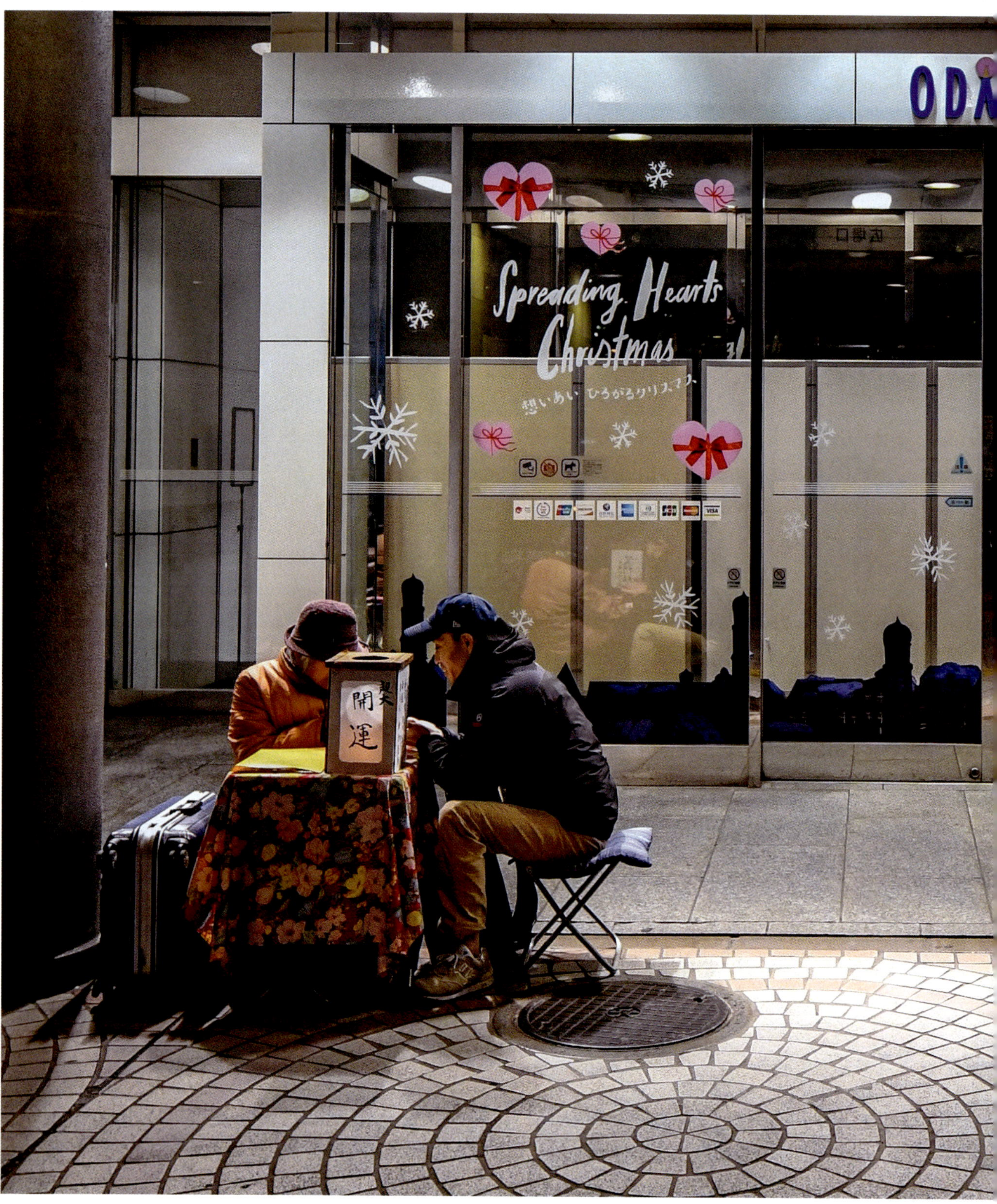

Spreading Hearts
Christmas
想いあい ひろがるクリスマス
開運
ODA
VISA

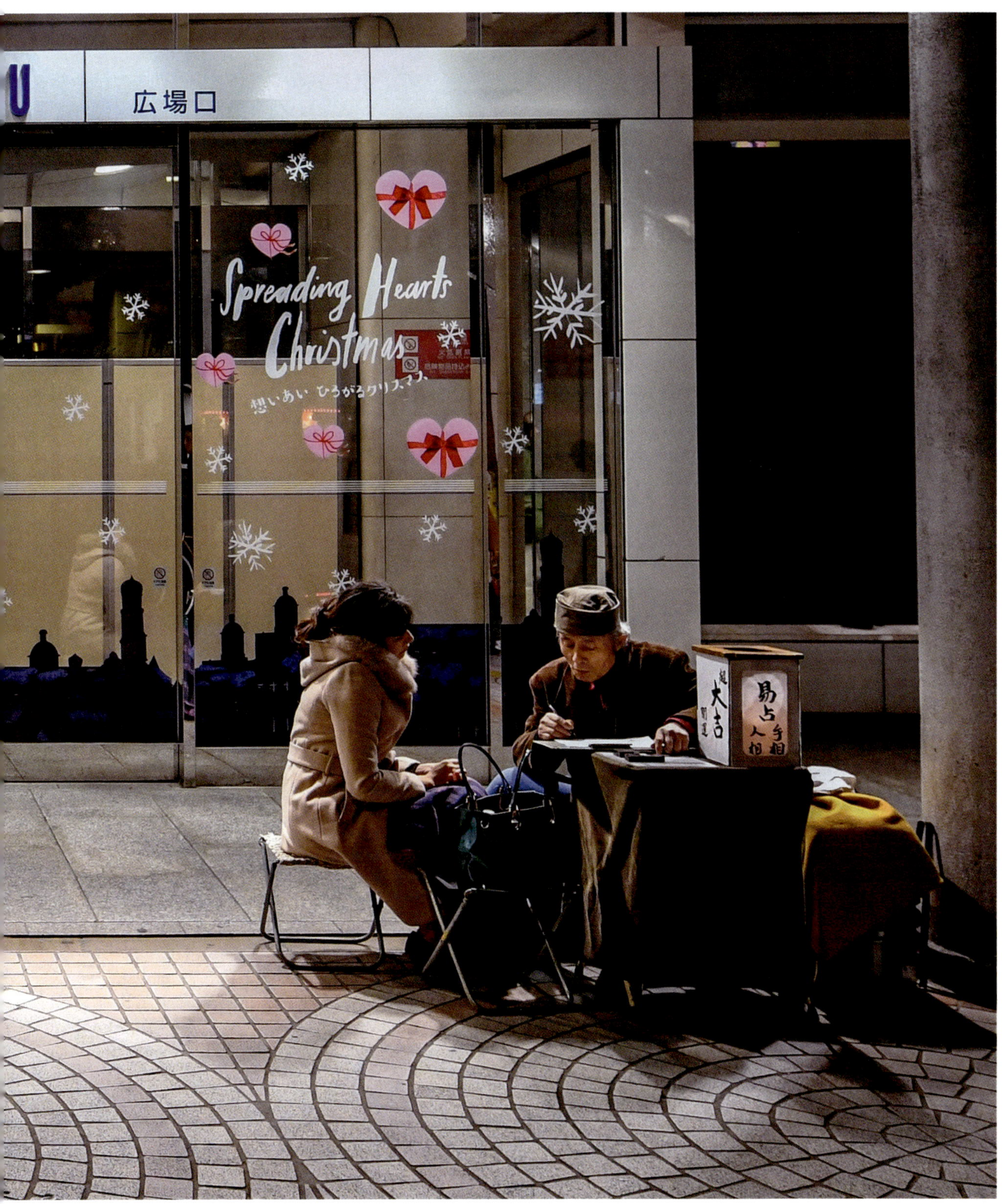

U
広場口
Spreading Hearts
Christmas
想いあい ひろがるクリスマス
大吉
開運
易占 手相
人相

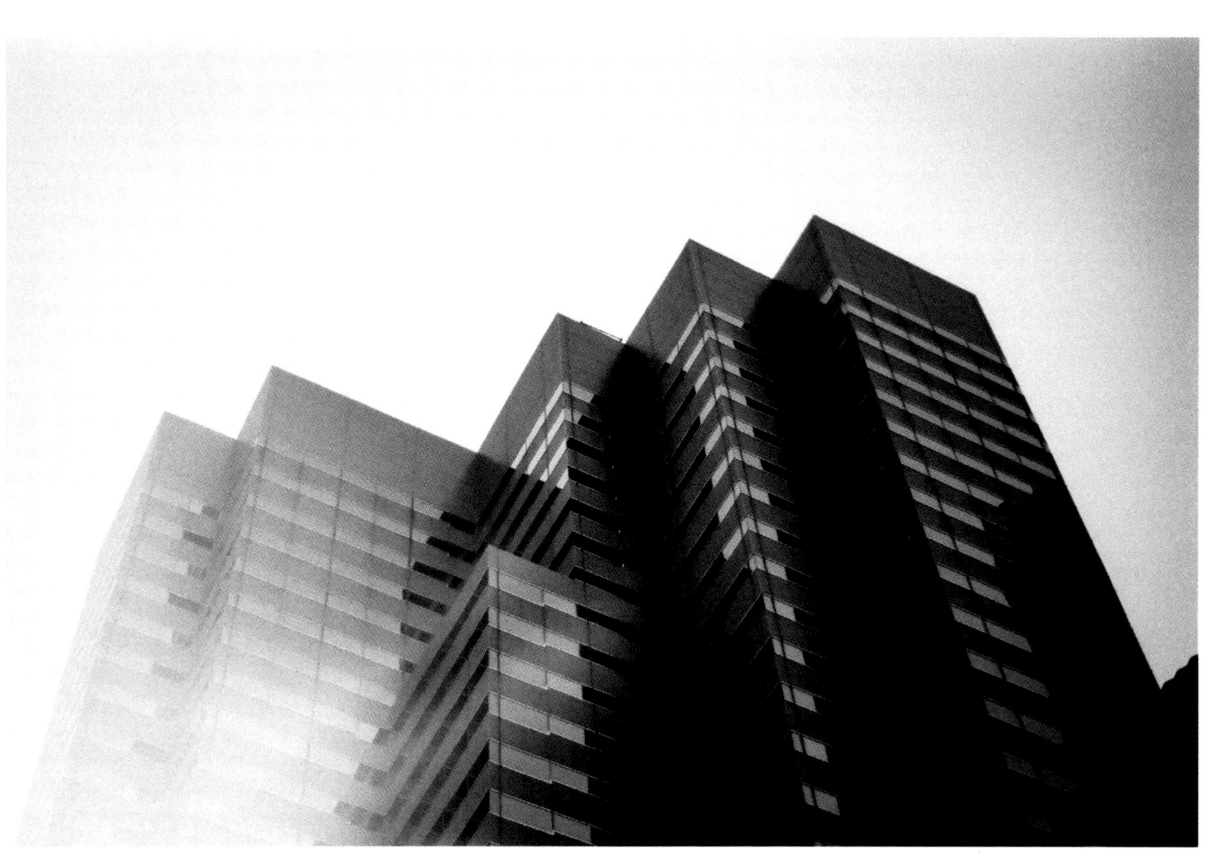

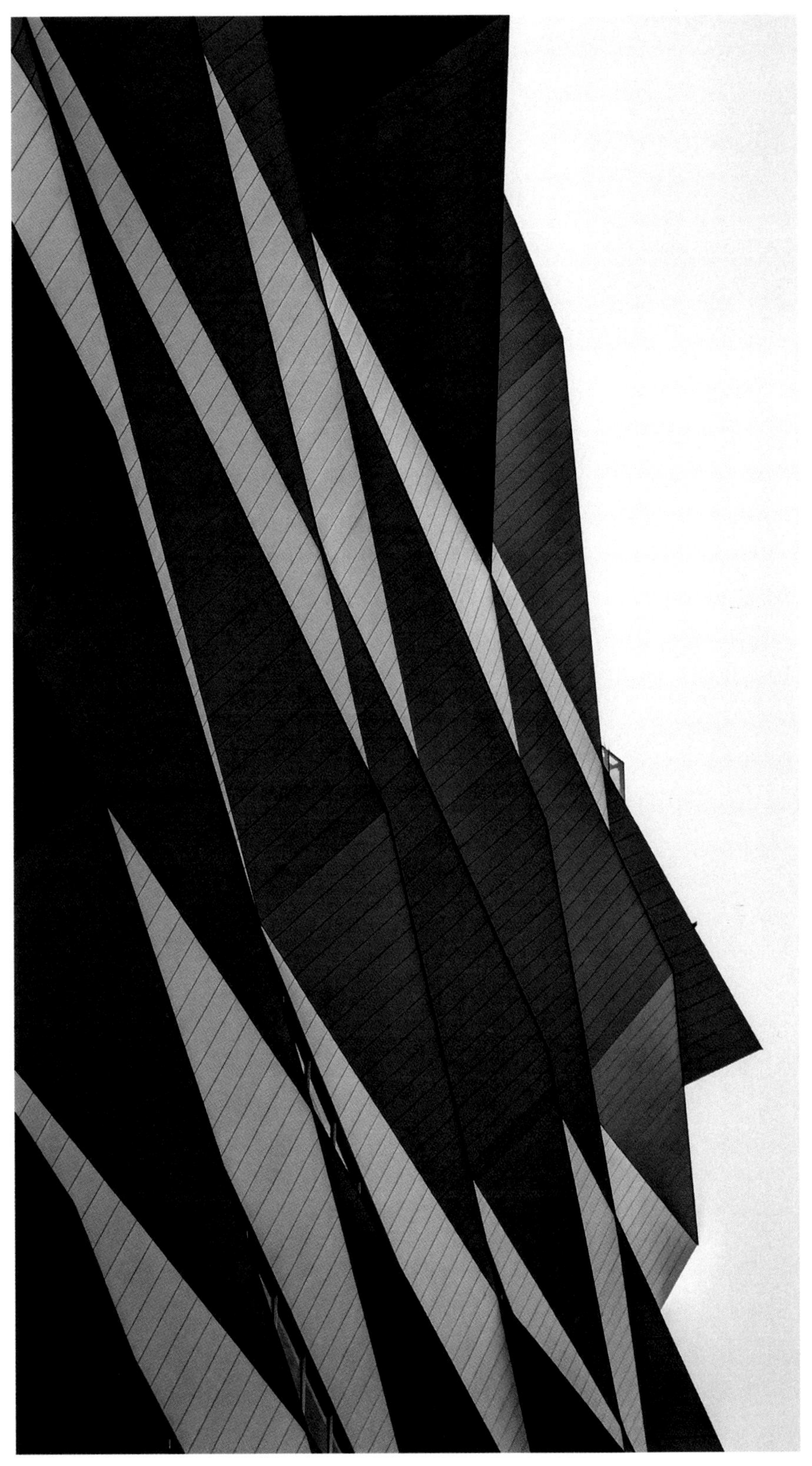

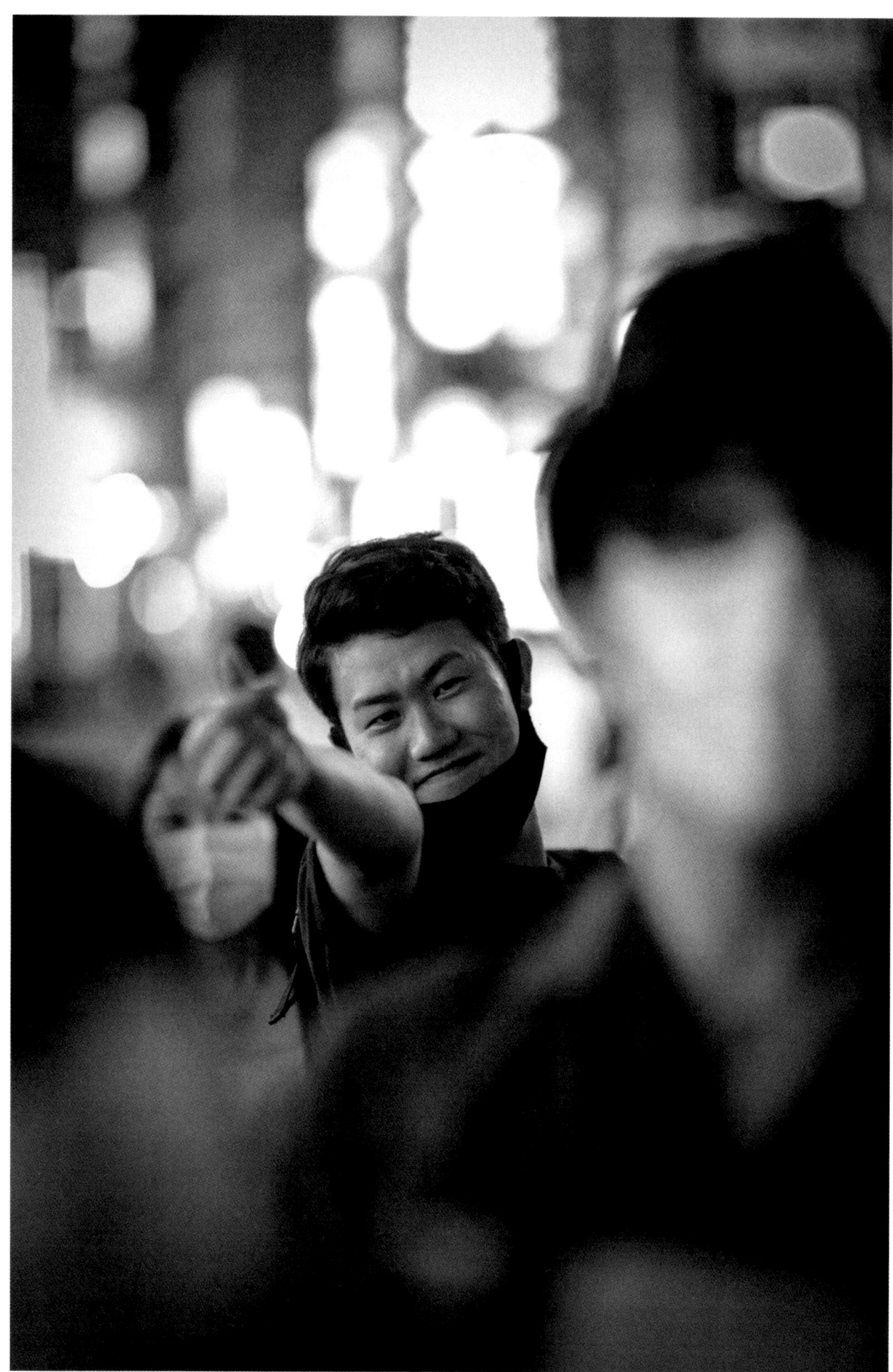

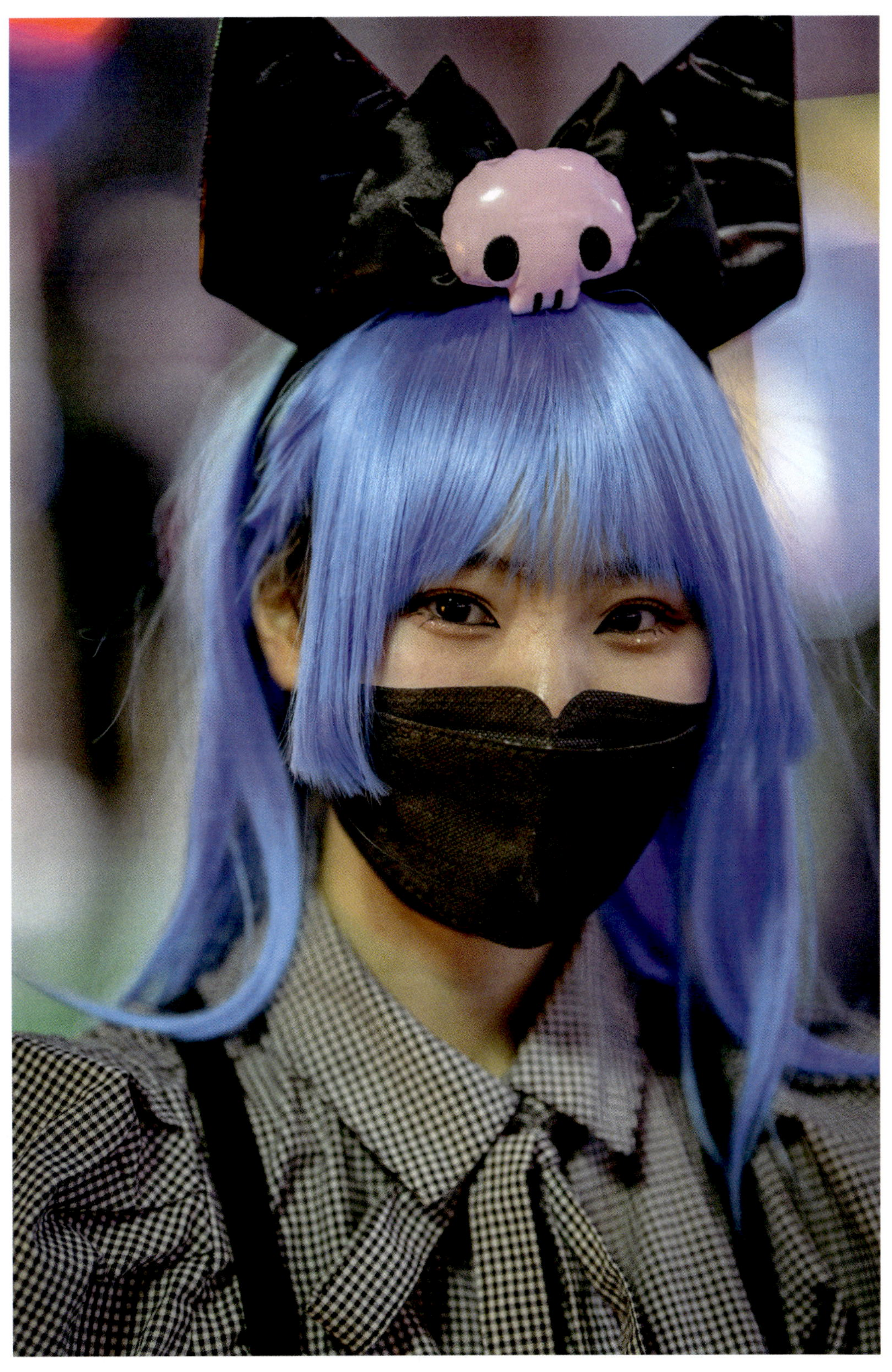

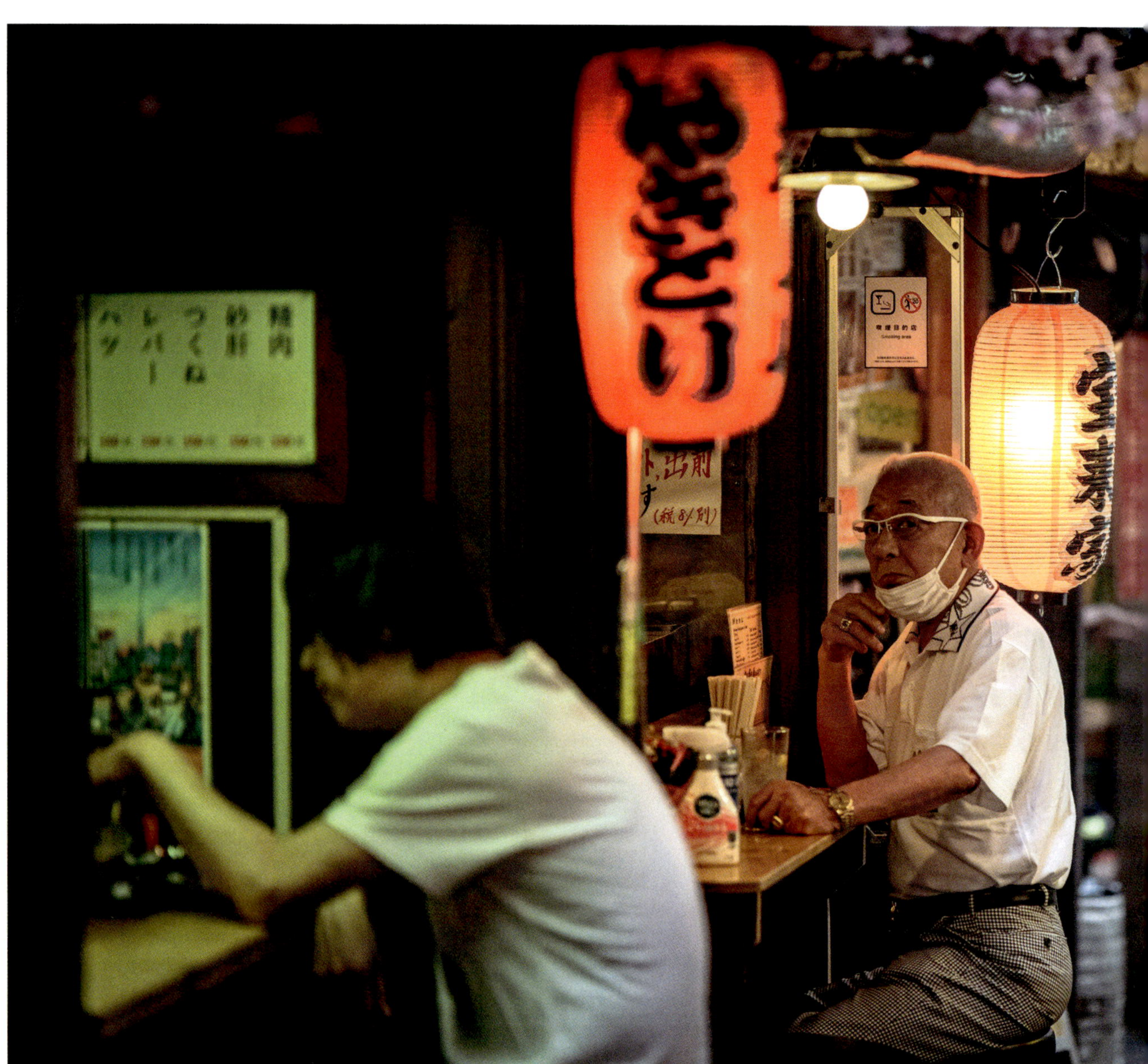
やきとり
精肉
めり
つくね
レバー
ハツ
ト、出前
す
(税8／別)
喫煙目的店
Smoking area

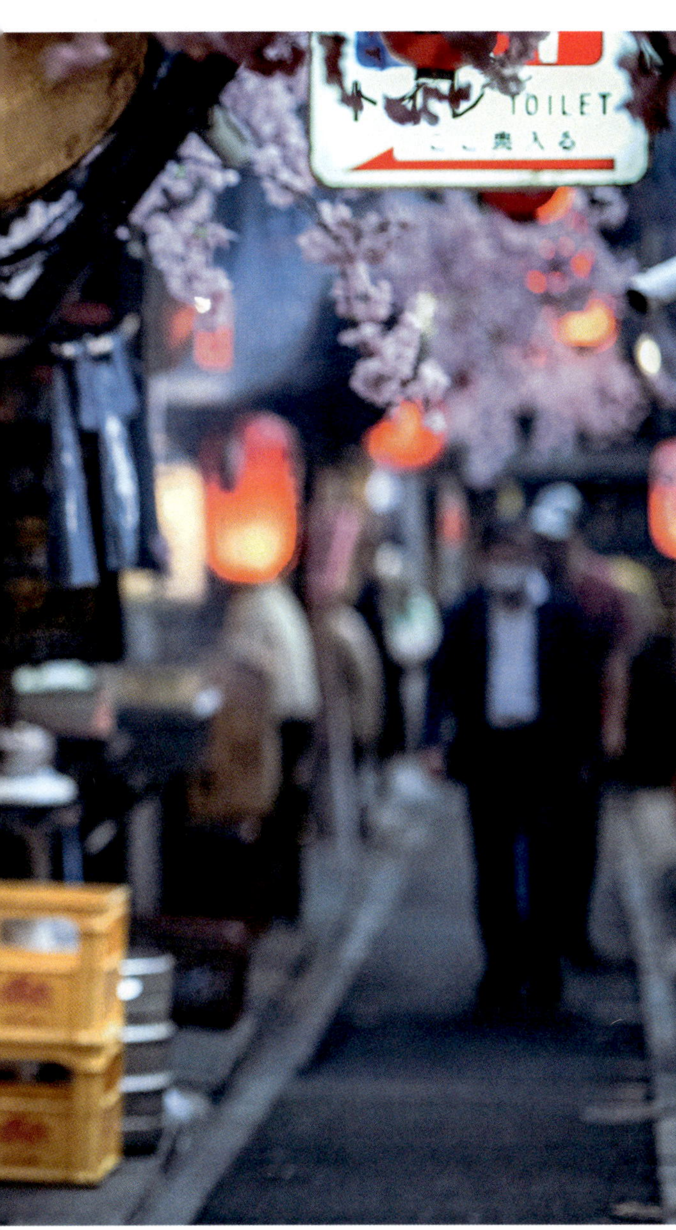
トイレ TOILET
ここ奥入る

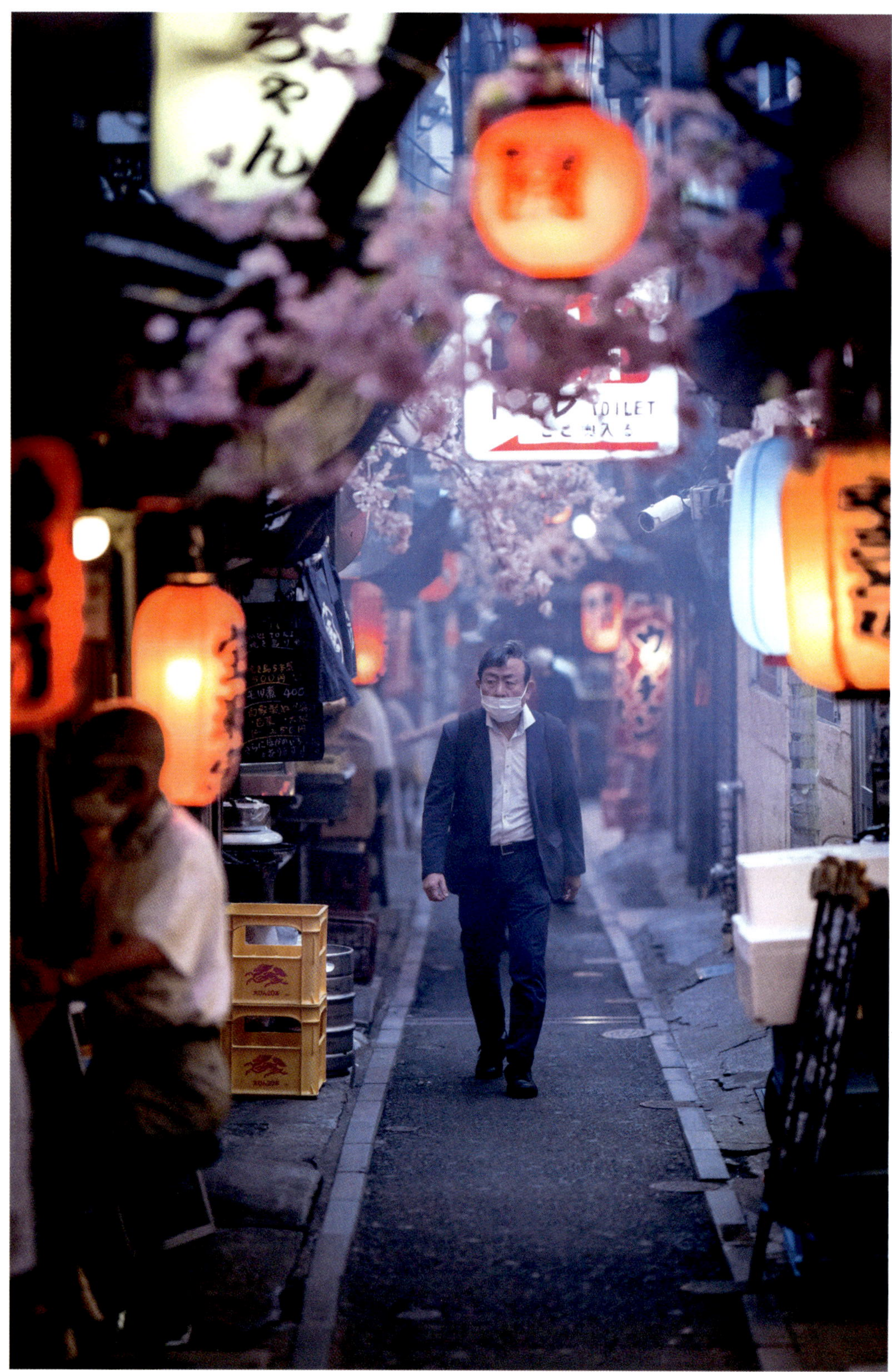
TOILET

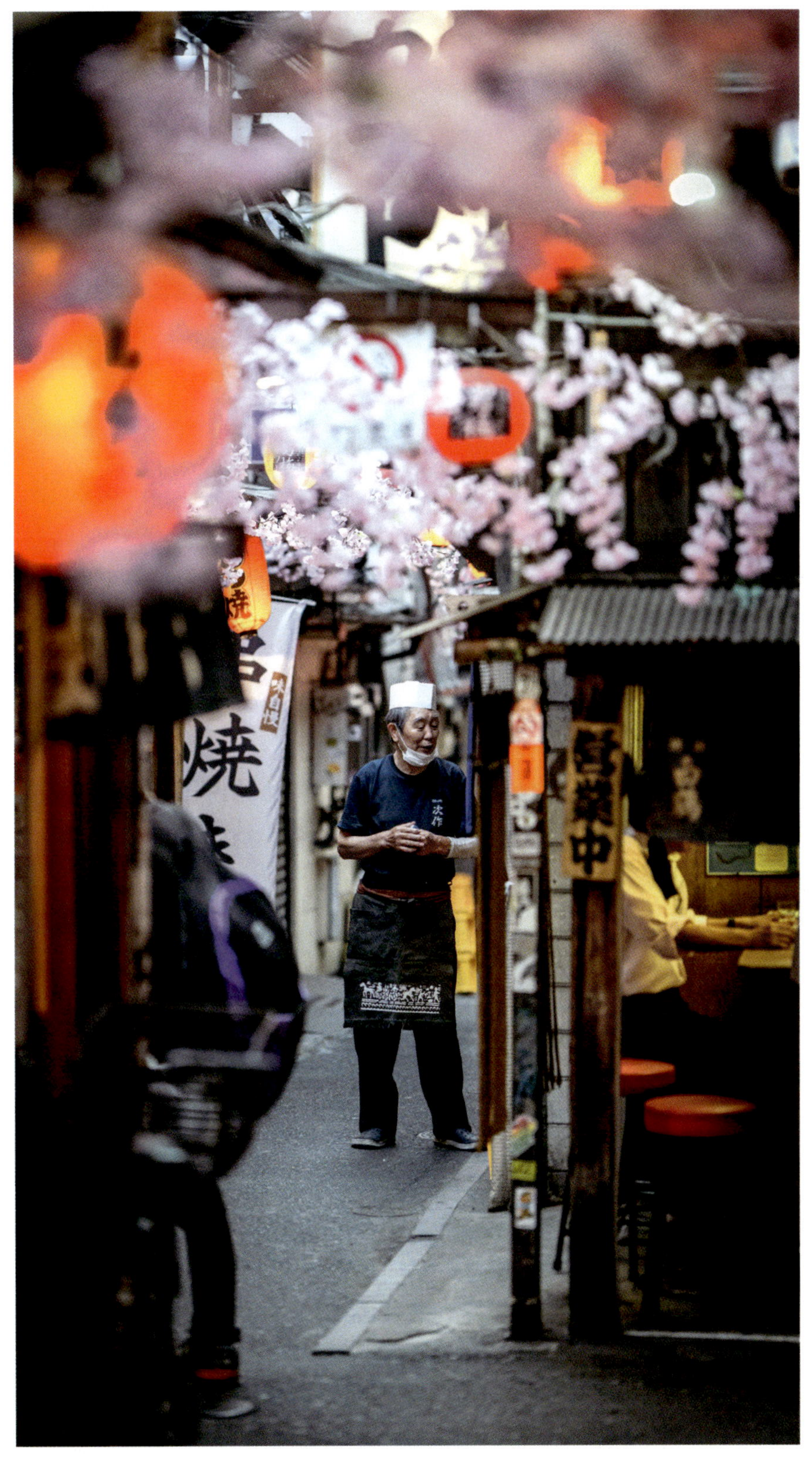

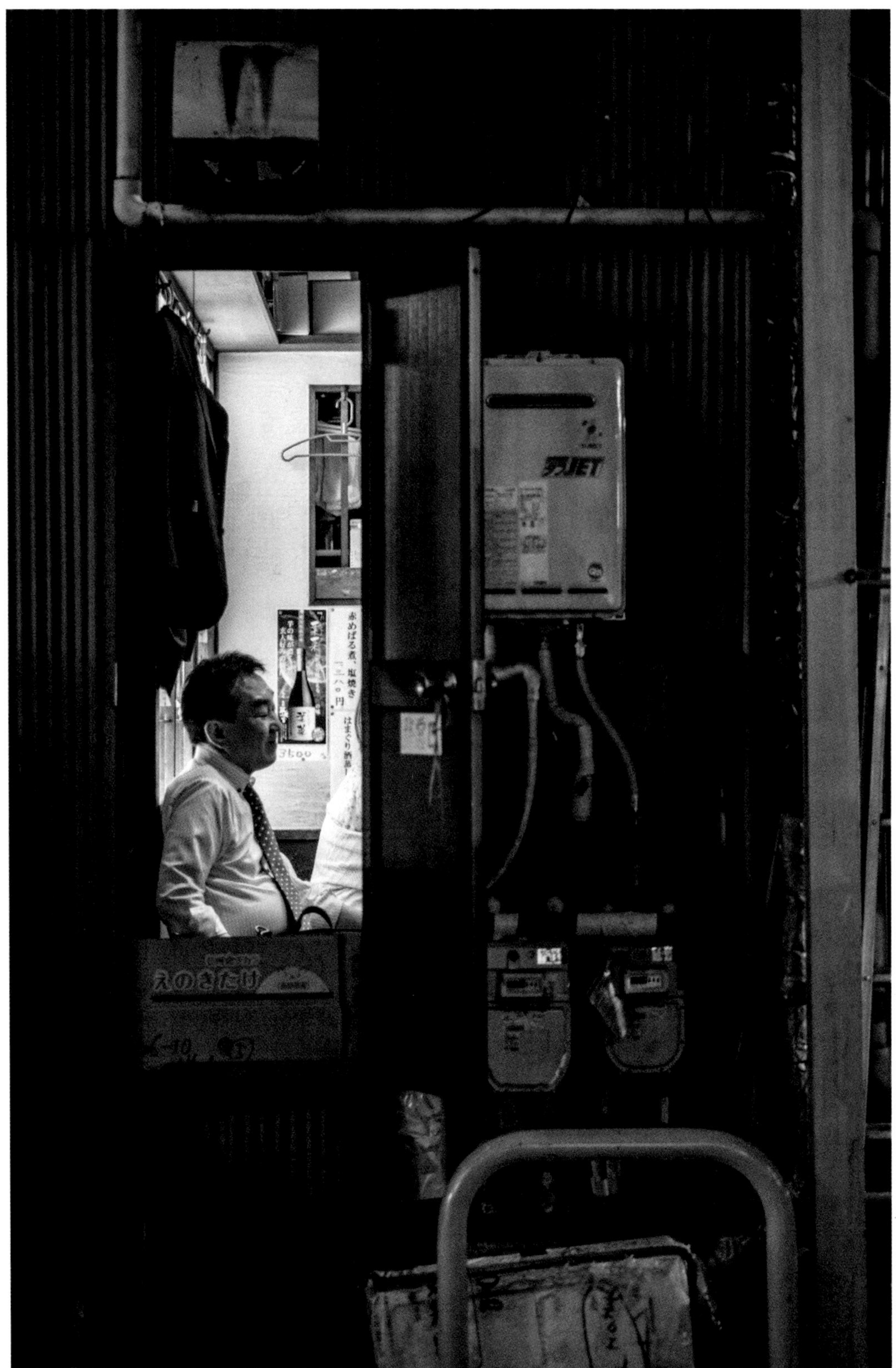

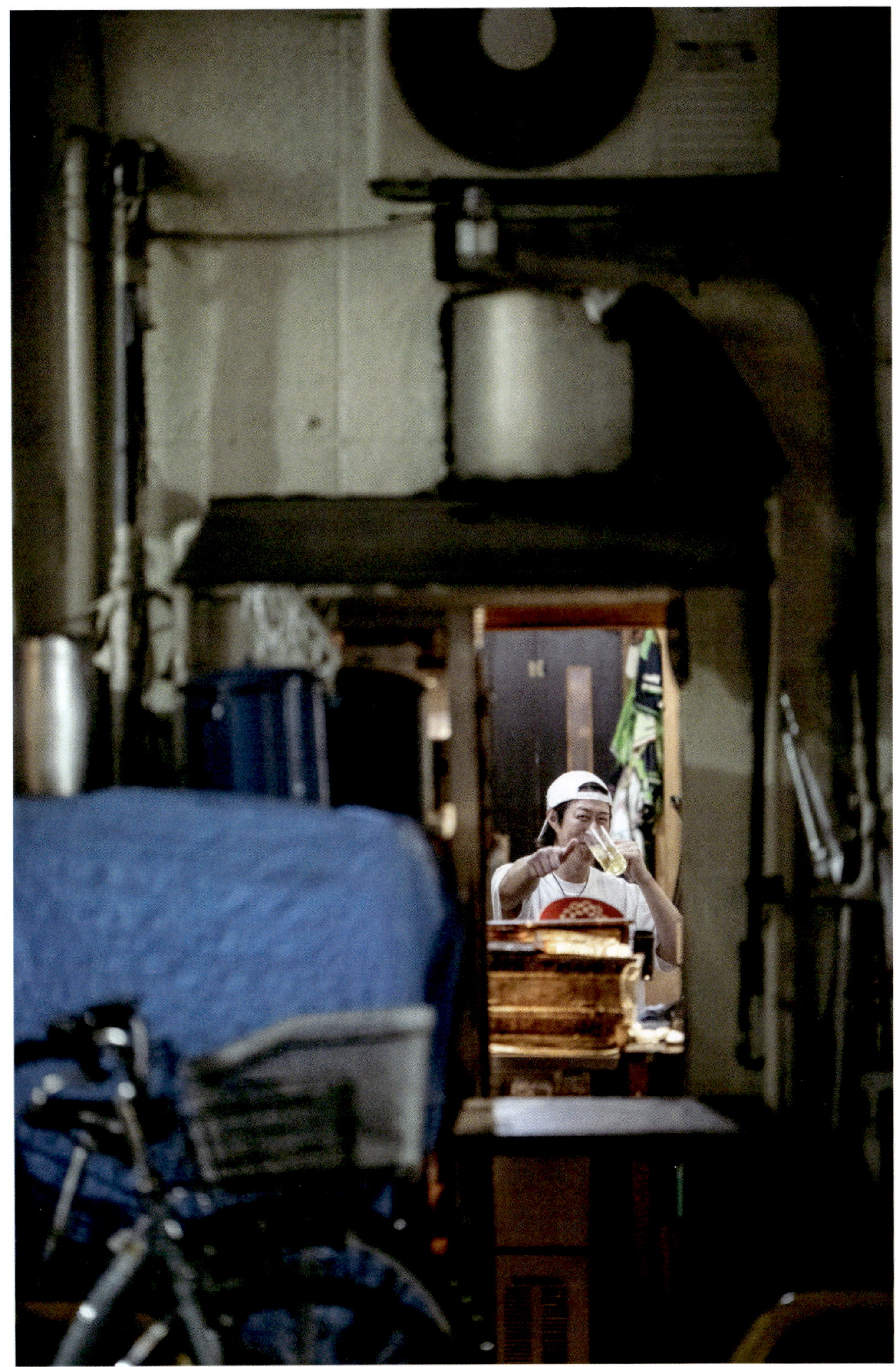

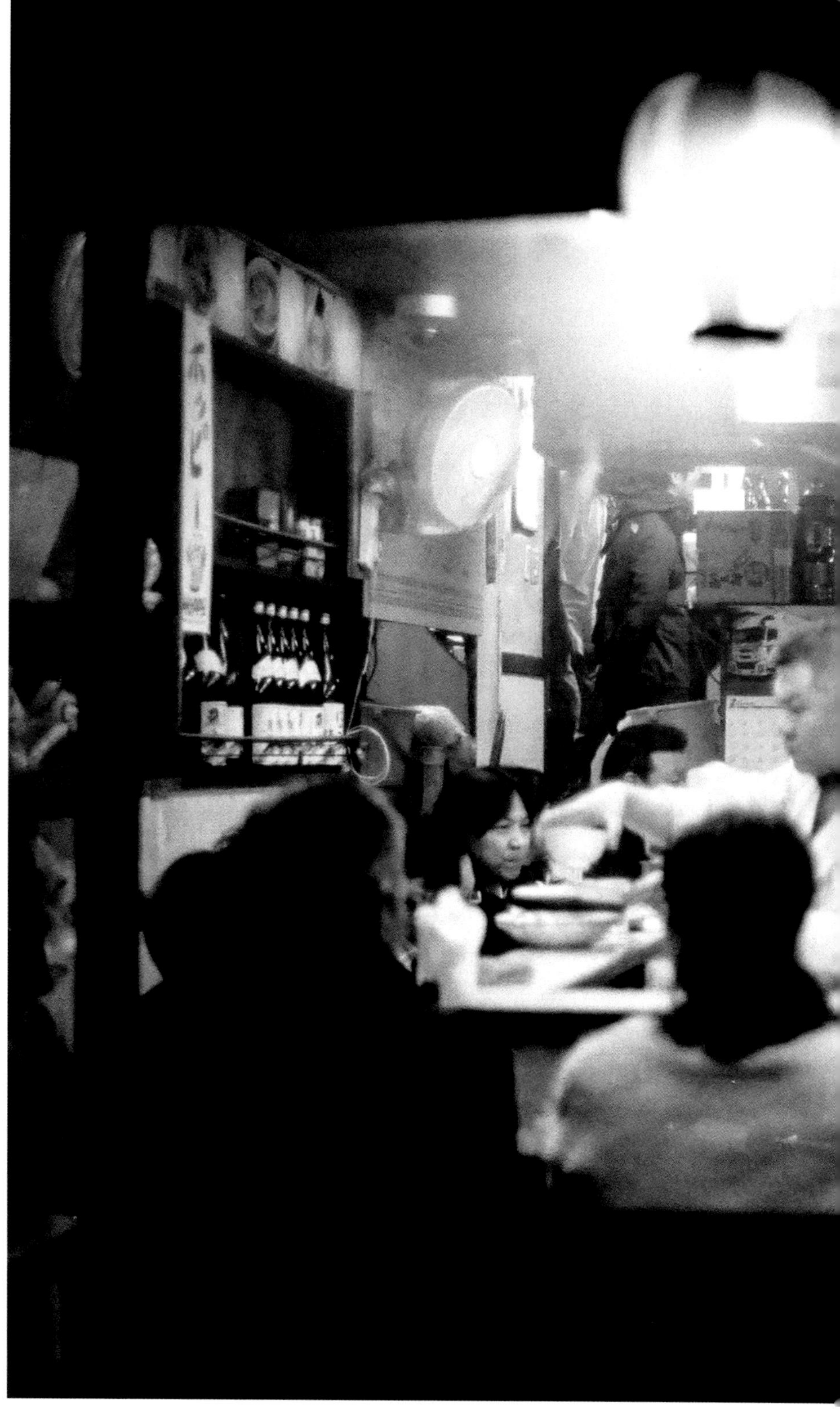

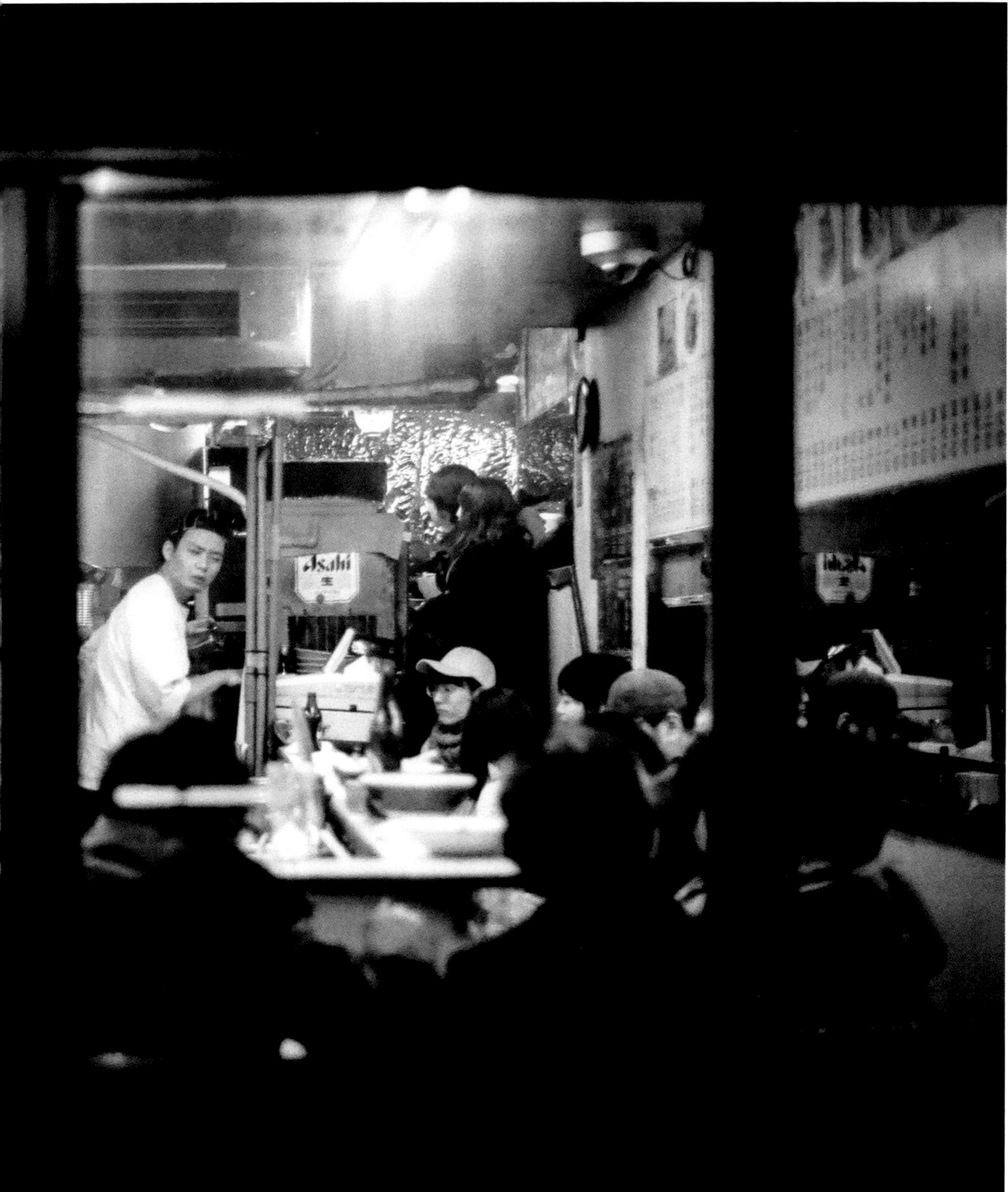

Asahi
生

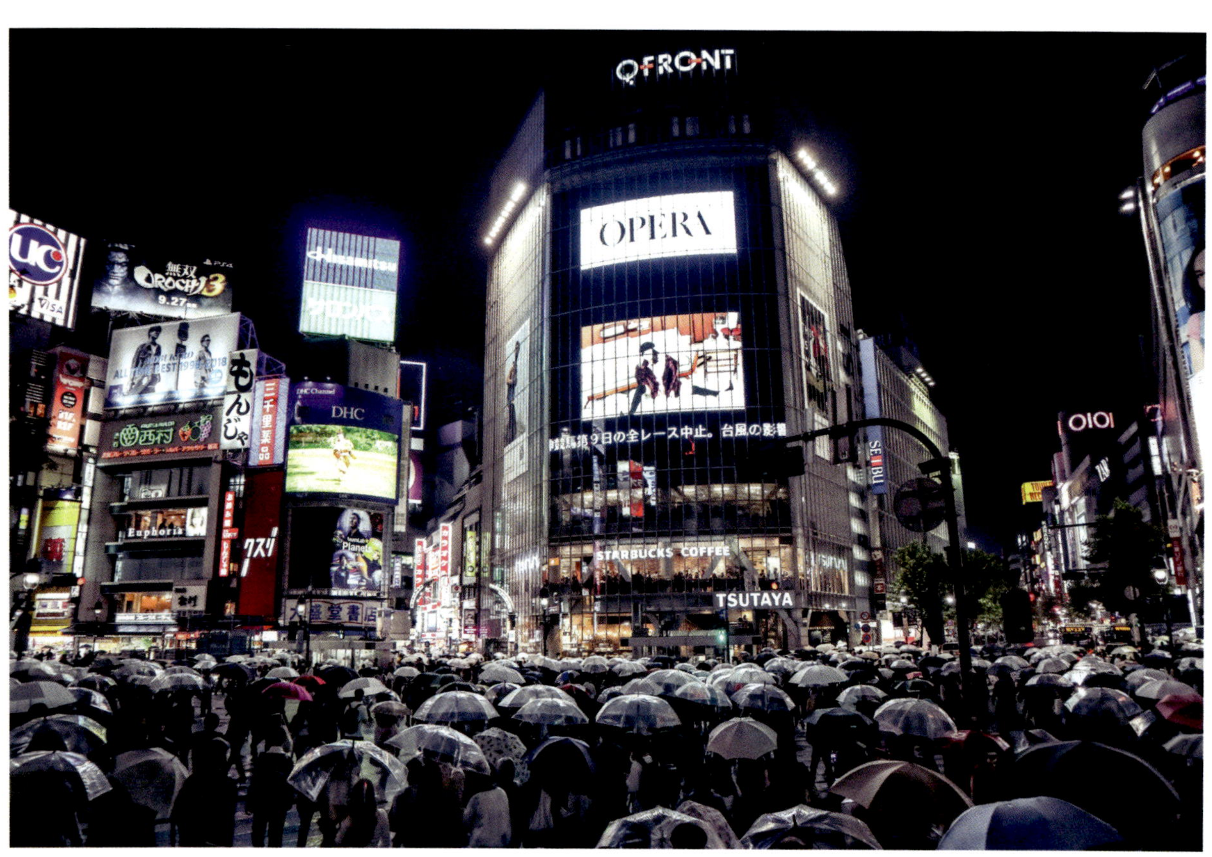
Q FRONT
OPERA
無双 OROCHI 3
9.27
DHC
西村
もんじゃ
クスリ
Euphoria
Planet
STARBUCKS COFFEE
TSUTAYA
SEIBU
OIOI

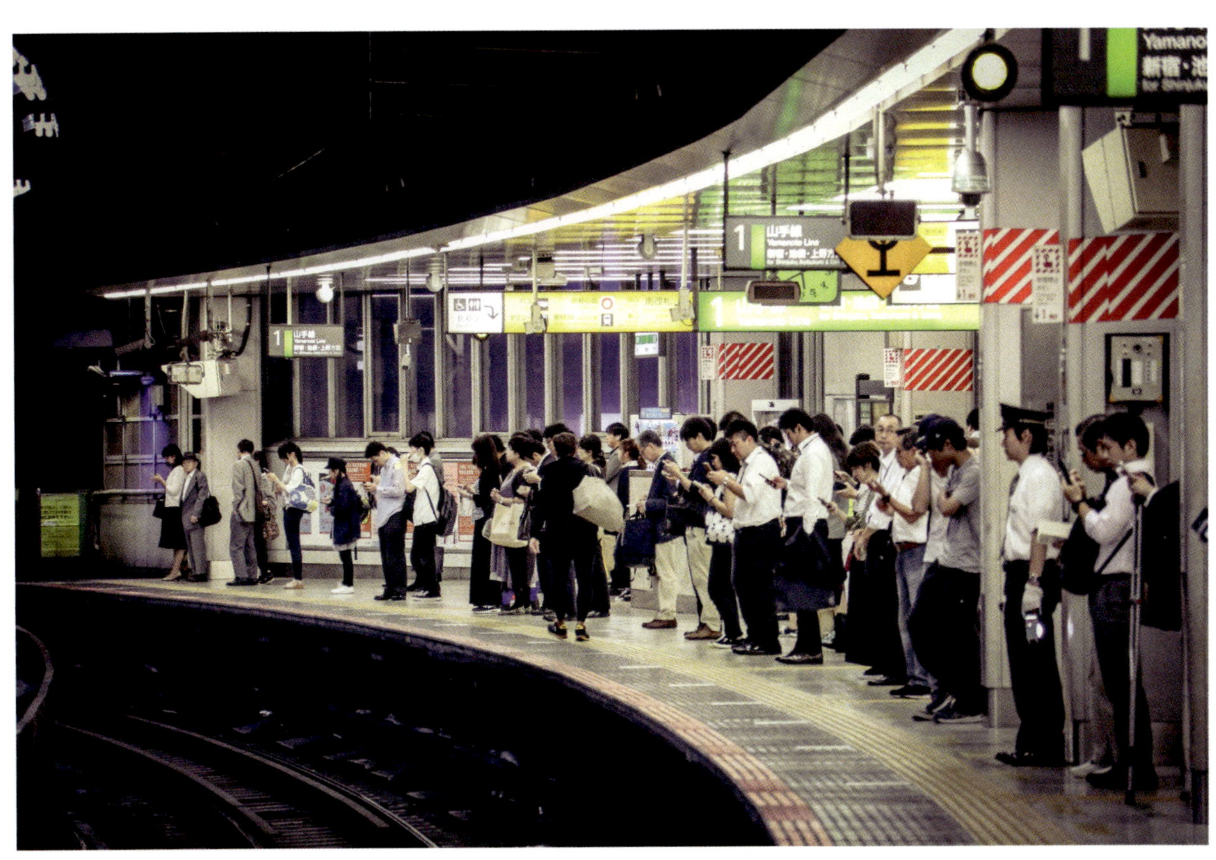

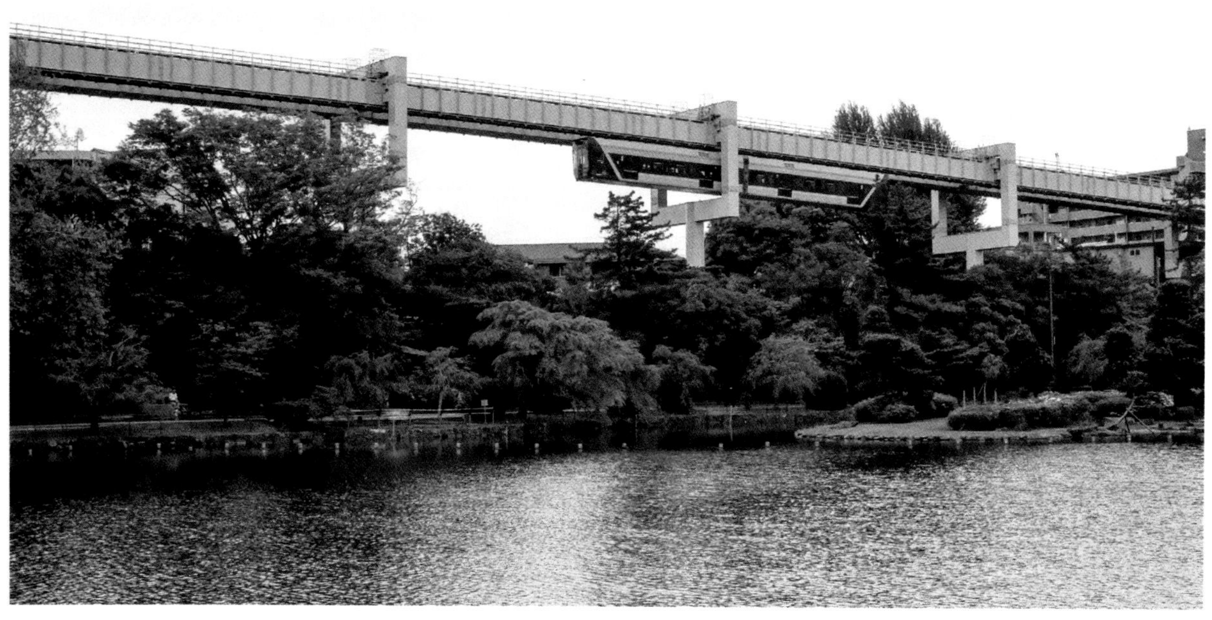

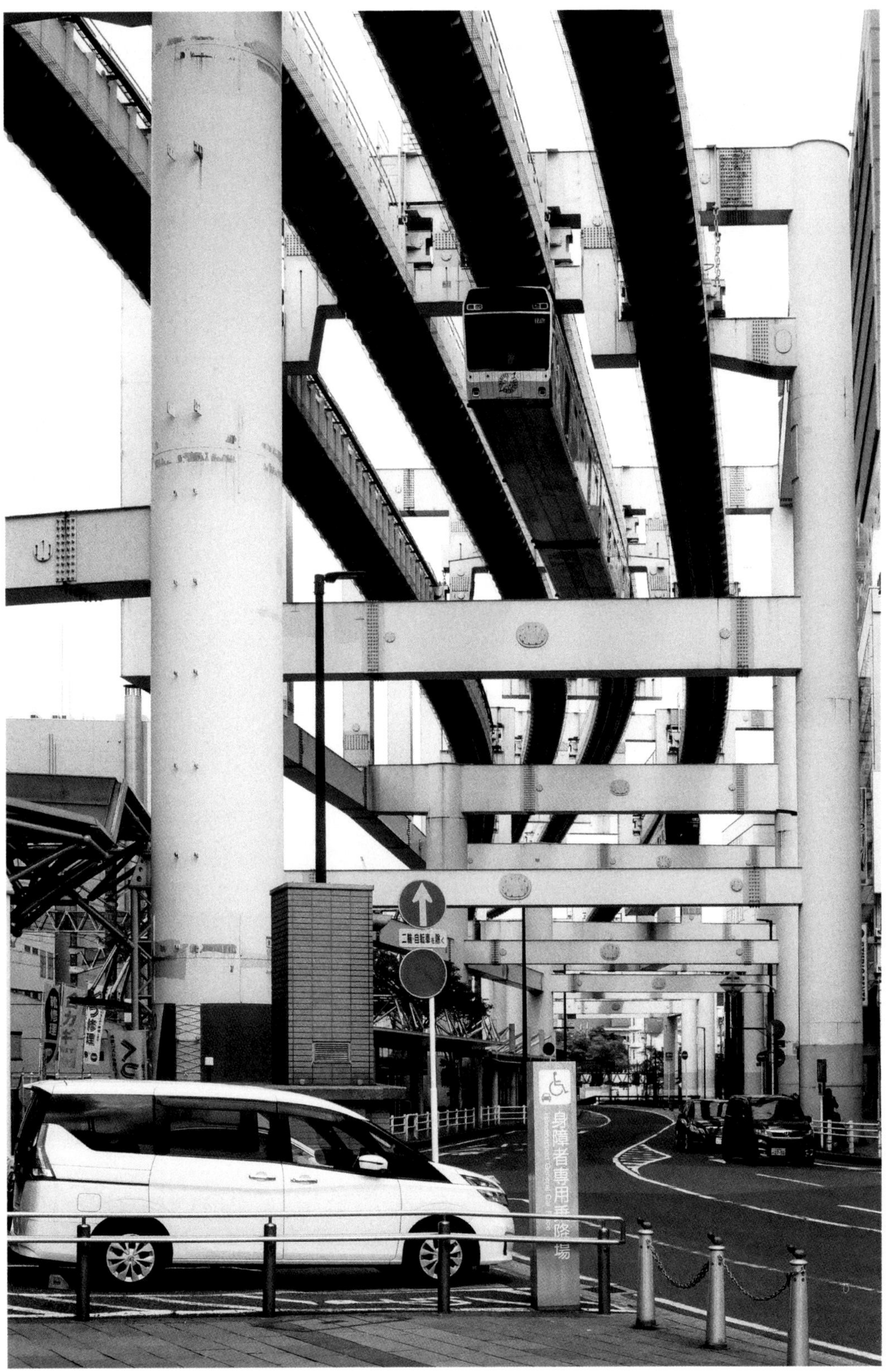

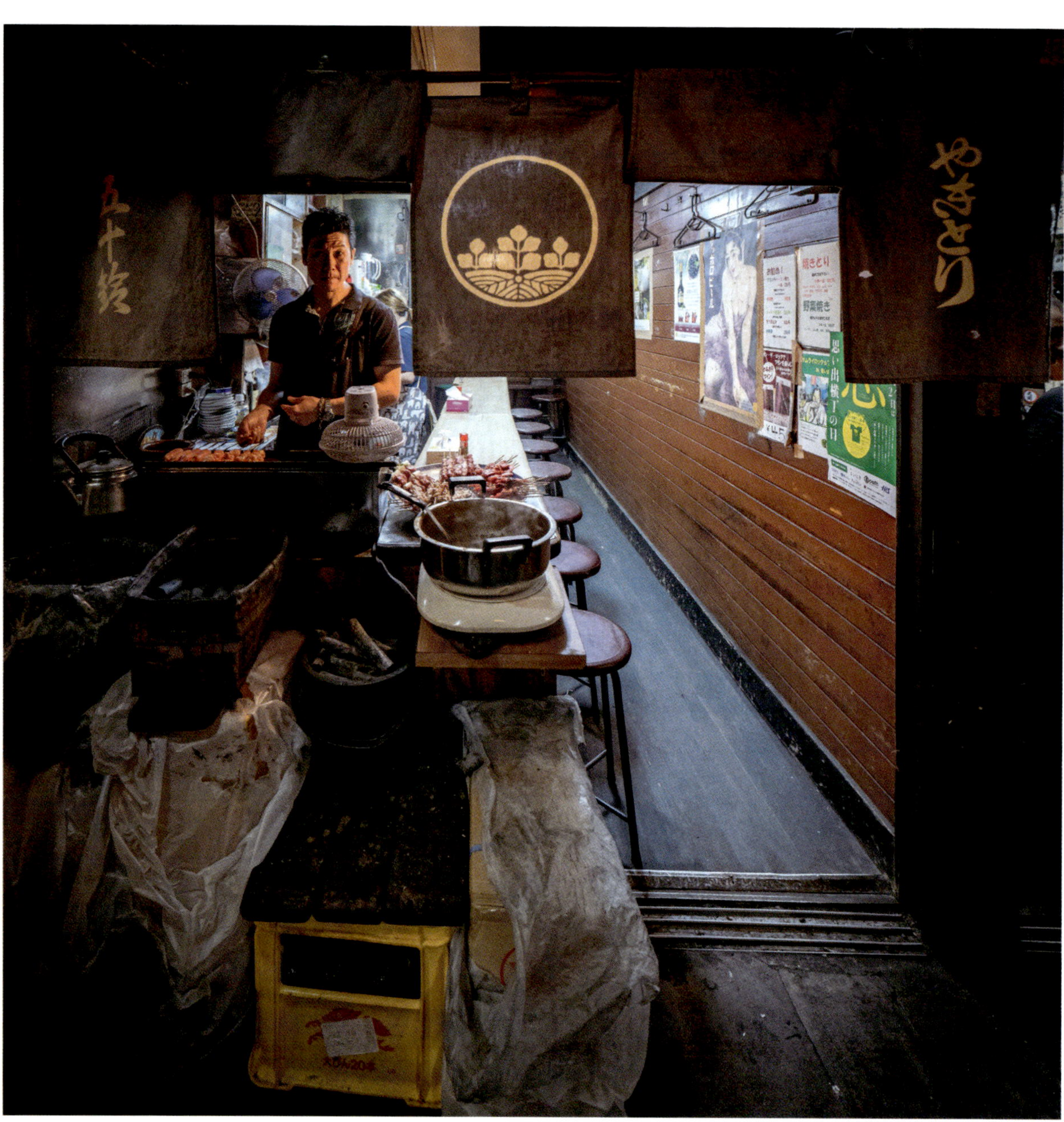
五十鈴
やきとり
焼きとり

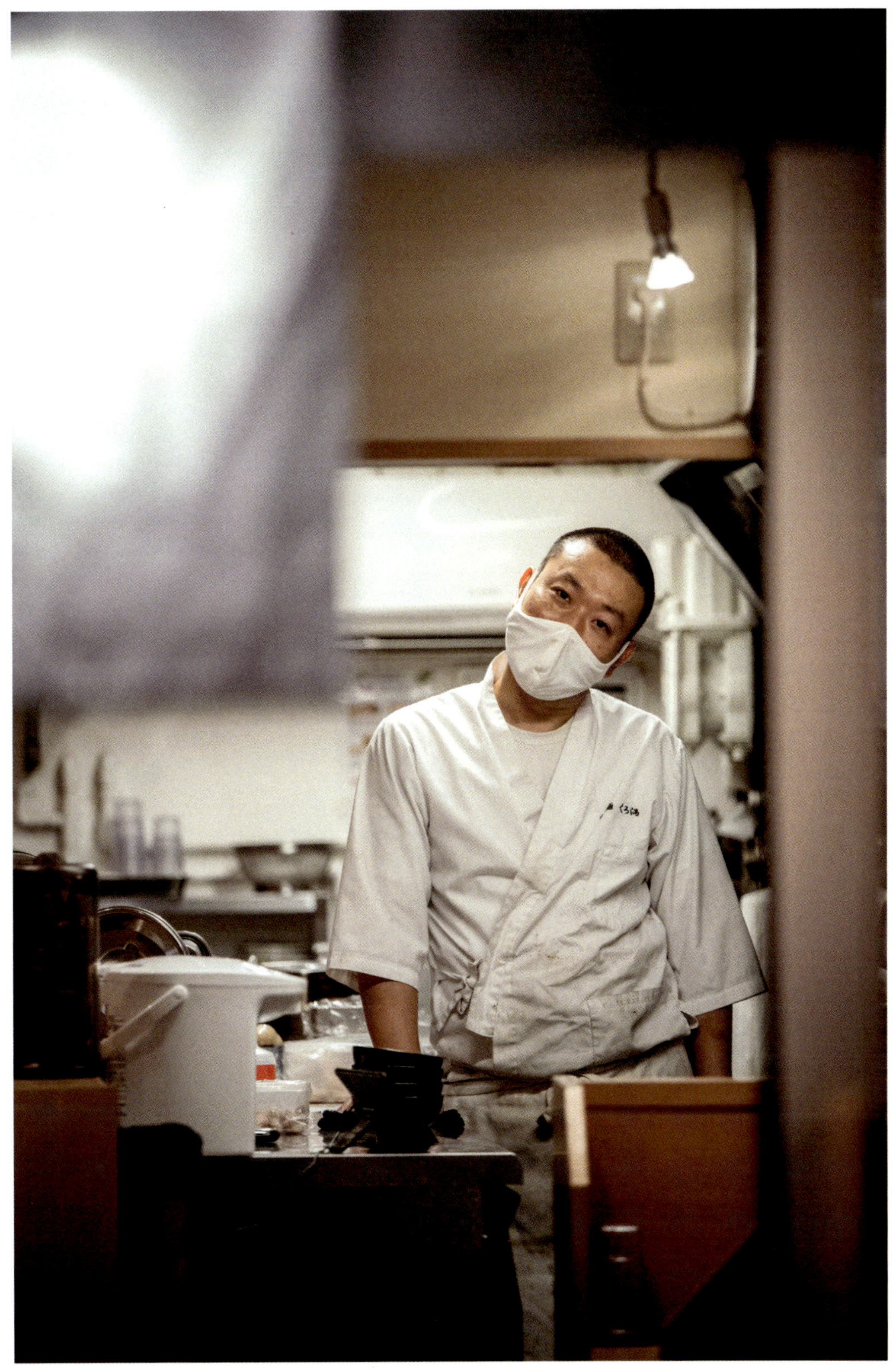

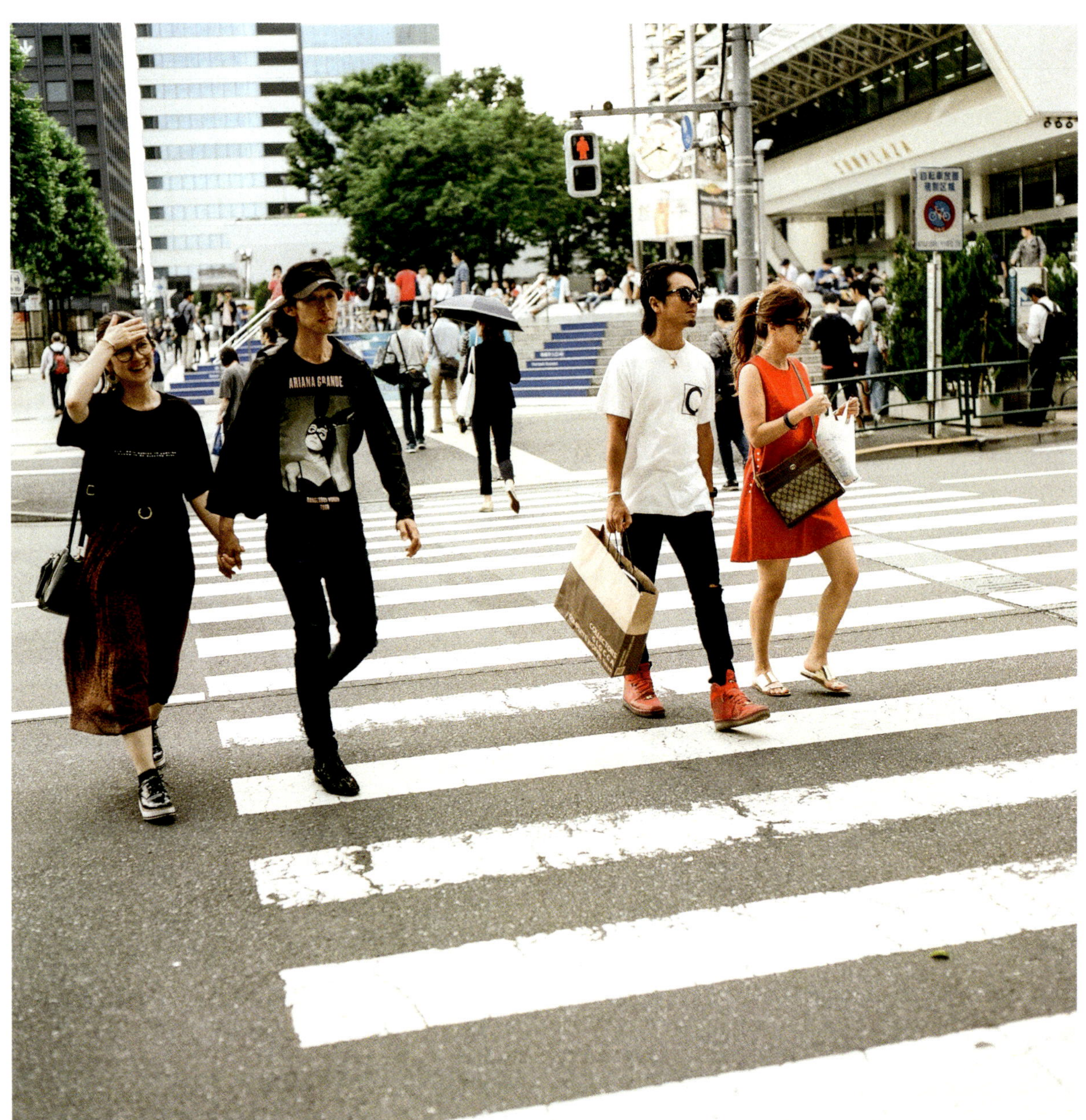

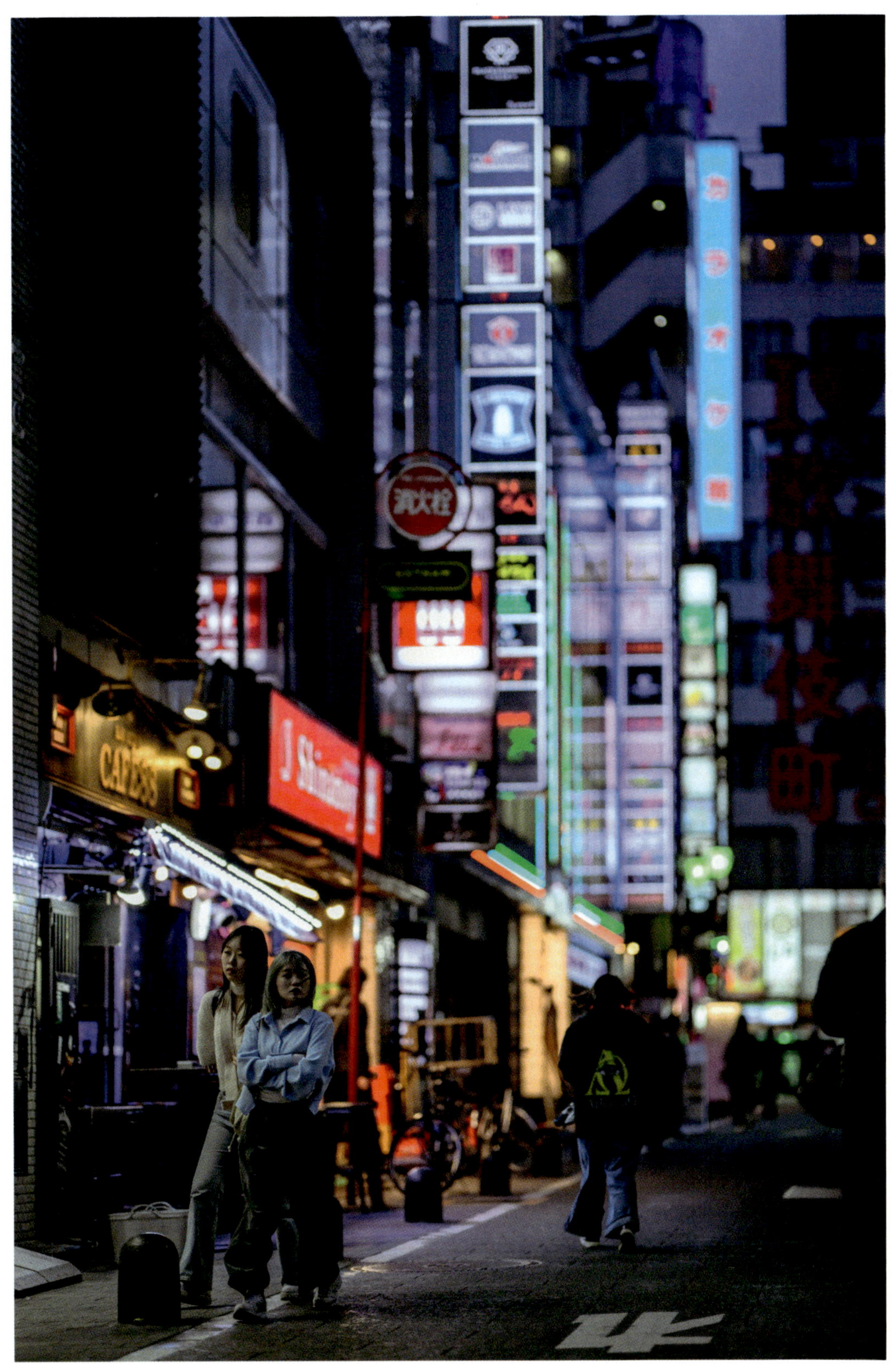
CARESS
Shimura
消火栓
歌舞伎町

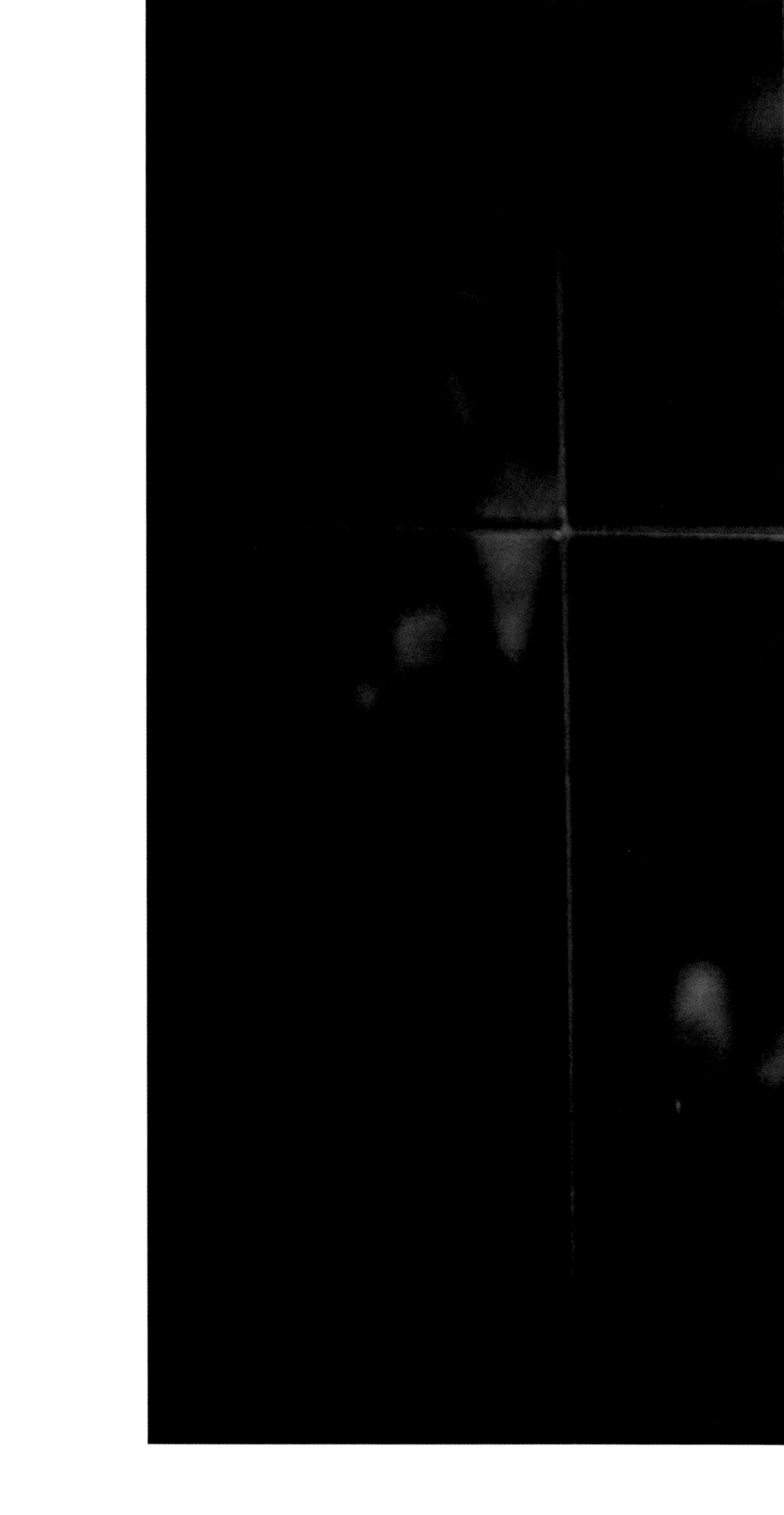

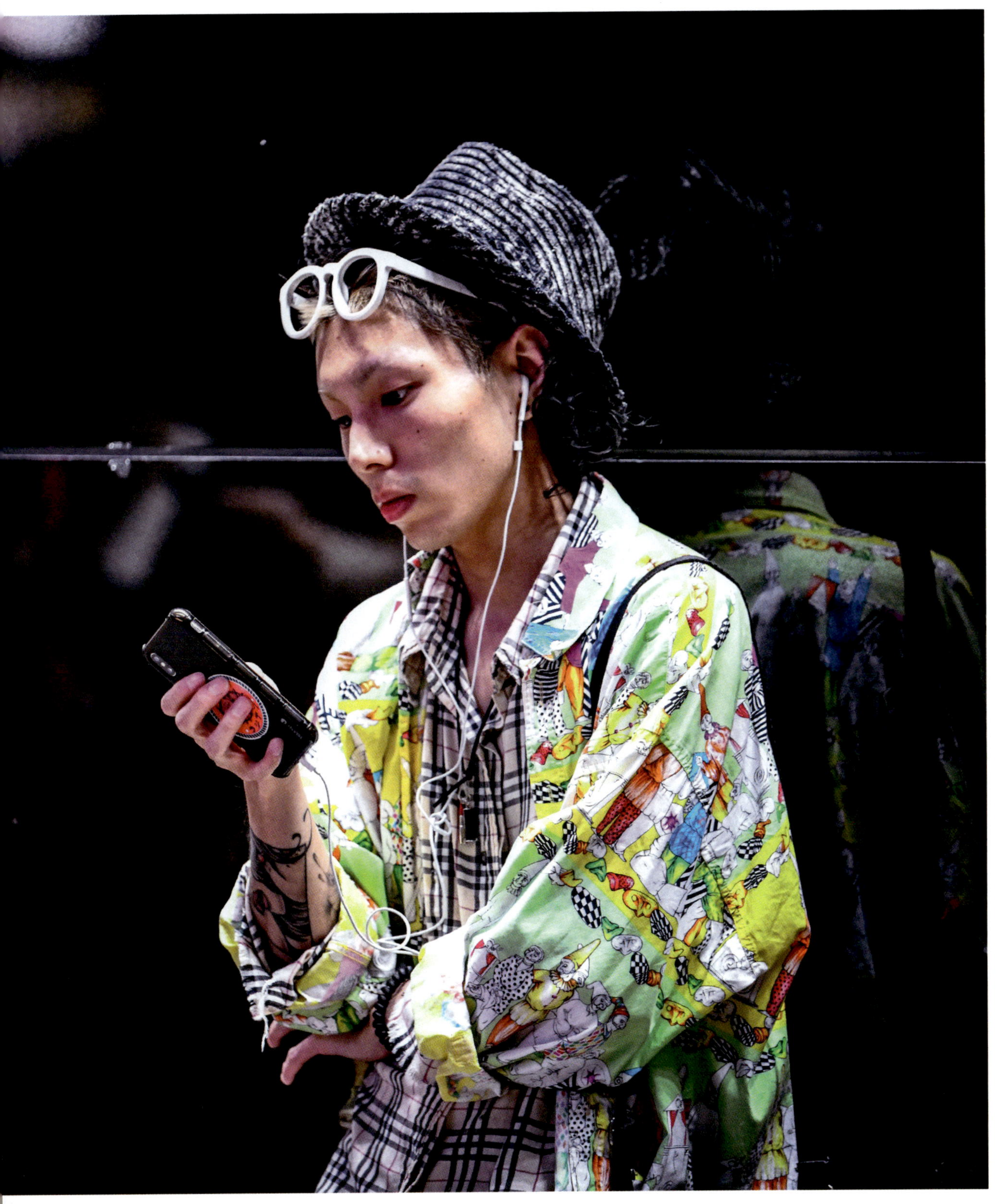

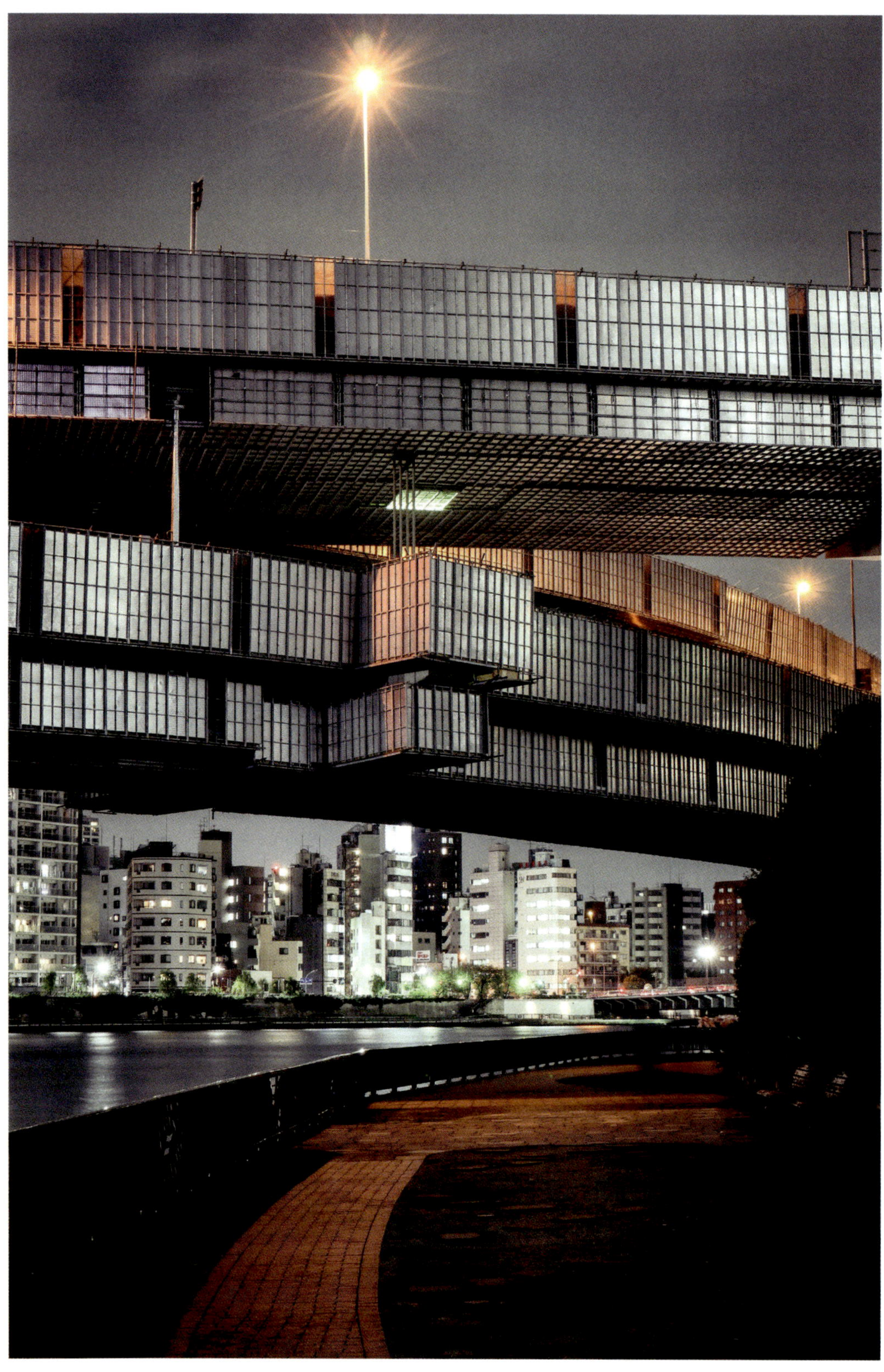

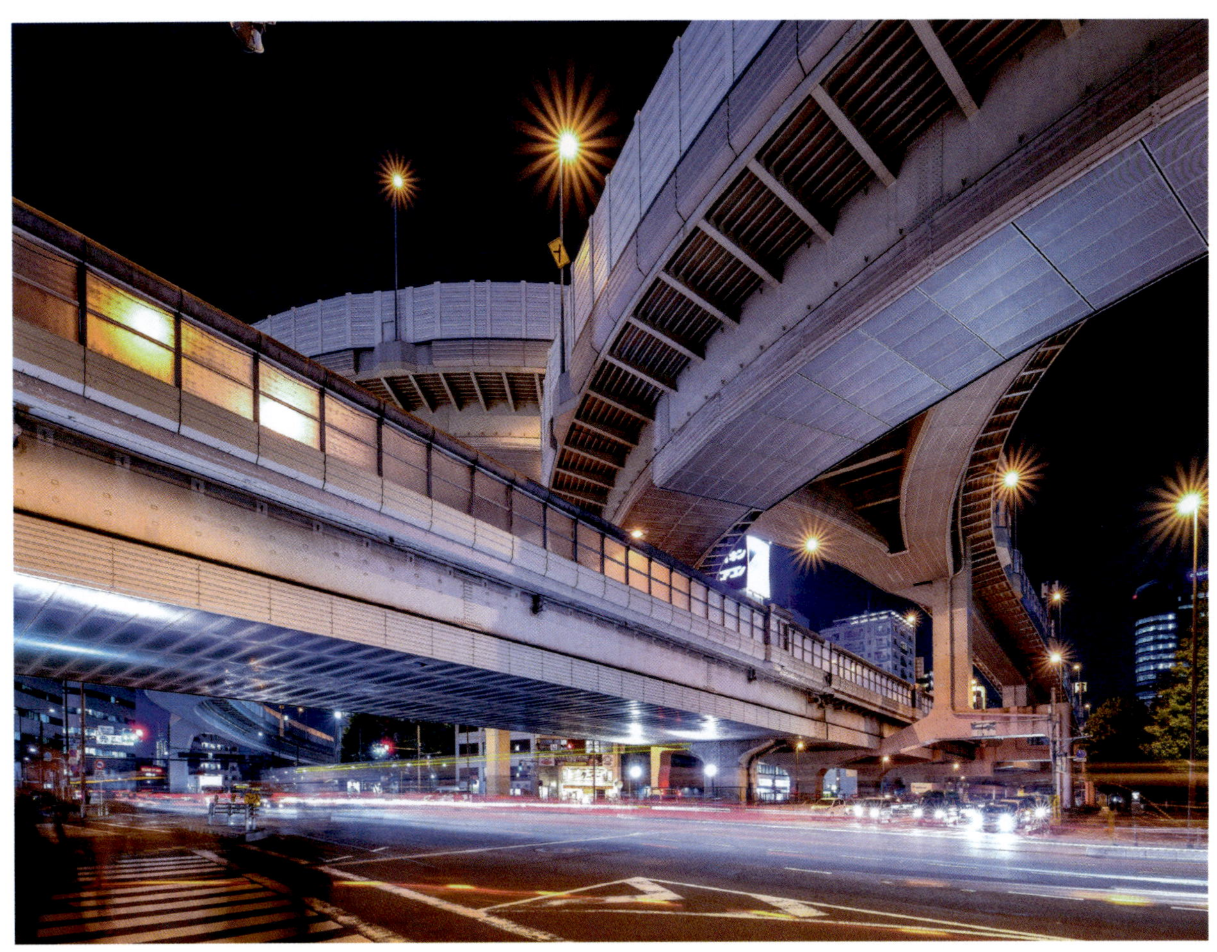

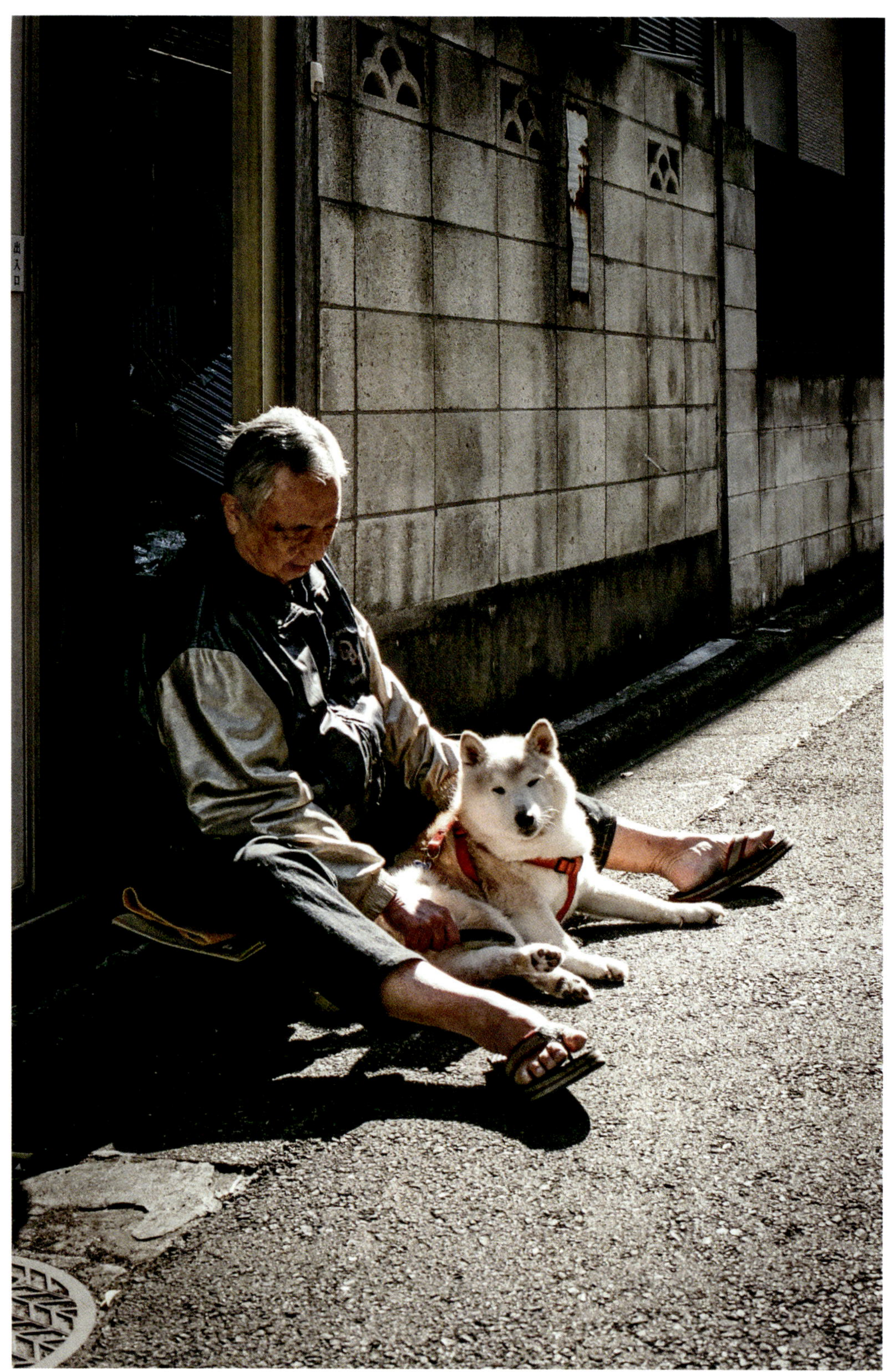
出入口

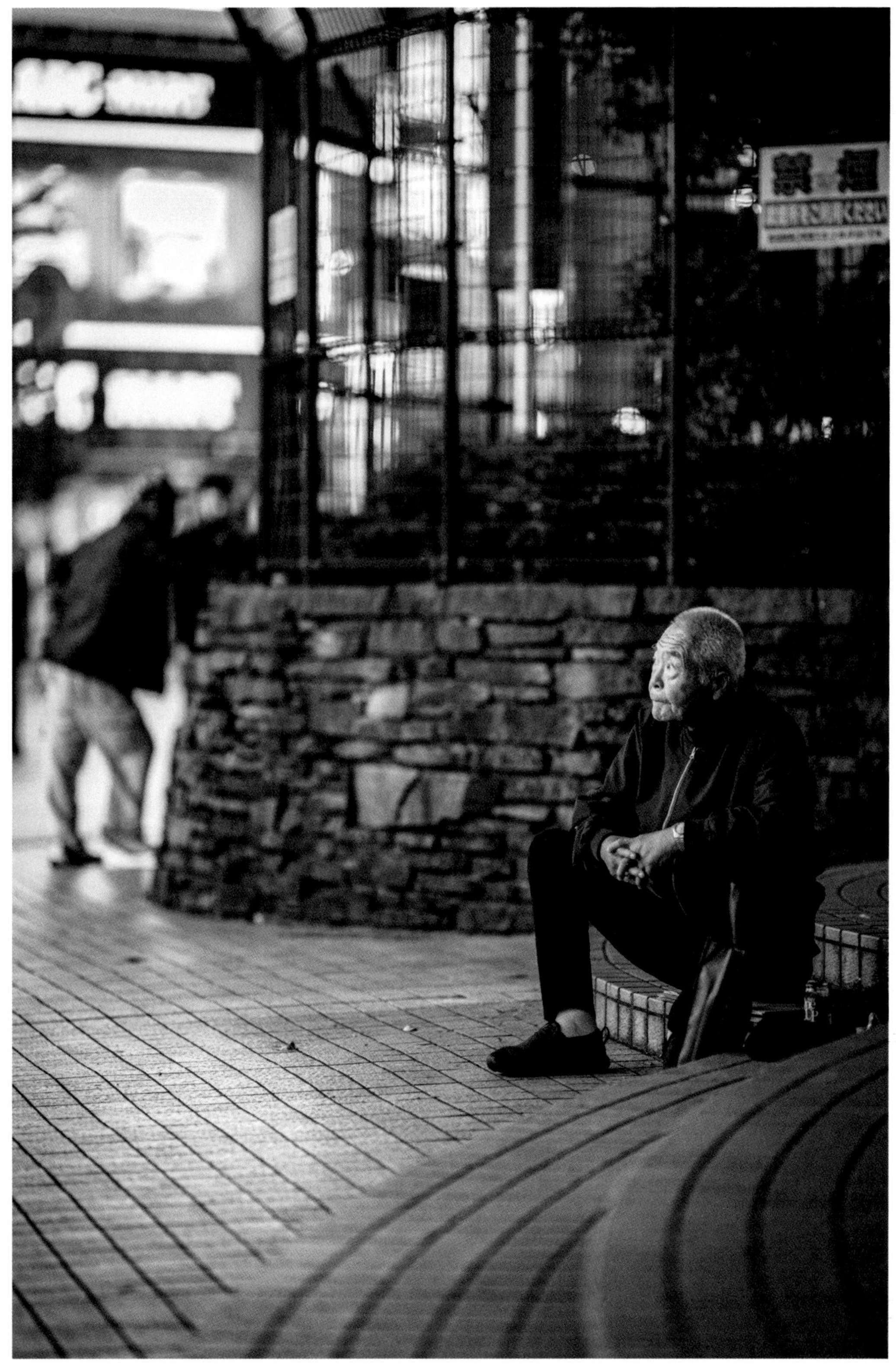

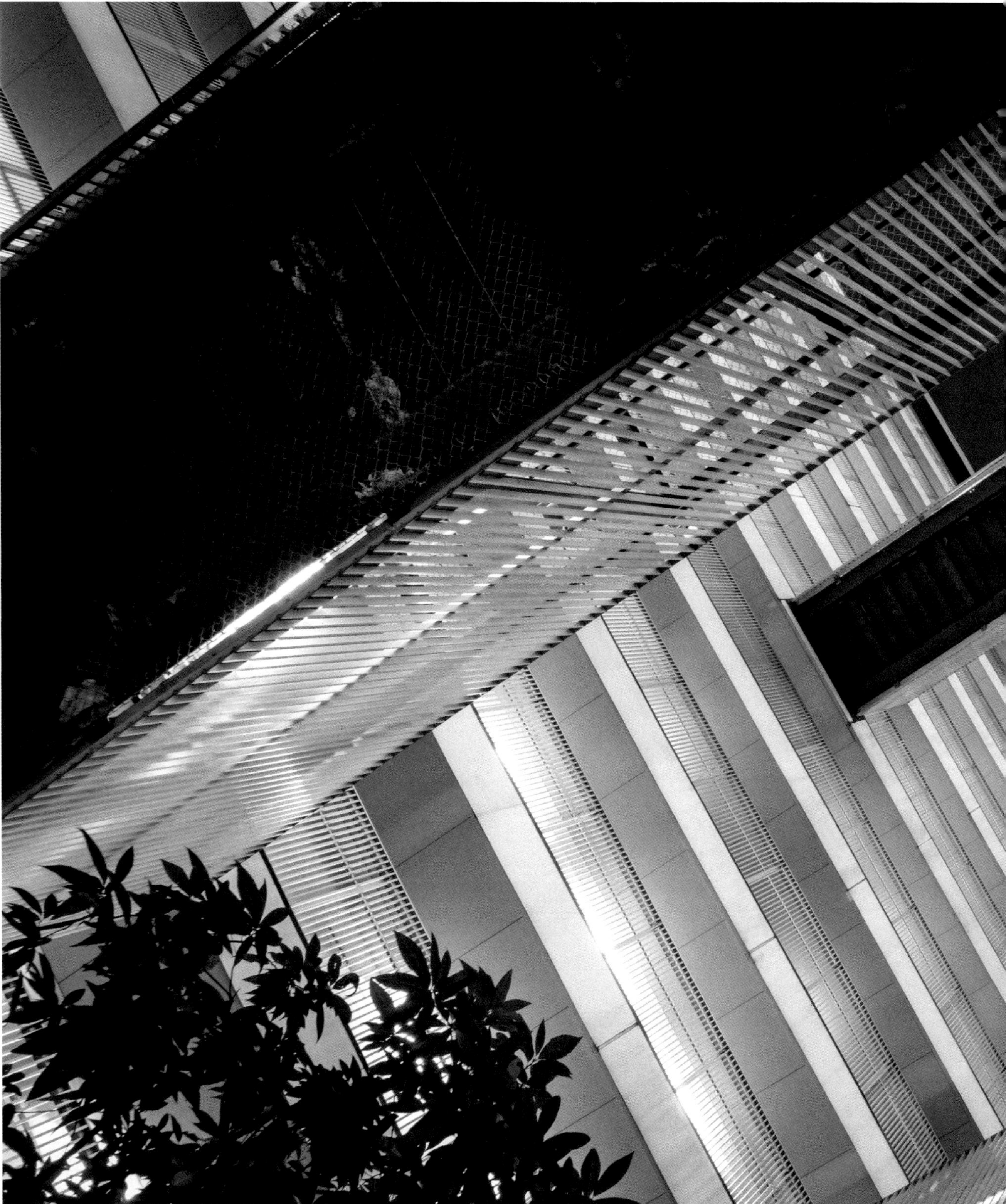

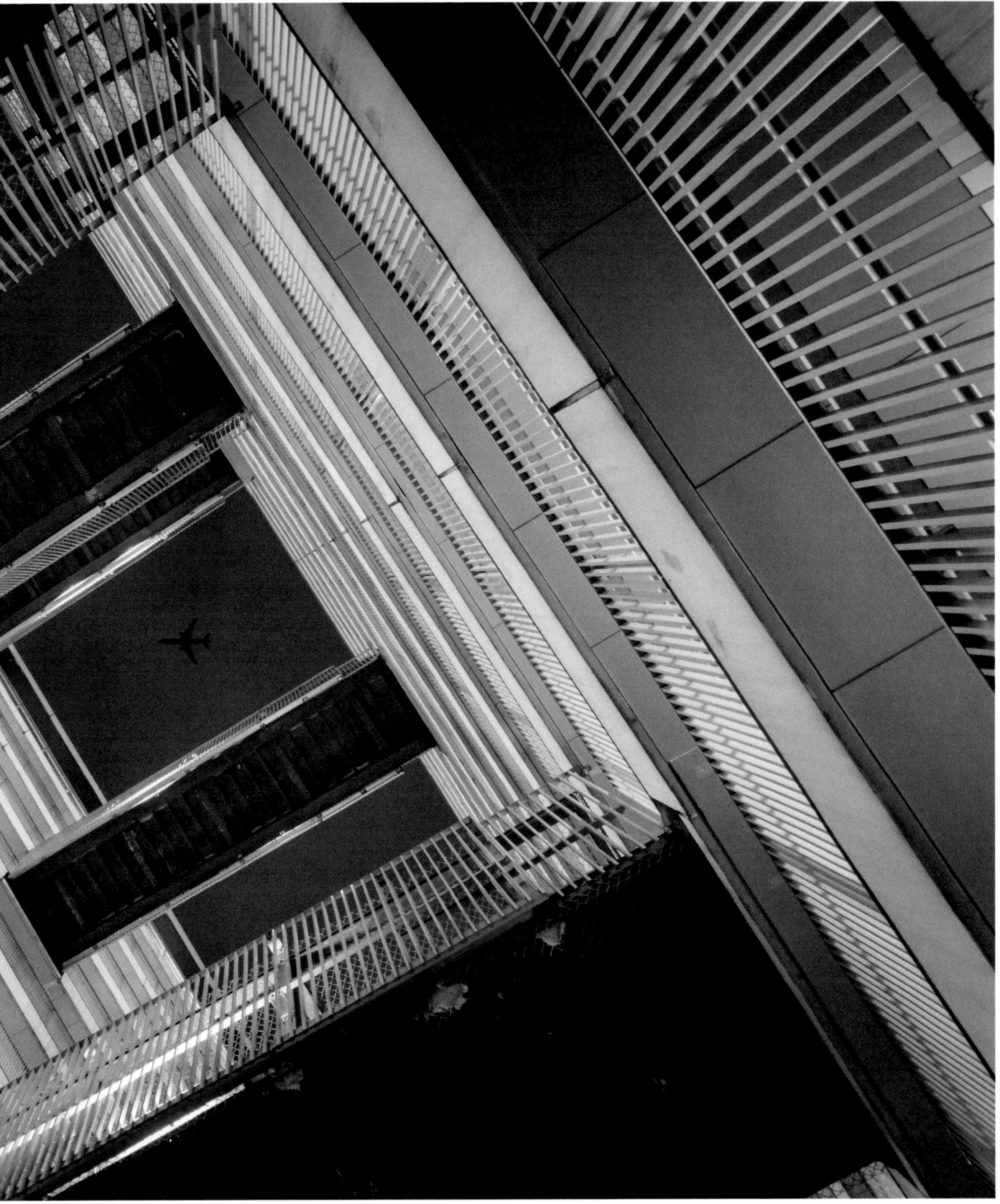

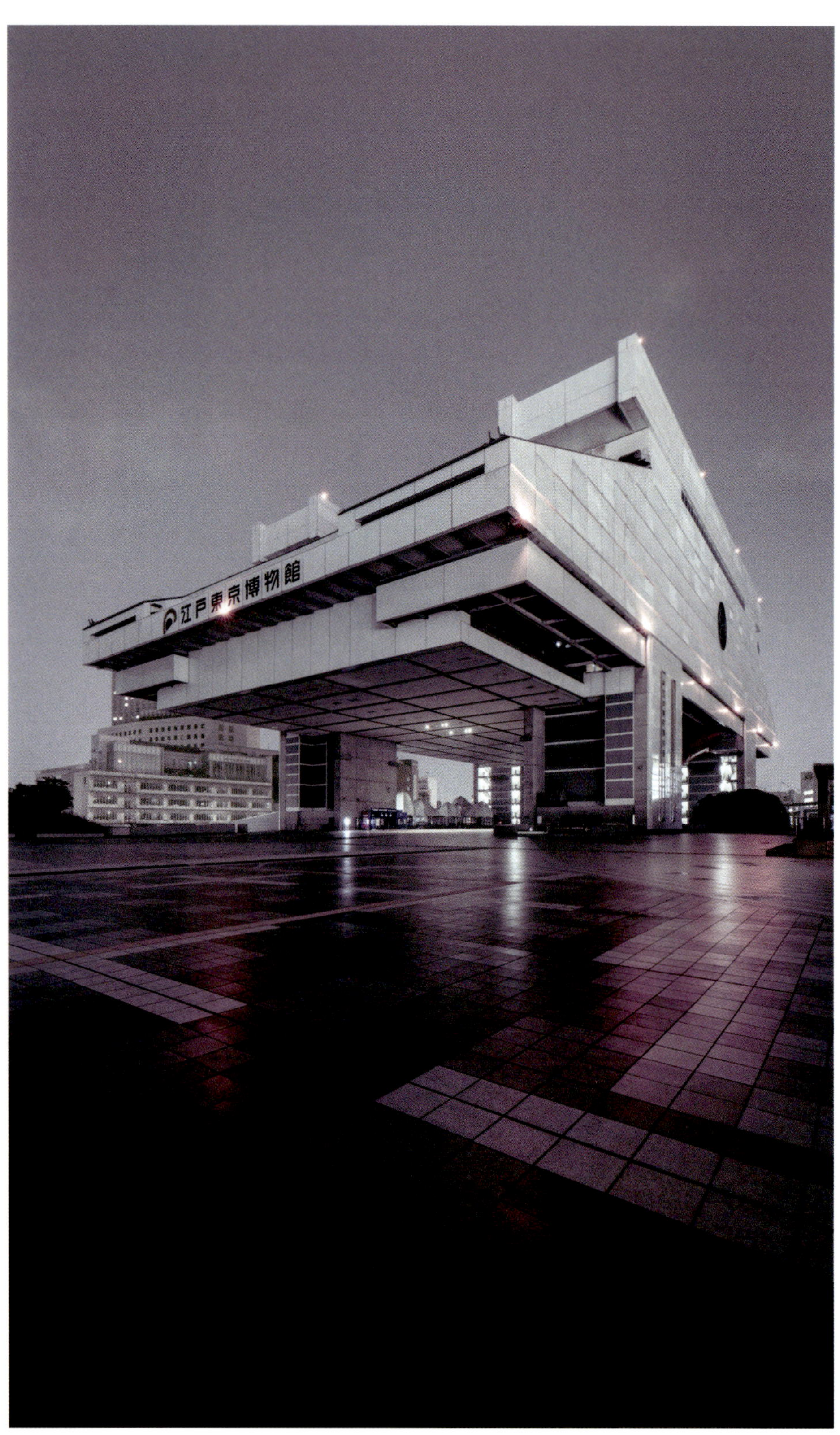

江戸東京博物館

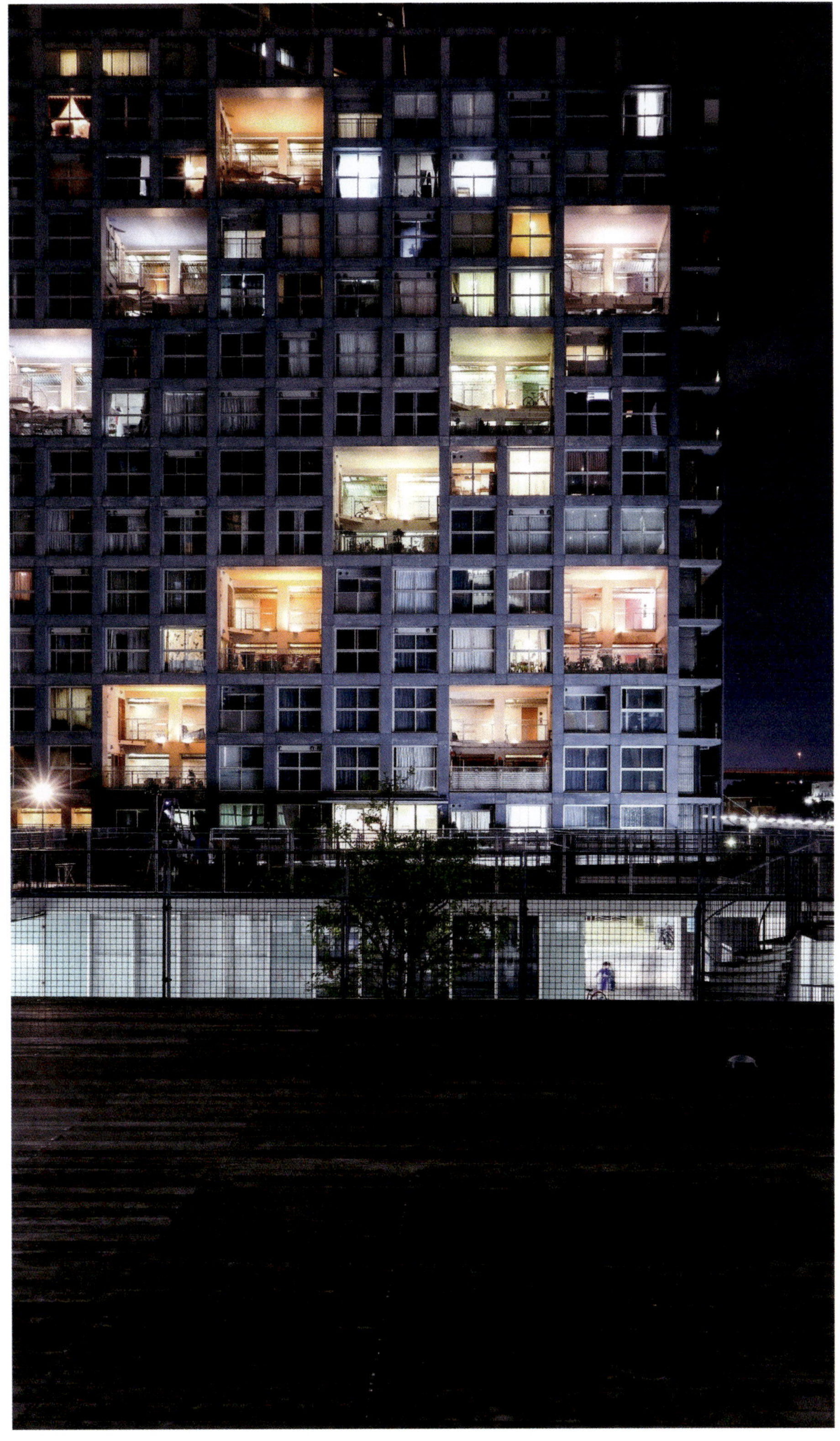

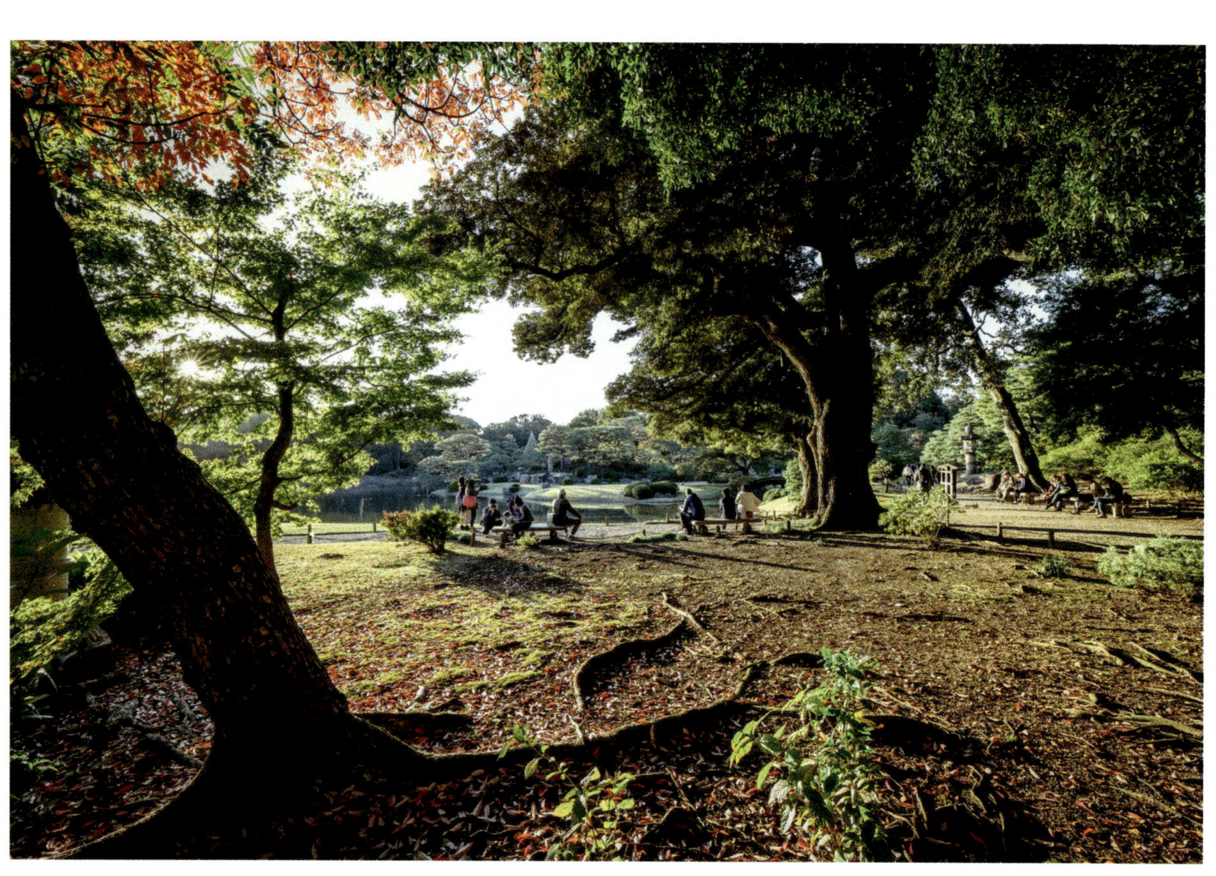

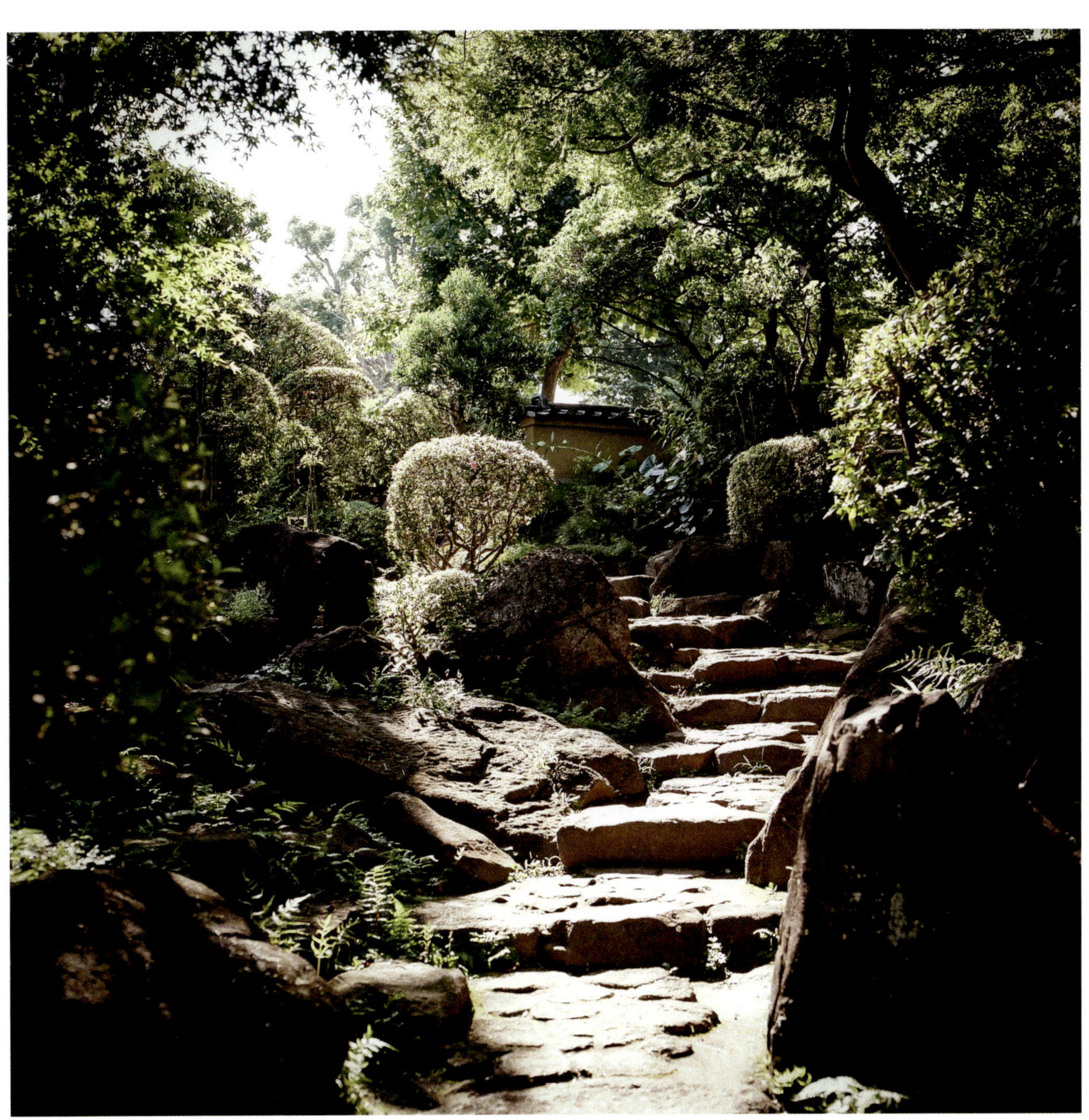

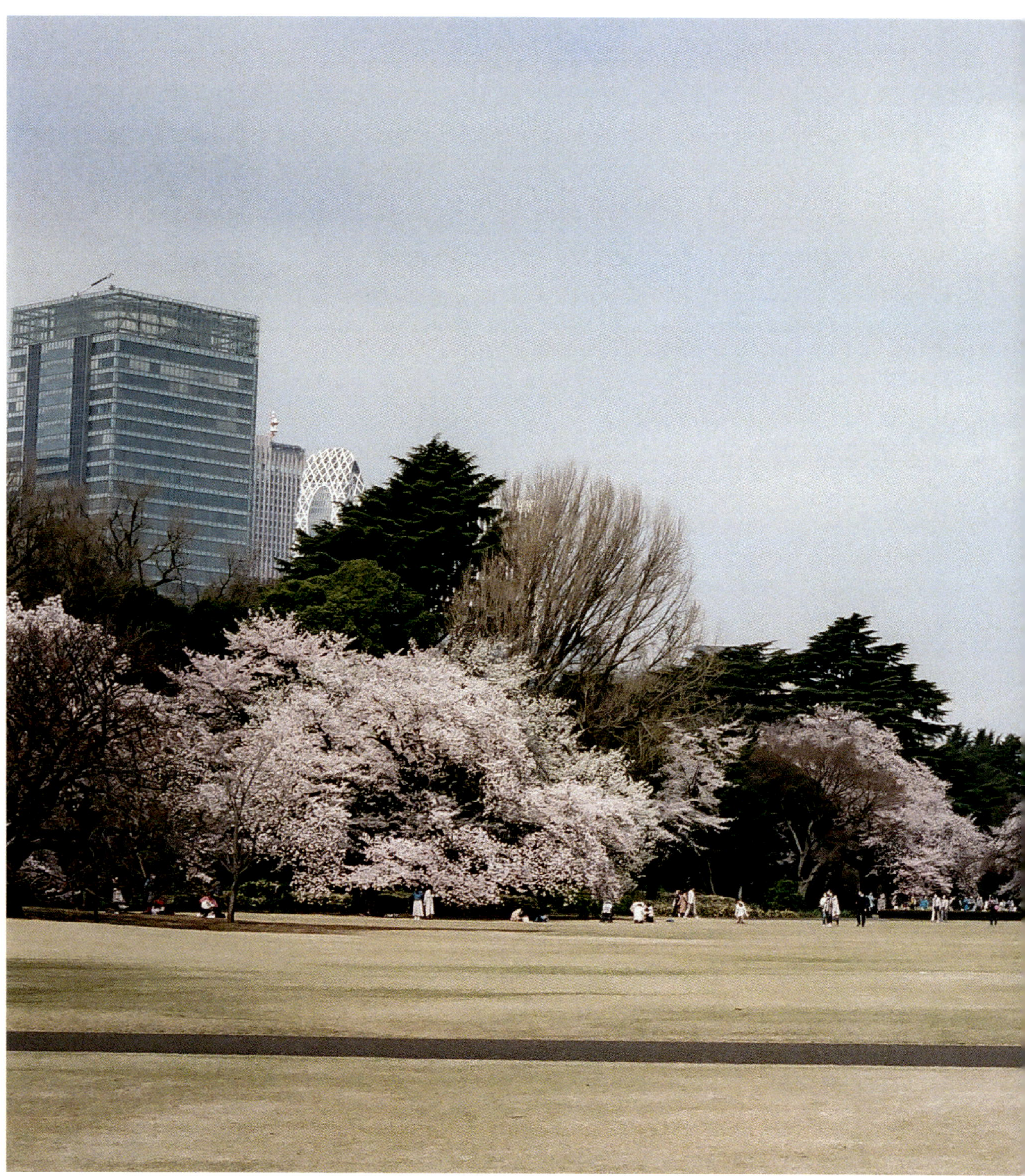

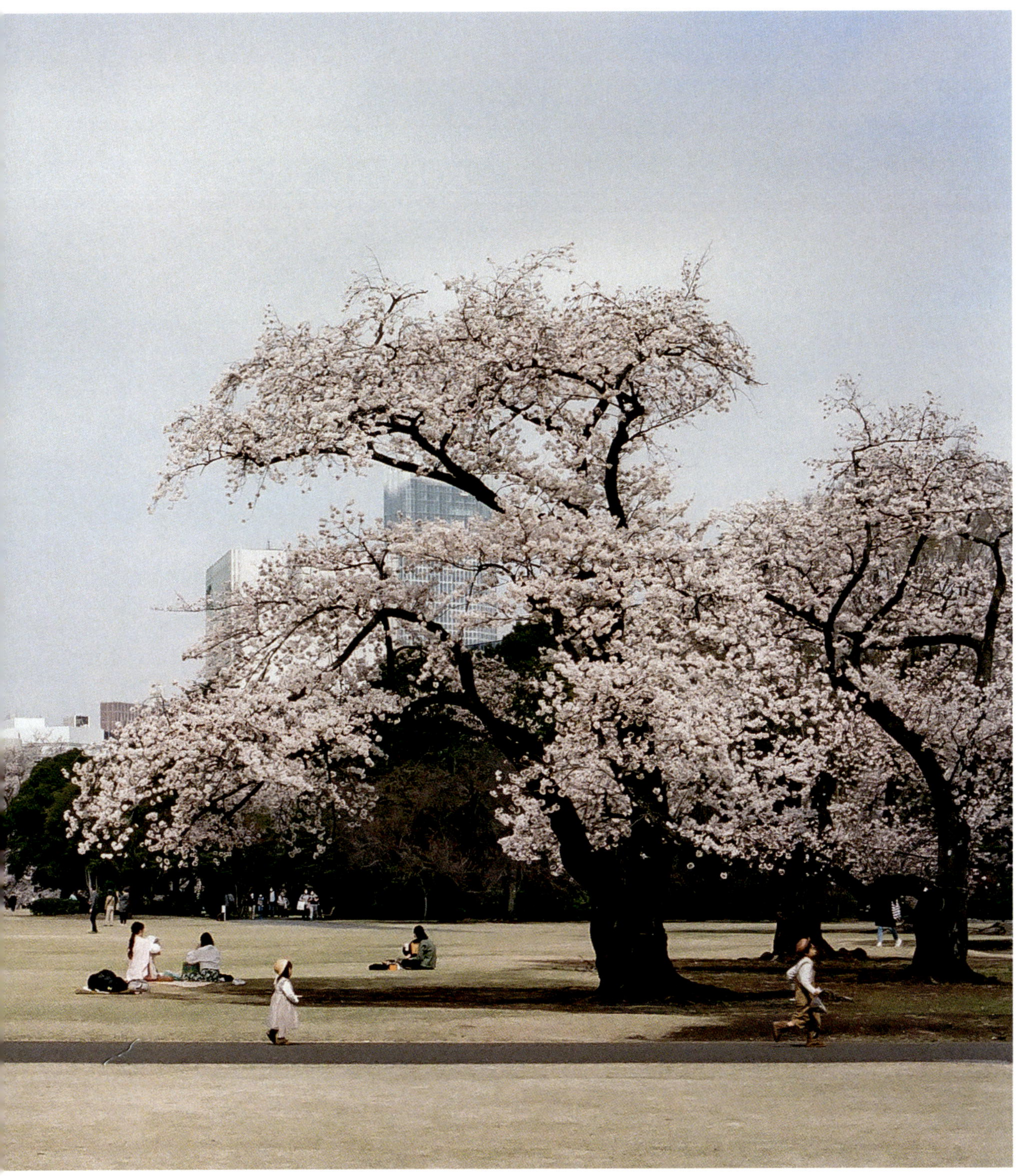

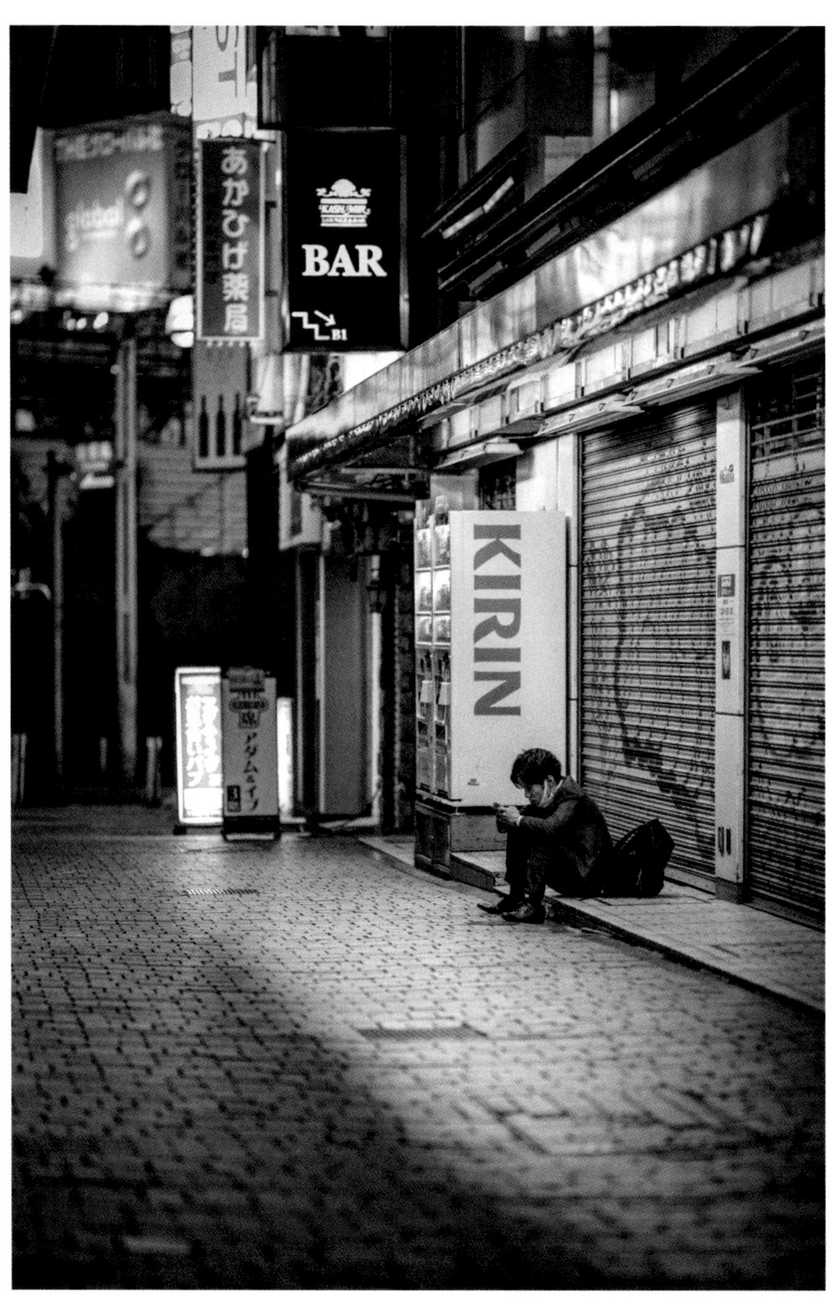
あかひげ薬局
BAR
B1
KIRIN

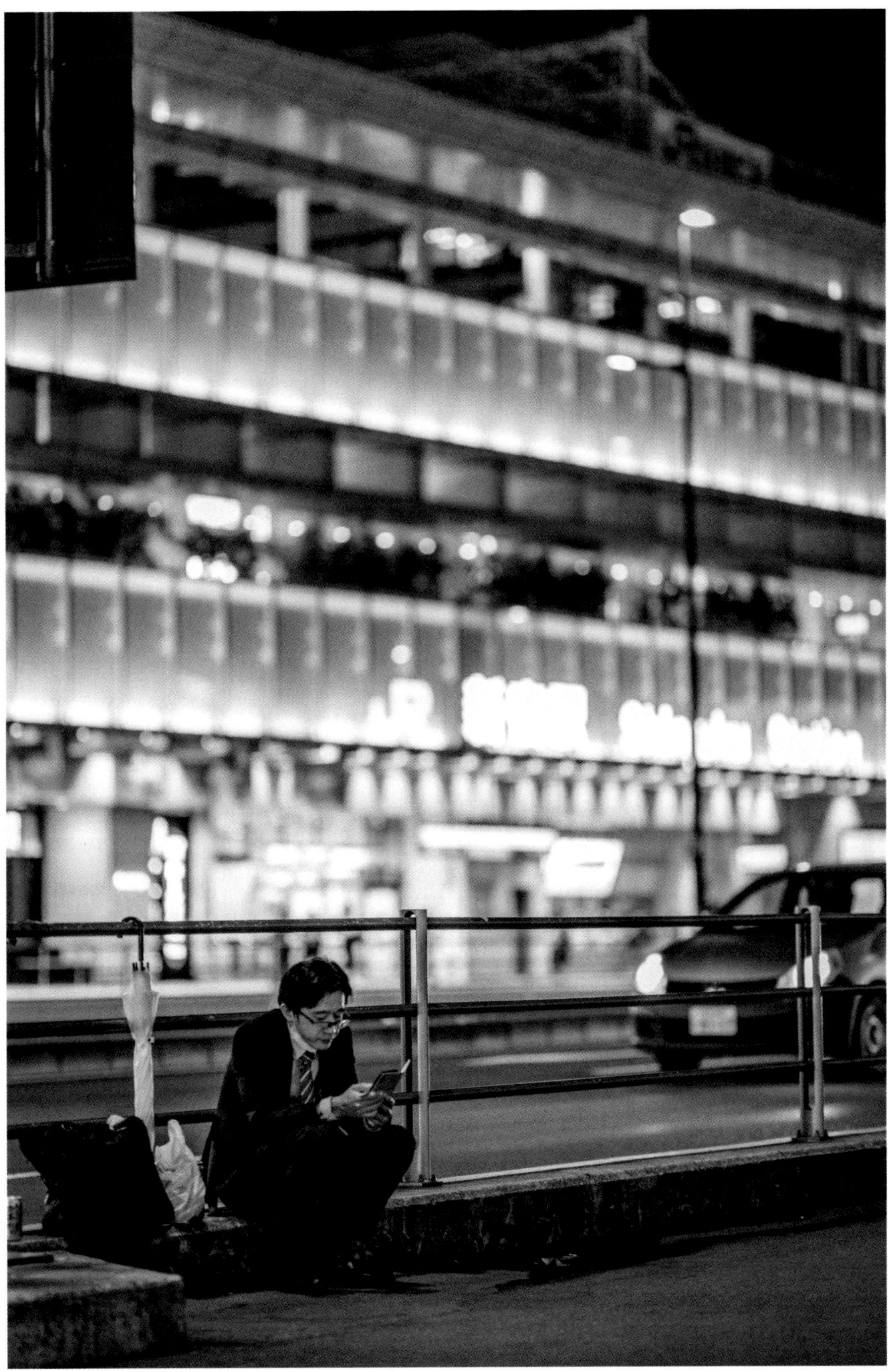

PART TWO: PHOTOGRAPHY AS THERAPY

Photography has become a fundamental part of my therapy. It is usually a solitary hobby, something which makes it even more precious. I have always been a loner. I'm not antisocial, nor am I a *hikikomori*, as they call it here in Japan; while I cherish time with friends and family, I deeply value my solitary moments. It's my way of restoring inner balance and resetting the system. I lived alone for several years, here in Japan and beforehand in Venice, and I cherish those memories. In Venice, I decided to live alone precisely because of the illness, not because I needed to. The university was a few kilometres from my parents' house; I could have commuted from there like I did for the first five years of study. But after graduation, and especially after the breakup with my ex, I needed my own space. I also wanted to hide my fragile state from my parents. They recognised my suffering but couldn't fathom the depth of the solitary hell I'd created for myself. In Venice, I could heal on my own, but I made the mistake of seeing a solution in work rather than in psychotherapy. The latter seemed like a long, uncertain path – not to mention costly – while work yielded immediate results. Upon reflection, I see how wrong I was.

In Venice, I divided my time between two architecture studios while immersing myself in university life through a research fellowship and two teaching positions. Though the studio work was unpaid, my university commitments provided my livelihood.

During my spare hours, I collaborated with friends on minor architectural competitions. These contests held the potential to alter the course of my career – though whether for better or worse remains uncertain. We garnered special mentions but never claimed first prize.

Living alone had benefits. At my parents' house, I lived with my brother and two sisters, and space sometimes felt limited even though the house wasn't small. I was suffocating beneath a role I could no longer sustain – I was anything but well. Though no one had dismissed my condition as mere moodiness, the fear of such dismissal haunted me. I masked my struggles to spare others worry, yet found myself desperately craving solitude like oxygen.

Now that I have a family of my own, time alone has almost totally disappeared, which has impacted my personality and mental state. I don't blame my family; it's just more challenging for me to manage domestic commitments. Everything requires more effort, and is too much to handle. Daily interactions become a burden, each moment of companionship deepening my despair. Yet paradoxically, I need more support than ever – a difficult thing to secure while maintaining the facade of a capable caregiver and parent. I generally like children a lot, but caregiving is an exhausting job, especially for those with chronic fatigue.

Sumire's parents still work, so we don't heavily rely on them for help with the children. A babysitter is also beyond our financial means. Everything falls on us, and especially on Sumire, who, in addition to taking care of them, often takes care of me too. She knows that in the worst moments, she has to let me sleep as much as possible. She'll go to a friend's place, taking the children with her. Between solitude and sleep, I slowly recover, and after a few days, I manage to start functioning again.

During my darkest bouts of depression, tension manifests physically – pockets of pain scattered throughout my body, from my heart to my ribs and back. These sharp aches signal a need to quiet my nerves and retreat into restorative solitude.

The doctor advised me to eliminate non-essential commitments beyond work and family. Though my schedule was already dominated by work, I learned to decline additional responsibilities and guard against new sources of stress. At first, my therapist viewed my photography excursions as frivolous strain – only later recognizing them as therapeutic respite.

Illness breeds a necessary selfishness, with solitude as its natural companion – a survival mechanism, much like the airplane safety protocol of securing your own oxygen mask before helping others. The body enforces its own boundaries: dialogue becomes taxing, concentration on others' words feels impossible, even with family. You retreat into a hermetic shell, instinctively rejecting anything nonessential to survival. This isn't mere self-centeredness, but rather a functional withdrawal.

In my deepest crises, solitude became vital. After work, I would wander the city streets, postponing my return home, dreading the weight of paternal and spousal responsibilities. I'd arrive late even when unnecessary, ensuring the children were already asleep – a calculated delay born of self-preservation.

The condition also impacts appetite. You eat too little or too much, and you eat without pleasure. You do minimal work, and the passions that once made you happy become mere routines.

Depression forces me to slow down – life unfolds in slow motion, as if you're underwater. I can accomplish only a few things each day, and even that feels like triumph. Achieving these modest daily goals becomes not just a challenge, but a calling.

When Covid forced most people into isolation, many struggled with the sudden seclusion. Yet in Japan, where restrictions were less severe, I found myself strangely adapted to this new reality. I hadn't socialised with friends for months, yet felt no significant void. The illness had already diminished my appetite for parties and celebrations – even before the pandemic, I struggled to summon genuine smiles at children's birthdays and anniversaries.

My wife Sumire struggles with loneliness and always needs people around her. She initially had some difficulty understanding why I needed my own space and moments of solitude, both at home and elsewhere. But once she understood my nature, she made every effort to ensure I was granted my time off, whenever I felt the need to be alone. Photography is part of my time off. In those moments, I have no worries, and I quickly recover from many hours of stress. It's not an easy hobby. It's expensive and requires hours of study and preparation. It's also physically demanding, especially when using certain cameras and lenses. Often my backpack weighs more than it should – a testament to my inability to leave any camera or lens behind. Each piece of equipment feels essential, despite the strain on my shoulders.

The parallel between my improving mental health and intensifying photographic practice is unmistakable. Visual expression has always been my natural language, beginning with drawing – a passion that led me through art school and ultimately to architecture. Though self-taught in photography, my architectural training proved invaluable, honing my eye for proportion, composition, and geometry. Whether capturing buildings or people, my architectural background reveals itself in every frame – a fact observers often note.

My photographic journey began in earnest during high school, learning from two talented friends who generously shared their expertise. The passion followed me to

Tokyo, where it intensified alongside my first encounters with depression in the city. When my old Canon failed, Ryo's impending arrival provided the perfect excuse for new equipment. We chose the Canon M6 – a versatile camera that could accommodate both Sumire's need for automatic settings and my preference for manual control, its compact size making it an ideal companion.

I had it with me even on the day of the accident. I crossed at the green light, my view obscured by construction barriers. A car ran the red, violently striking the back of my bike and throwing me several metres. My unprotected head struck the road, blood pooling beneath me. Olympic Stadium construction workers rushed to help, along with the driver who'd hit me. When the paramedics arrived, the language barrier loomed – until an African construction worker stepped forward. Through his translation from Japanese to French, I managed to communicate using my rusty high school French. A few days in the hospital and several stitches later, I was released, grateful that scans had revealed no internal bleeding.

The driver of the car worked for a wedding agency that had a dedicated office for inconveniences, a kind of complaints office. The head of department was a middle-aged man who sat by my bedside throughout the hospital stay, apologising to me. It didn't matter if I told him everything was okay; he wouldn't leave, and every time I turned around, he would bow and apologise for what had happened to me because of one of their employees.

Unfortunately, the camera along with the two lenses I had with me were broken beyond repair. Insurance covered all damages, and I decided that with the compensation I would buy a Nikon D850, which was my workhorse until recently, when I bought the new Nikon Z8. Later, I discovered the allure of film photography and acquired a Hasselblad 503cx. The camera has become my constant companion, central to many of my photographic projects.

My father passed down his Olympus OM1n, a 35mm camera that had sat unused for years. I was accumulating a collection of cameras, spanning from past to present.

Japan, with one of the world's highest suicide rates, proves a complex environment for someone battling depression – a situation further intensified by Covid-induced isolation. During my second year in Tokyo, near Kasai Rinkai Koen station, I witnessed a man end his life on the train tracks. I turned away at the last moment, but the incident haunted my dreams for weeks. Even now, when darker thoughts surface, my mind returns to that stranger and his final moments.

My own encounters with suicidal ideation take different forms, ebbing and flowing with the severity of my depression. These thoughts aren't born of desperation, but rather emerge from overwhelming fatigue – a desperate longing to flip an internal switch, to find ultimate solitude.

In dreams of self-destruction, I always find myself either falling into emptiness or sinking beneath waters – methods my mind perhaps perceives as merciful endings. Even in these darkest imaginings, I shy away from violence or pain; there's an ironic fear of suffering in contemplating such a final act. Though these thoughts have subsided for now, my doctor remains vigilant, watching for what he terms 'red flags'.
Behind the lens, I find perfect isolation – regardless of location or crowd. I call it Shooting Therapy. The ritual is simple: hold breath, slow down heartbeat, press eye to viewfinder, capture moment. Everything stops.

I discovered this technique one late afternoon in Shinjuku, when the setting sun aligned with the main street, gilding the towering commercial facades. A panic attack struck, and my medications lay just out of reach in my backpack. Desperate, I raised the camera to my eye and released the shutter. The effect was immediate – my racing heart steadied, the sweating subsided, my facial tremors stilled. The photograph proved unremarkable, but I'd stumbled upon something remarkable: a remedy that required no chemicals.

Some might dismiss this as mere placebo, but few understand the suffocating reality of panic attacks: the accelerating heartbeat, the cold sweat, vision narrowing to a tunnel, disorientation tangled with nausea. Body temperature seems to revolt – alternating between fierce heat and bone-deep chill. Traditional anti-anxiety medications, with their dulling side effects, only compound my existing exhaustion.

This camera-as-anchor has become my constant companion. The actual photography is secondary; it's the viewfinder's restricted perspective that helps steady my world, easing dizziness and calming palpitations. My therapist endorses this unconventional approach, noting enough progress to reduce my medication.

Shooting Therapy transcends its role as panic attack antidote – it has become a wellspring of energy and purpose. As depression dimmed my architectural passion, a fervour that once defined me, photography rekindled something I thought I had lost. Where architecture once consumed my reading, guided my travels, and shaped my worldview, it has now settled into simply being my profession. Antidepressants can't resurrect that former intensity; they merely flatten the emotional landscape.

But through the viewfinder, I've rediscovered that spark of passion, that warmth of genuine engagement that architecture once ignited. Photography also offers what my desk-bound profession cannot: physical movement, outdoor exploration. On precious days off, I roam the city with my camera, these long walks in open air contributing as much to my mental health as any prescription. In this way, Shooting Therapy fills the void left by purely pharmacological treatment, offering a form of self-directed healing that medication alone cannot provide.

Though I've begun accepting freelance photography work, I resist transforming this passion into a primary career. The logic is clear: as a hobby, photography remains therapeutic; as a profession, it would bend to market demands, losing its power to grant inner peace. Architecture remains my vocation, while photography sustains my emotional equilibrium.

My photographic practice is solitary by design. While I'm naturally drawn to solitude, this choice stems from preserving Shooting Therapy's effectiveness. Group outings with fellow enthusiasts or friends, though enjoyable, dilute the practice's essential gift: that profound sense of peace and complete relaxation I find only in solitude.

The illness eventually found a new voice: psychosis. My reality began filling with visitors – utterly convincing hallucinations of strangers, accompanied by stretches of lost time. I would interact with these apparitions until the moment their unreality became clear. They manifested differently: sometimes mere voices or shadows, but often as flesh-and-blood people who engaged me in conversation.

Distinguishing reality from illusion proves challenging. When a stranger materializes in my living room, I can recognize the deception and maintain distance.

But in public spaces, the line blurs. Recently, in the office elevator, I found myself conversing in English with an elderly man who wasn't there – my colleagues entered to find me speaking to empty air. The realization brought crushing embarrassment.

My doctor, characteristically understated, responded by adjusting my 'anti-visitor' medication. I had begun calling these apparitions 'visitors' rather than hallucinations – a term he found so apt that he now uses it with other patients.

Of all my symptoms, psychosis has shaken me most profoundly. These episodes felt like evidence of 'madness' – a thought that filled me with such shame that I hid this aspect of my illness from friends and colleagues. The very act of acknowledging these experiences seemed to confirm my deepest fears.

My psychiatrist's guidance gradually shifted this perspective. 'Would you feel judged if you had cancer?' he asked during one session. 'Depression and psychosis are no different – conditions that can affect anyone. People mistakenly label brain disorders as madness, but you're not crazy; you're a patient requiring treatment, like any other.' Though his words felt more consoling than clinically precise, they offered a framework for acceptance.

Now I discuss these experiences more openly, even finding humor in them. This frankness has freed me from the exhausting charade of excuses and unnatural behavior. Yet part of me still questions my psychiatrist's cancer analogy – was it truth, or merely a comfortable fiction designed to ease my mind?

My condition has influenced my approach to photography, and life more generally. I see melancholy in my work, especially in shots taken in the coastal town of Chiba, the mountainous small city of Nikko, and commuters in central Tokyo. These photographs are not intentionally taken to express my illness, but it somehow transpires on the page.

Many of my shots are 'street photography'. I enjoy capturing people at night, without them knowing they are being photographed – especially in Shinjuku using a 200mm, a 105mm or an 85mm, keeping me at an optimal distance from the subjects.

Occasionally people notice me, or often I will be asked to photograph someone in areas like Shibuya and Shinjuku. Being a foreigner has unexpectedly aided my street photography in Tokyo. When I approach people with my camera, they often see me as just another Western tourist capturing their city. This works in my favour – the same request from a Japanese photographer might raise eyebrows or make people uneasy. Instead, my obvious foreignness seems to put people at ease, making them more open to being photographed. It's an odd privilege that's helped me document daily life here more freely.

Around the stations Tokyo and Shinjuku remain my main focus. When I'm with family, the dynamic shifts completely – I leave my cameras at home and use my phone instead. I've tried forcing myself to use the Nikon or Hasselblad for family moments, but it never feels right. These cameras are tools for my shooting therapy, instruments for processing my mental state through street photography. They belong to that world, separate from the simple joy of capturing family memories on my phone.

My solo weekends have become a ritual of restoration, with photography naturally woven into them. These quiet explorations have birthed projects like 'Chiba Coast Village', 'Enoshima', and the series from Iwate and Shimane Prefectures, as well as Lake Chuzenji. I deliberately seek out less-travelled destinations, avoiding the tourist crowds that would disrupt the solitude I need. The projects themselves often take shape later, emerging as I review the images at home. I set out simply to breathe and observe, camera in hand, with no fixed destination or subject in mind. It's a form of wandering meditation – just me, my camera, and wherever the day leads.

My work has found its way to gallery walls three times now – twice in Japan and once in my Italian hometown, where the town hall exhibition drew unexpected attention from both public and press. The most recent showing was 'Detour' at Gallery Tiers in Tokyo's Omotesando district. I chose this title deliberately – 'detour' meaning a departure from the expected path – because these images capture the moments when I break from my regular commute or step away from work to clear my head. My routes to and from the office vary, shaped by my need to escape routine and release accumulated stress. Each alternative path becomes an opportunity for both photography and mental decompression.

My commute has evolved into an intentional wandering – I choose longer routes and unexpected turns, always searching for new images. The 'Detour' exhibition drew from this daily exploration, weaving together pieces from my Shinjuku series, Enoshima wanderings, Tokyo Rivers, and cityscapes. The space came alive through an unexpected collaboration with Hinoqi-Tokyo's pop-up perfume store. Their team helped curate the selection, ensuring the photographs complemented their product display. The final layout ranged from statement A2 prints to A3+ pieces, with one wall transformed into a mosaic of postcards. Those postcards, surprisingly, resonated most with visitors. The

sales not only covered my printing costs but left me with something extra – a small but meaningful validation.

'Detour' carries a double meaning for me. It's the literal wandering from my daily path, but also the emotional divergence from illness and stress. Life rarely follows a straight line – it's shaped by these detours, each unexpected turn adding depth to our story. I've come to view my own illness as such a detour. It pulled me away from work's consuming rhythm and, surprisingly, drew me closer to my family. There's a strange gratitude in this recognition. Without this forced departure from my planned route, I might never have slowed down. Without my demons, I might never have found my way to photography. Sometimes the path we resist leads us exactly where we need to go.

Of my four cameras – two analogue, two digital – each serves a different purpose in my photography. Sometimes I choose based on practicality, grabbing the lighter one for spontaneous walks. Other times, I select the camera that best fits my subject matter. Even my phone has earned its place in my practice – some of the most popular postcards from the Detour exhibition began as smartphone captures.

The choice between film and digital shapes each image differently – film with its characteristic grain, digital with its precise rendering. Some viewers suggest I should develop a more consistent style, that these variations pose a problem. But I see these differences as authentic reflections of my changing moods and perspectives. The variety in my work mirrors the complexity of who I am.

Seeing my son's growing interest in photography brings its own kind of joy. When I gave him his first toy camera, he immediately made it his mission to document every family gathering and celebration. He especially loves photographing his little sister. Now I dream of future photo walks together, but for now, watching him discover the magic of capturing moments is enough.

Life tested our resilience just before Suzu's birth when Sumire tested positive for Covid. With my wife in hospital and Ryo testing negative like me, we faced two weeks of quarantine together. Despite my anxiety about managing alone, given my condition, we turned it into an adventure. The living room became our basecamp, complete with a pop-up tent barely big enough for two. My construction measuring tape transformed into a magical fishing rod for catching puppet sea monsters. We created our own world of flashlight expeditions to the kitchen and nightly calls to Mum. Sumire's pride in my handling of the situation meant everything – especially since it coincided with a delicate period in my illness. This unexpected challenge helped rebuild my confidence.

When Suzu arrived, her calm nature felt like a gift. Unlike her energetic brother, she took easily to both bottle and breast, and blessed us with long stretches of sleep. Now three years old, she continues to bring us joy. The children's growing independence has eased our family dynamics considerably.

The 'visitors' and voices that once dominated my days began fading, first appearing less frequently, then disappearing altogether. Months have passed now without hallucinations. For the first time in years, I can genuinely say, 'I am fine.' I'm aware this isn't necessarily permanent – depression often returns at least once in a lifetime. But this knowledge doesn't frighten me anymore. I have my shooting-therapy and my family's support. I can face whatever comes.

When friends and family question why I chose to publish this book, my answer is simple: it's my way of stepping into the light with my condition. While bipolar disorder has undeniably challenged both my career and personal life, it has also opened unexpected doors to growth. Through sharing these words and images, I hope to reach others walking similar paths. Perhaps they'll find something of their own story in mine.

This isn't perhaps a complete 'coming out,' as I write under the name Abele Navin – meaning 'new breath of life.' This choice isn't born from shame or fear of judgment, but from a father's instinct to protect. Children can be cruel in their innocence, and I won't risk making my family vulnerable to schoolyard taunts. Had I been writing only for myself, my choice might have been different.

I understand that anonymity is fragile, and my identity might eventually surface. If that day comes, I hope my children will understand that this book grew from a place of hope – hope that sharing my story might help others while protecting them. To Ryo and Suzu: if you're reading this one day, please know that every word, even those written under another name, came from a place of love.

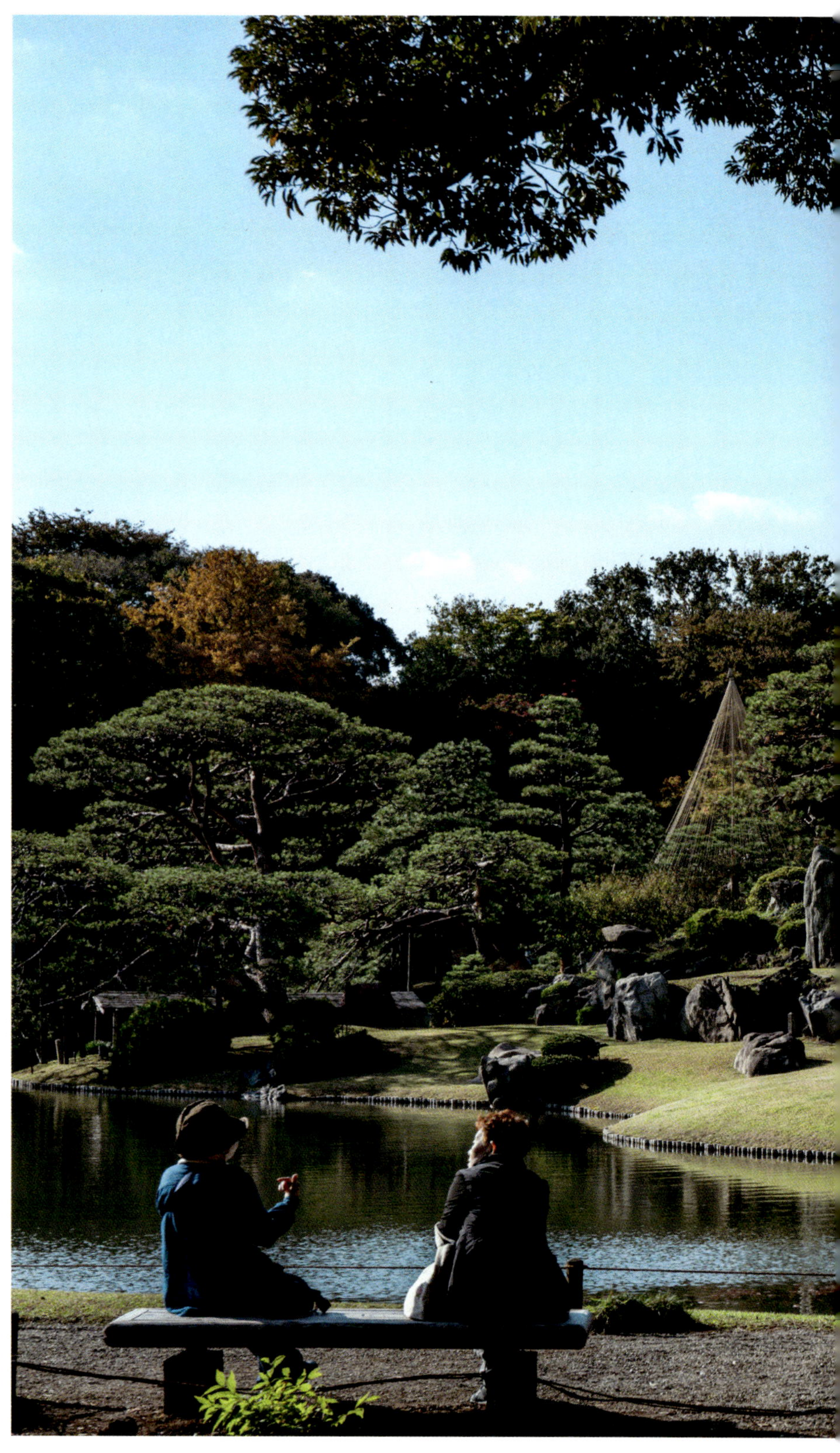

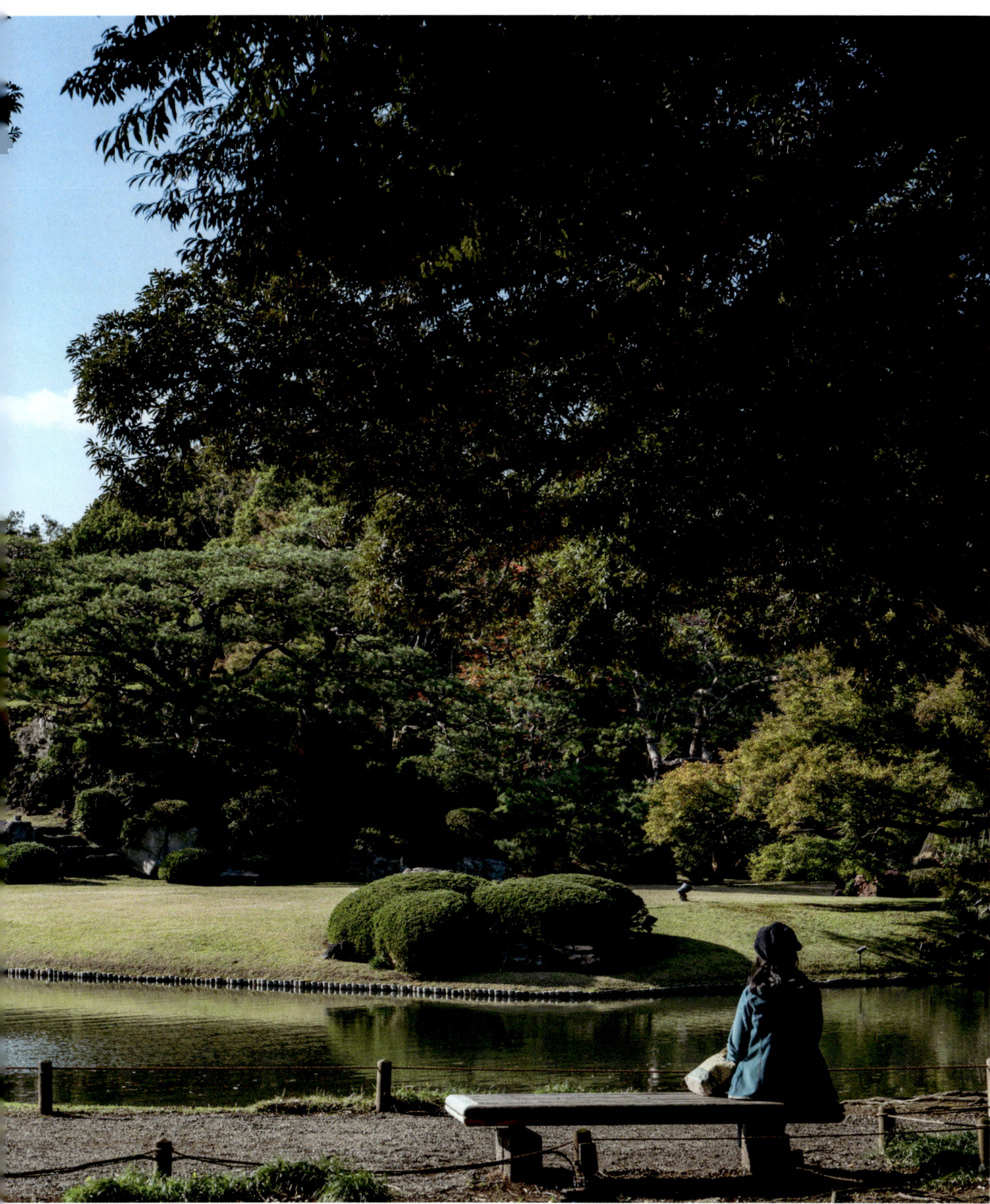

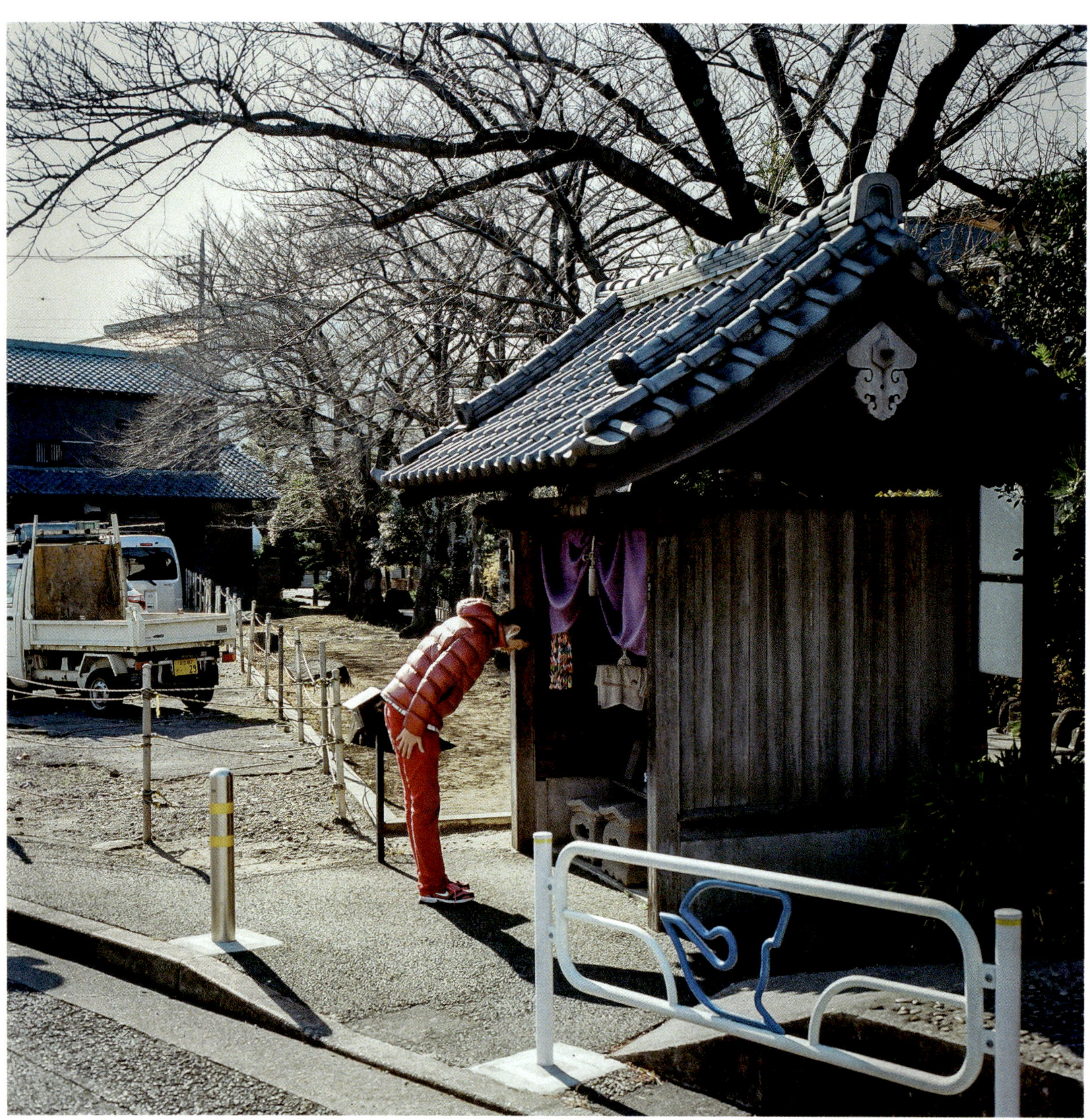

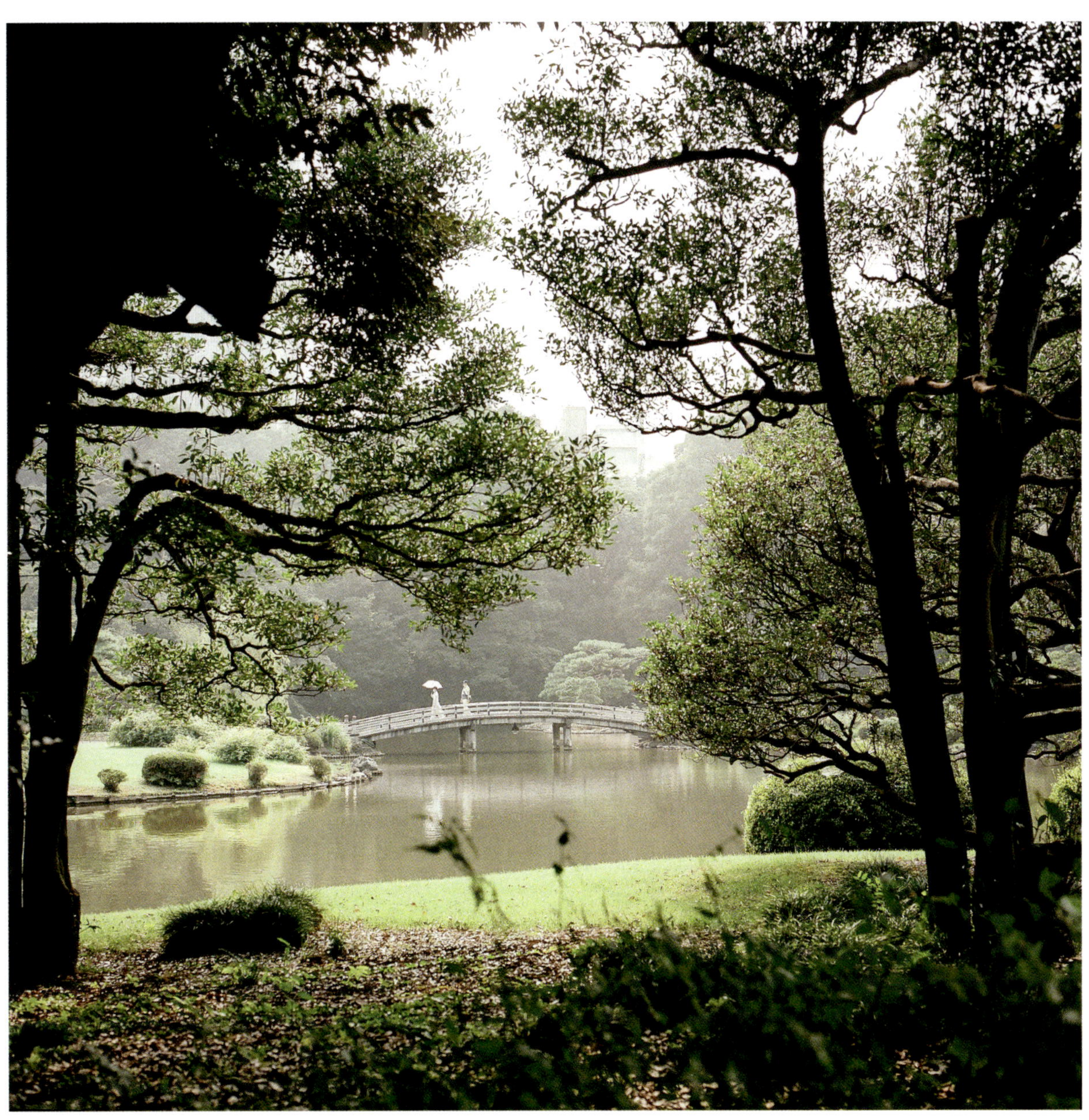

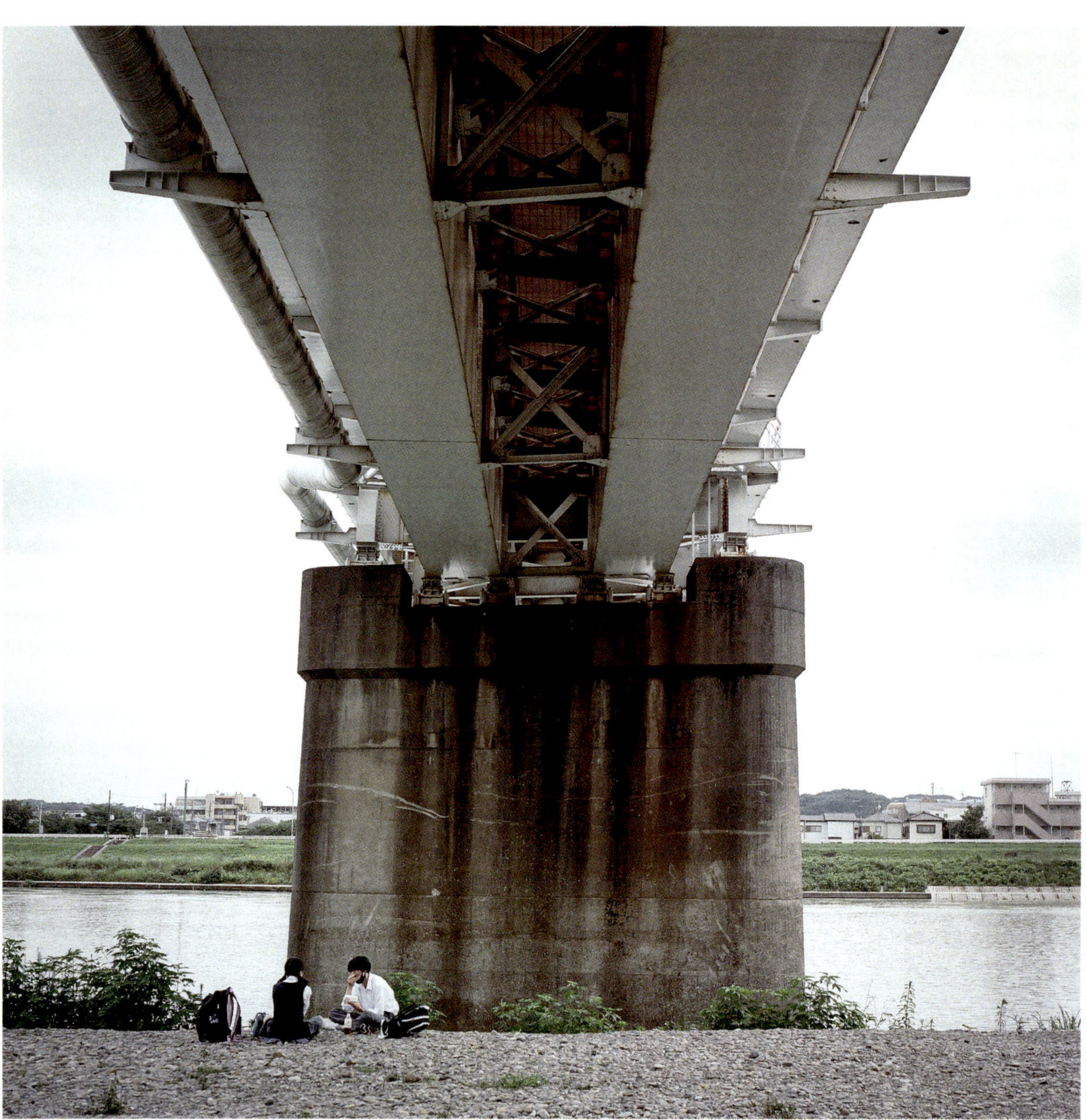

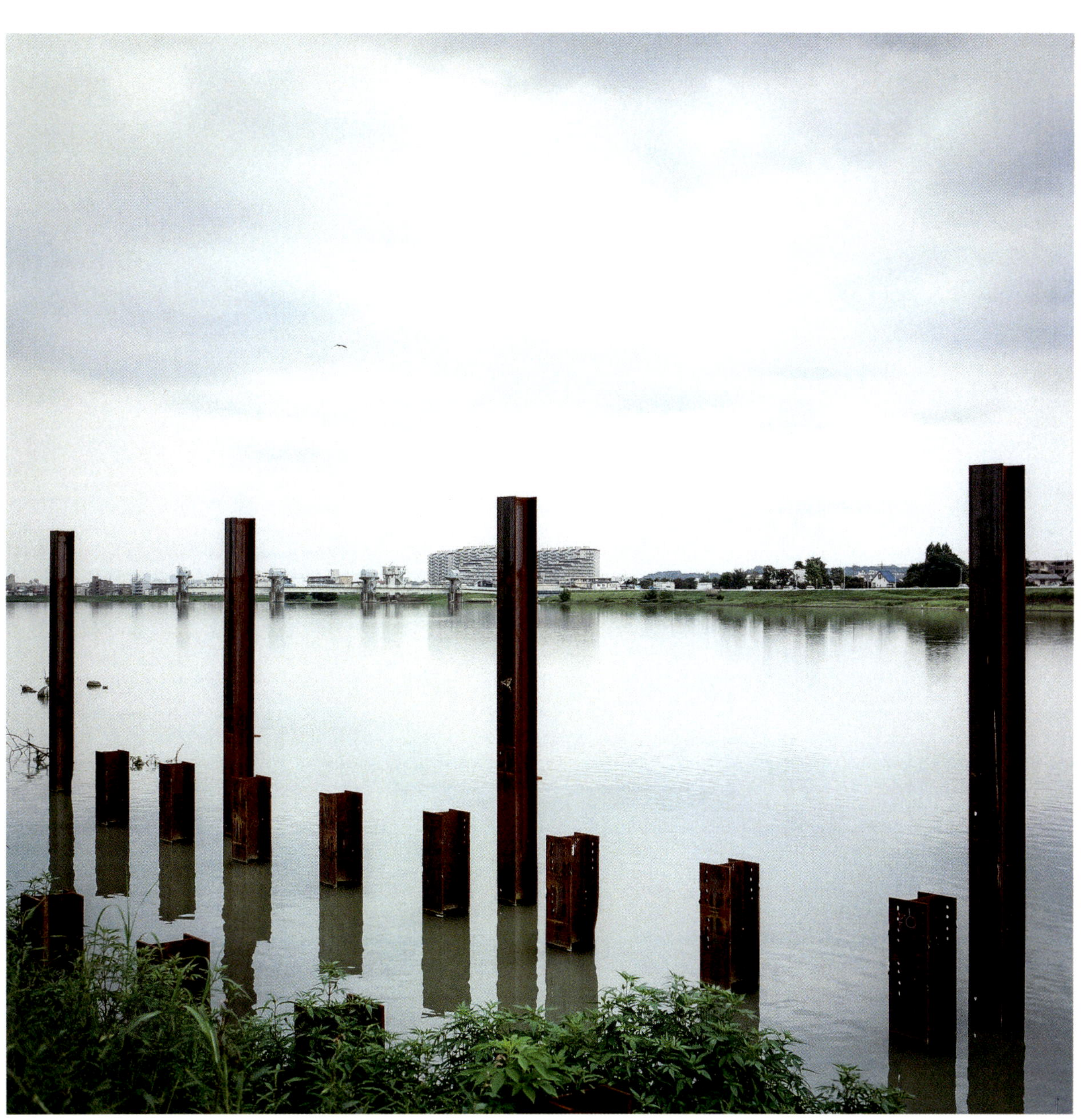

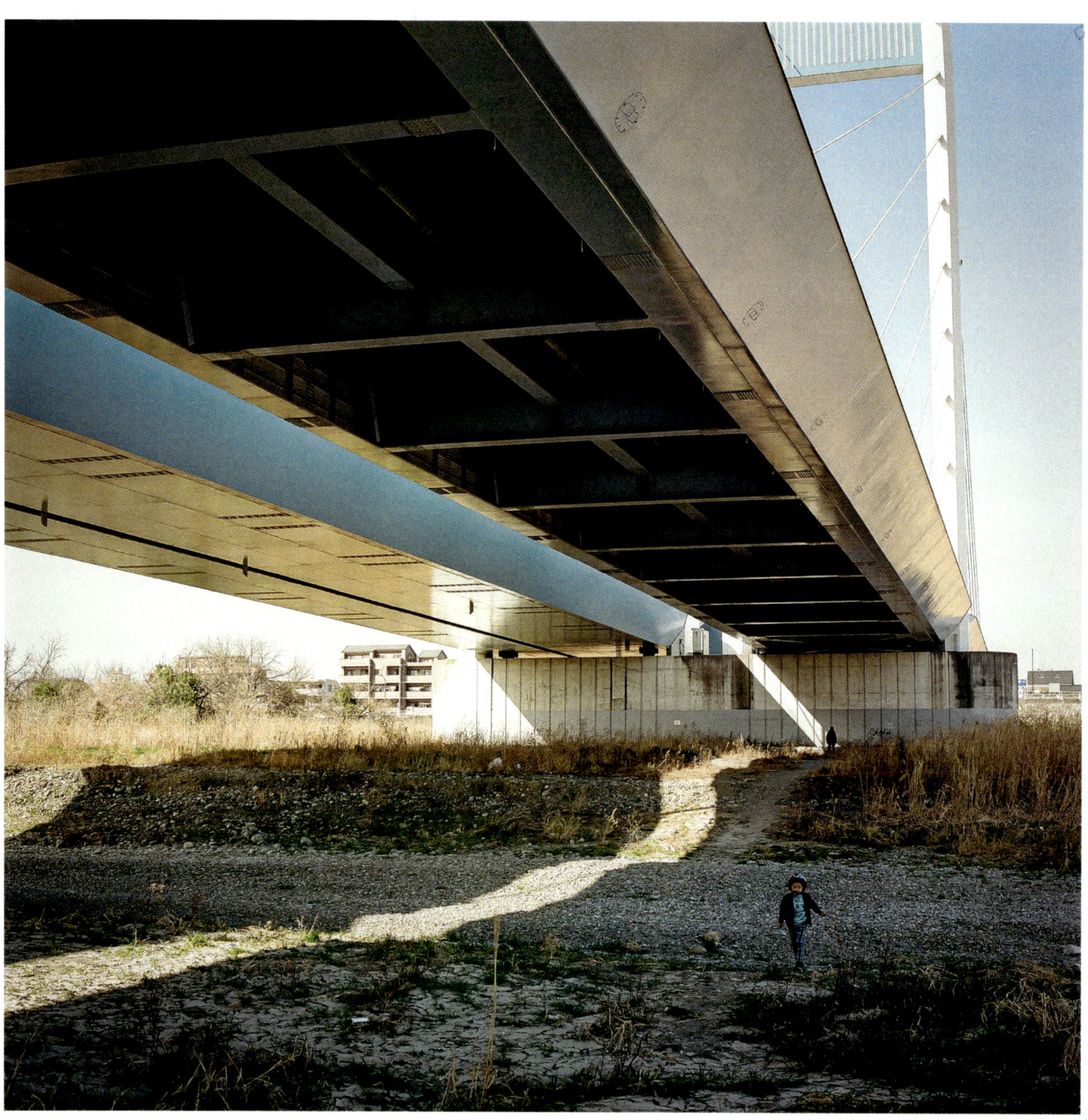

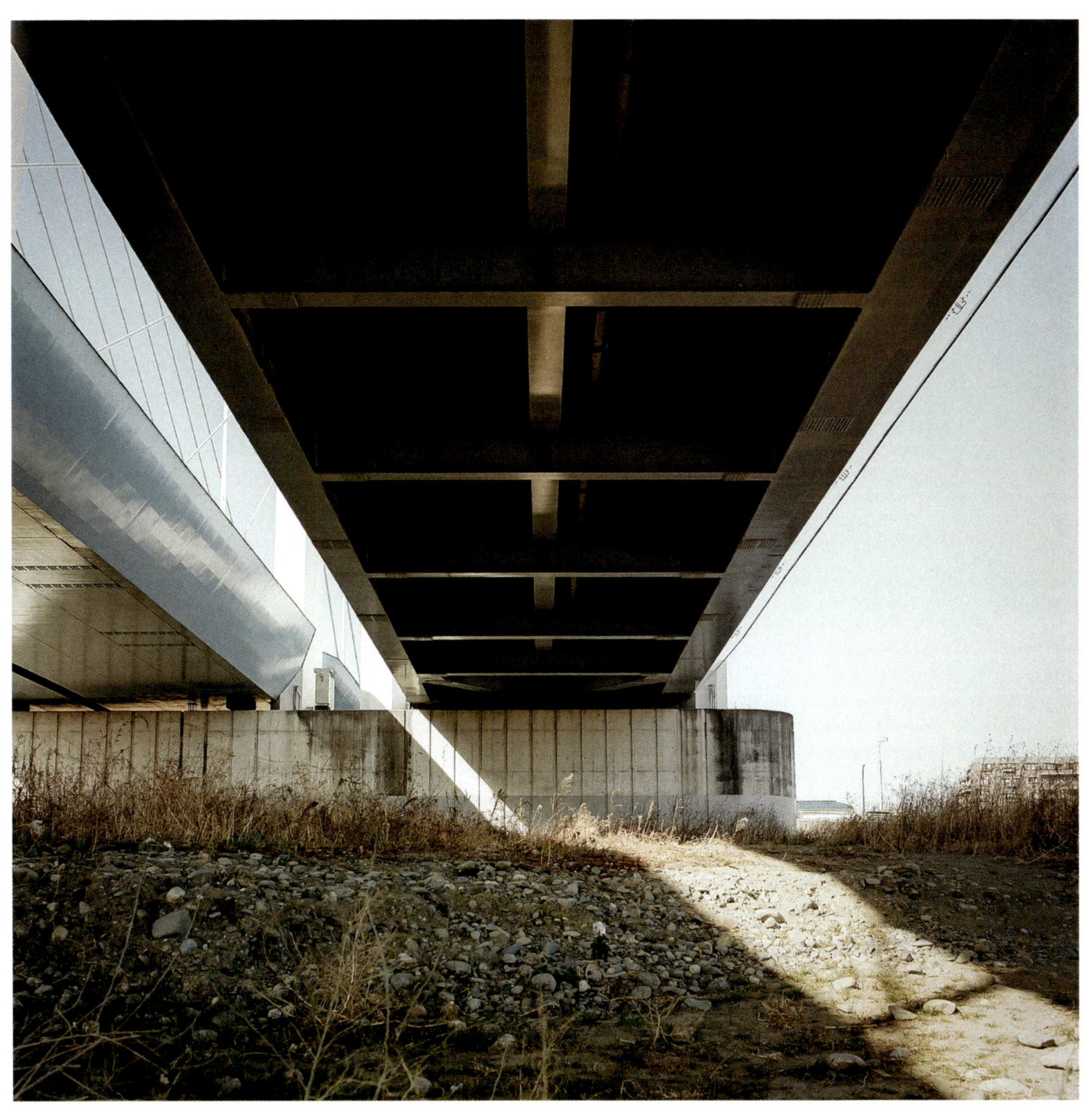

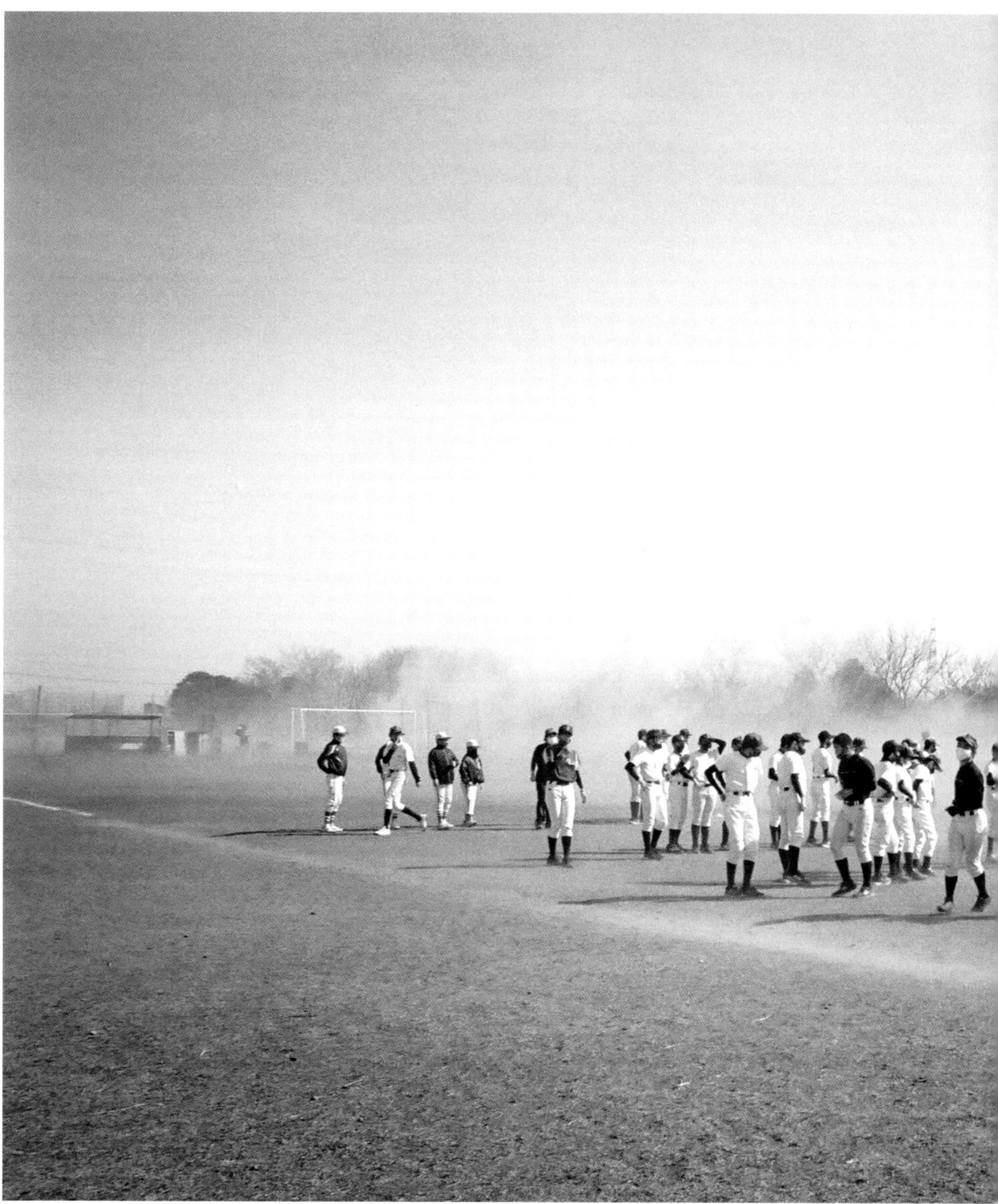

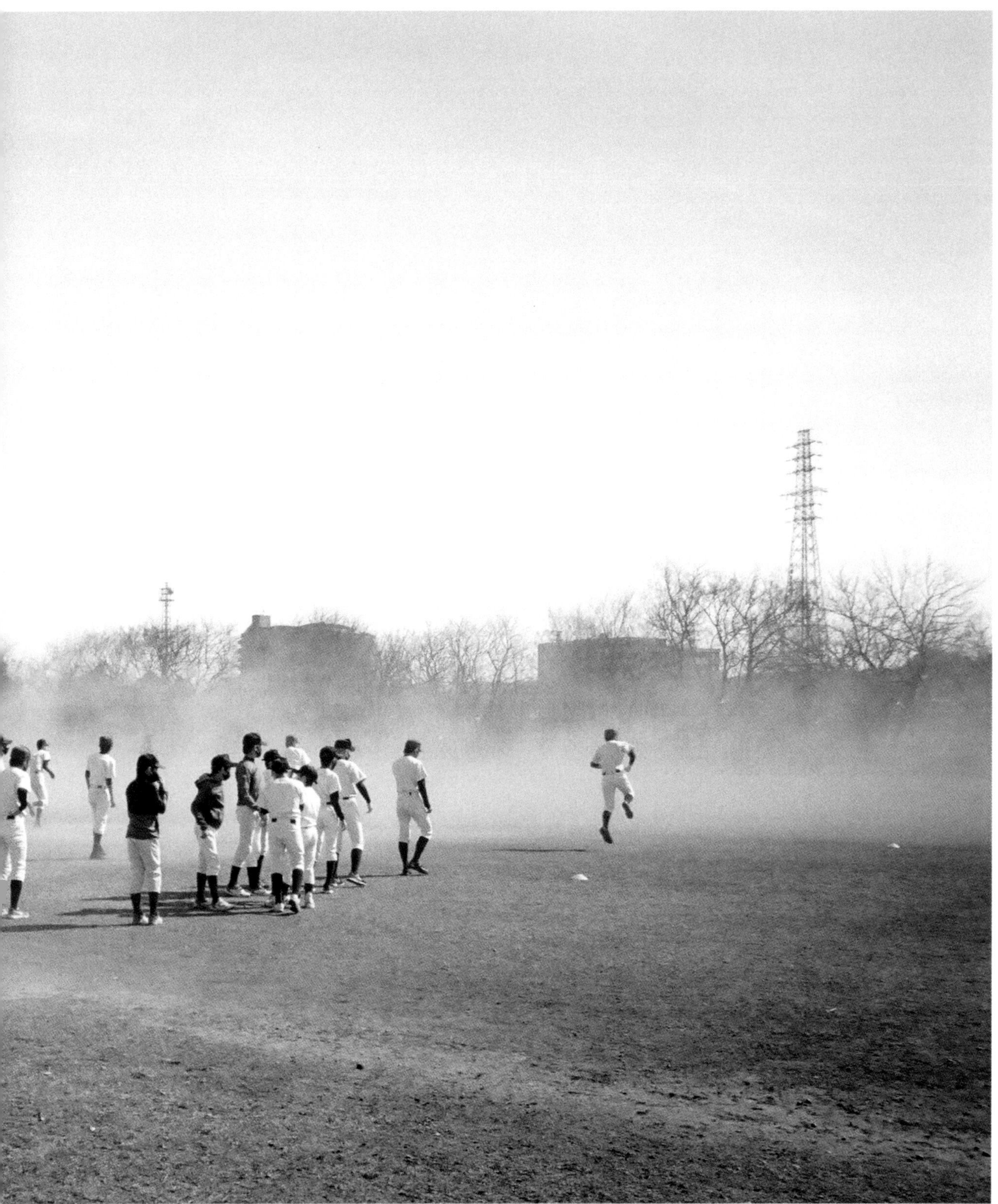

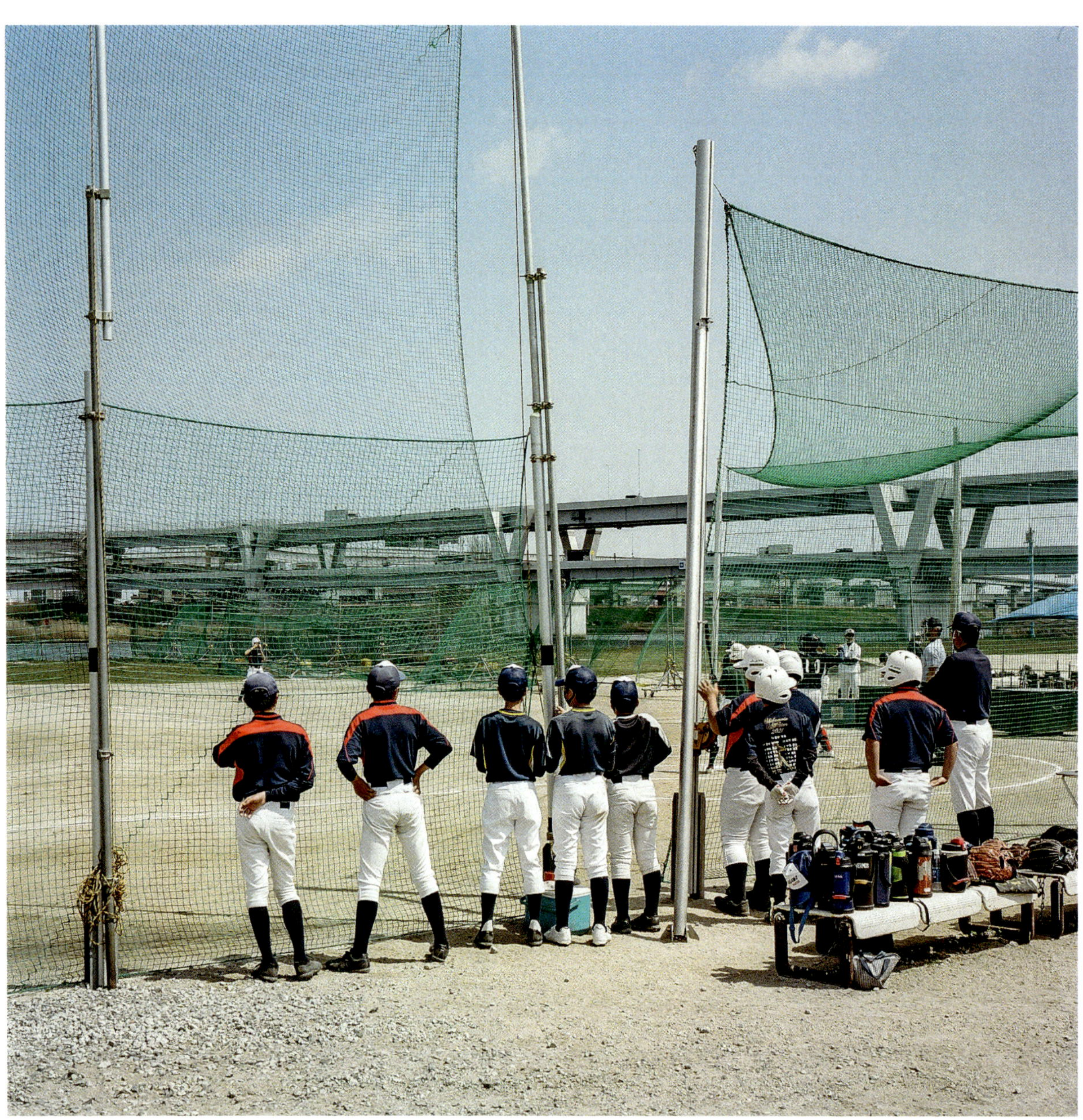

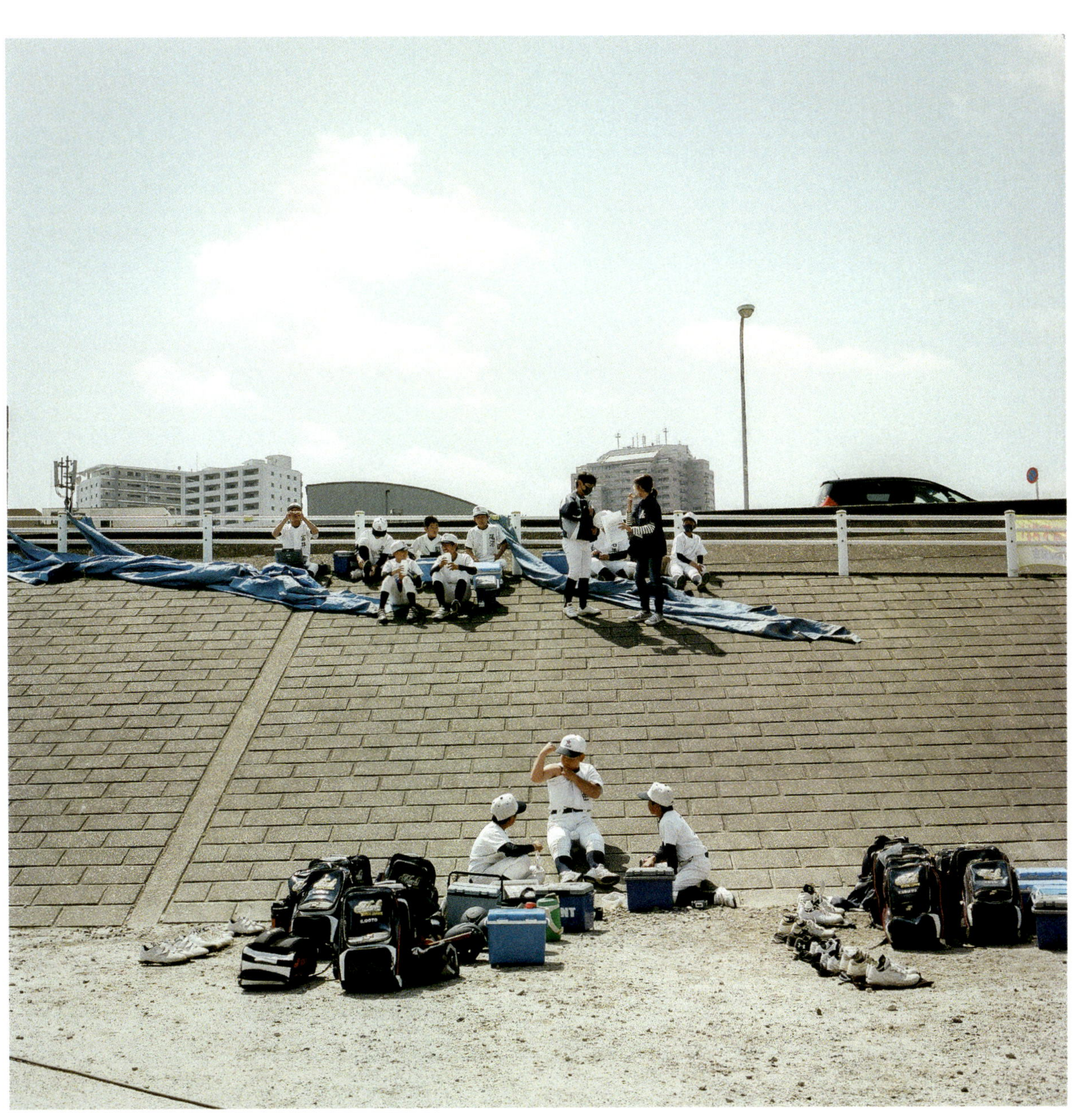

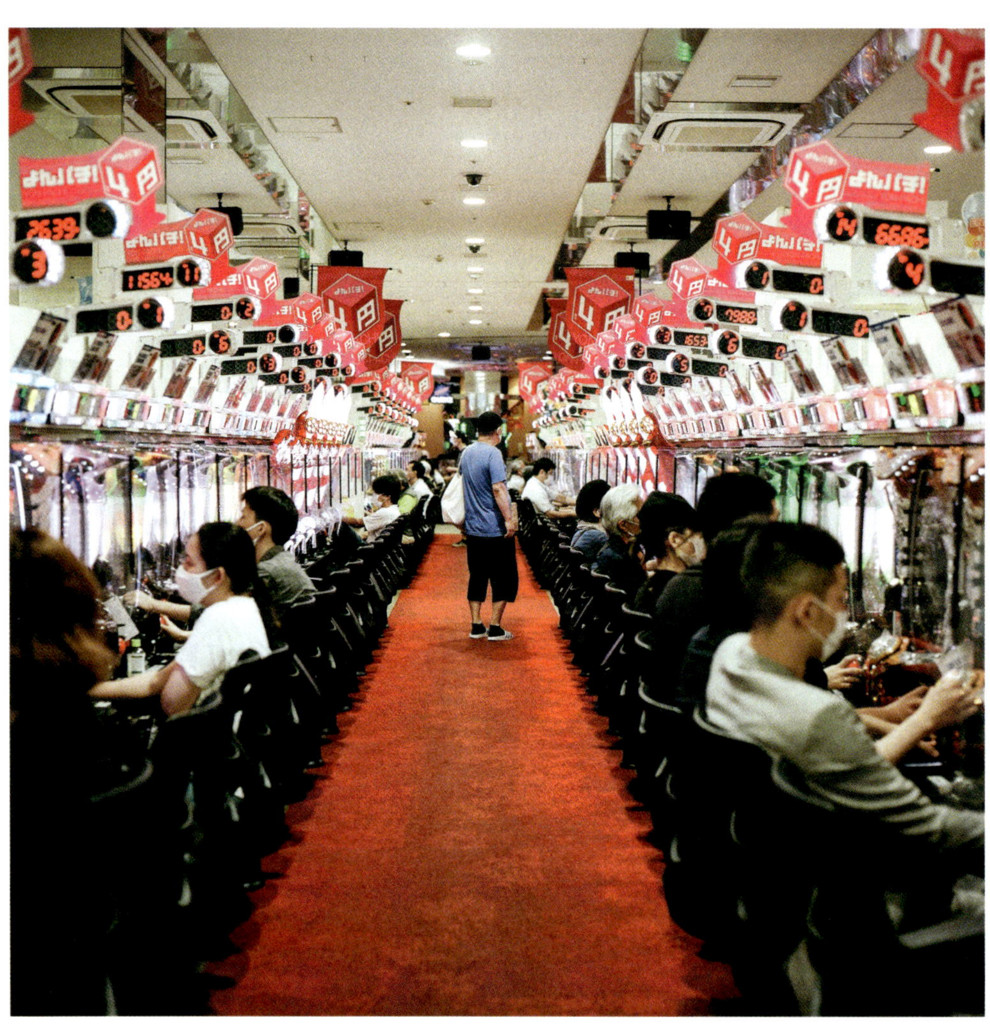

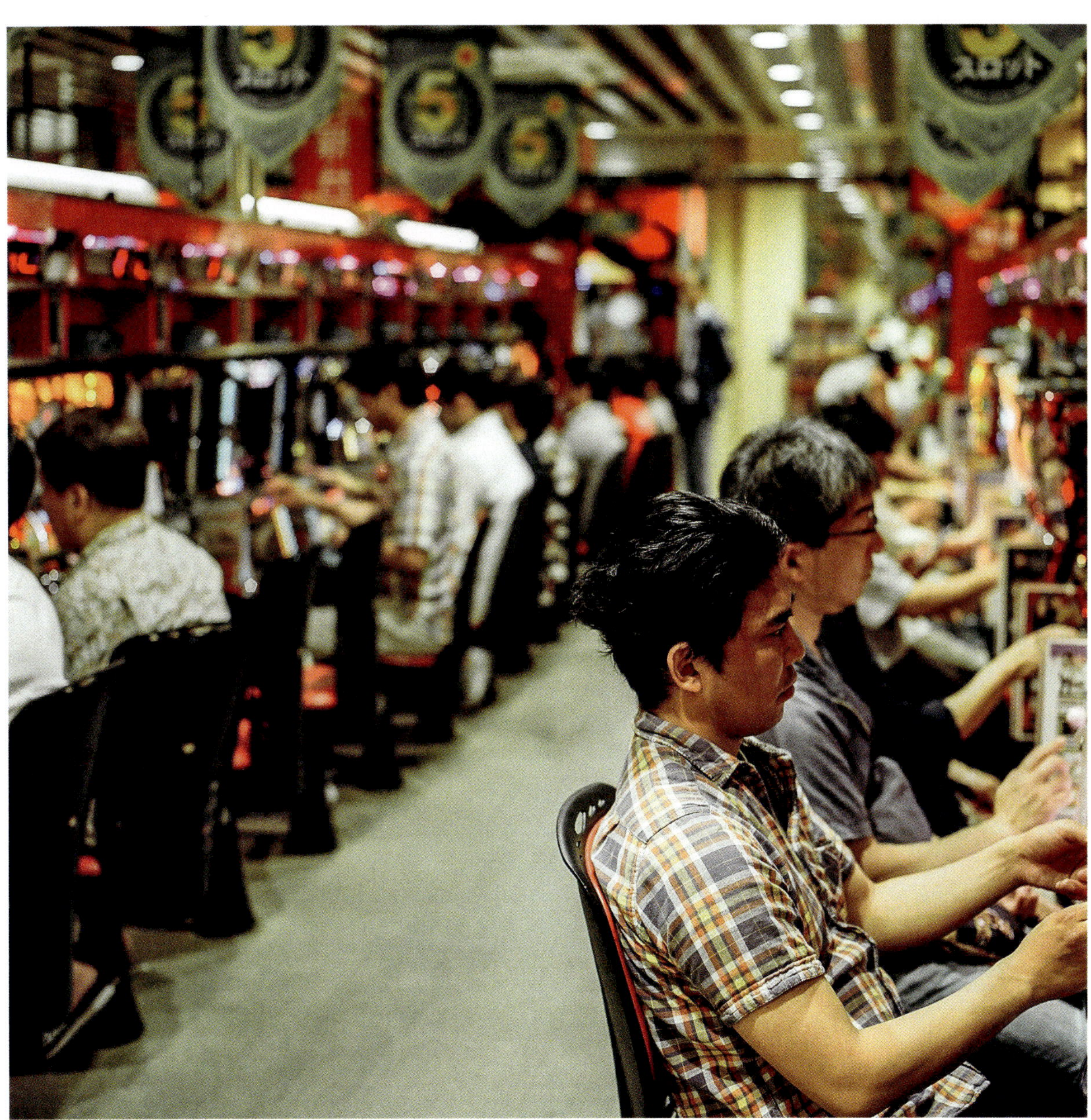

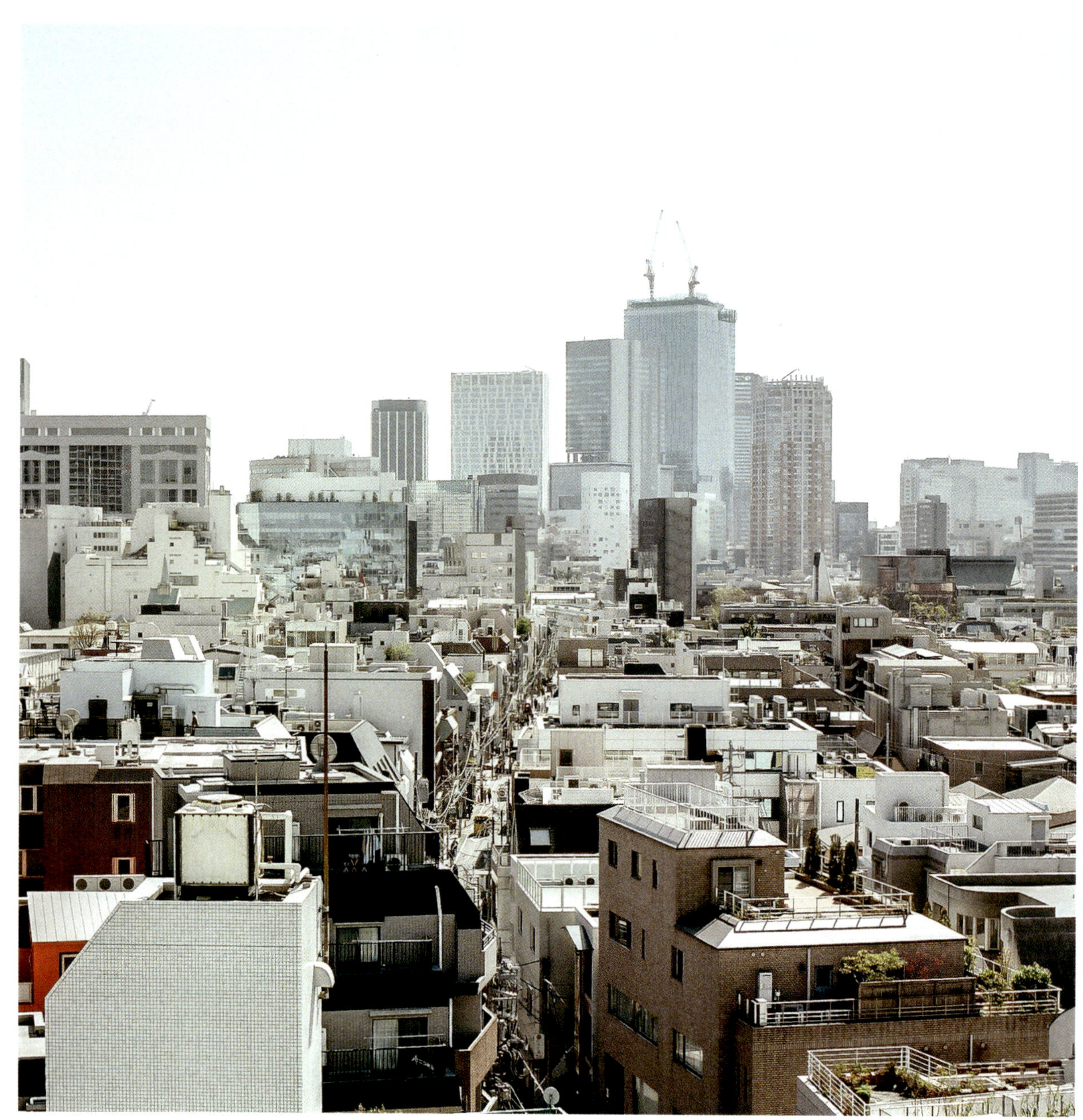

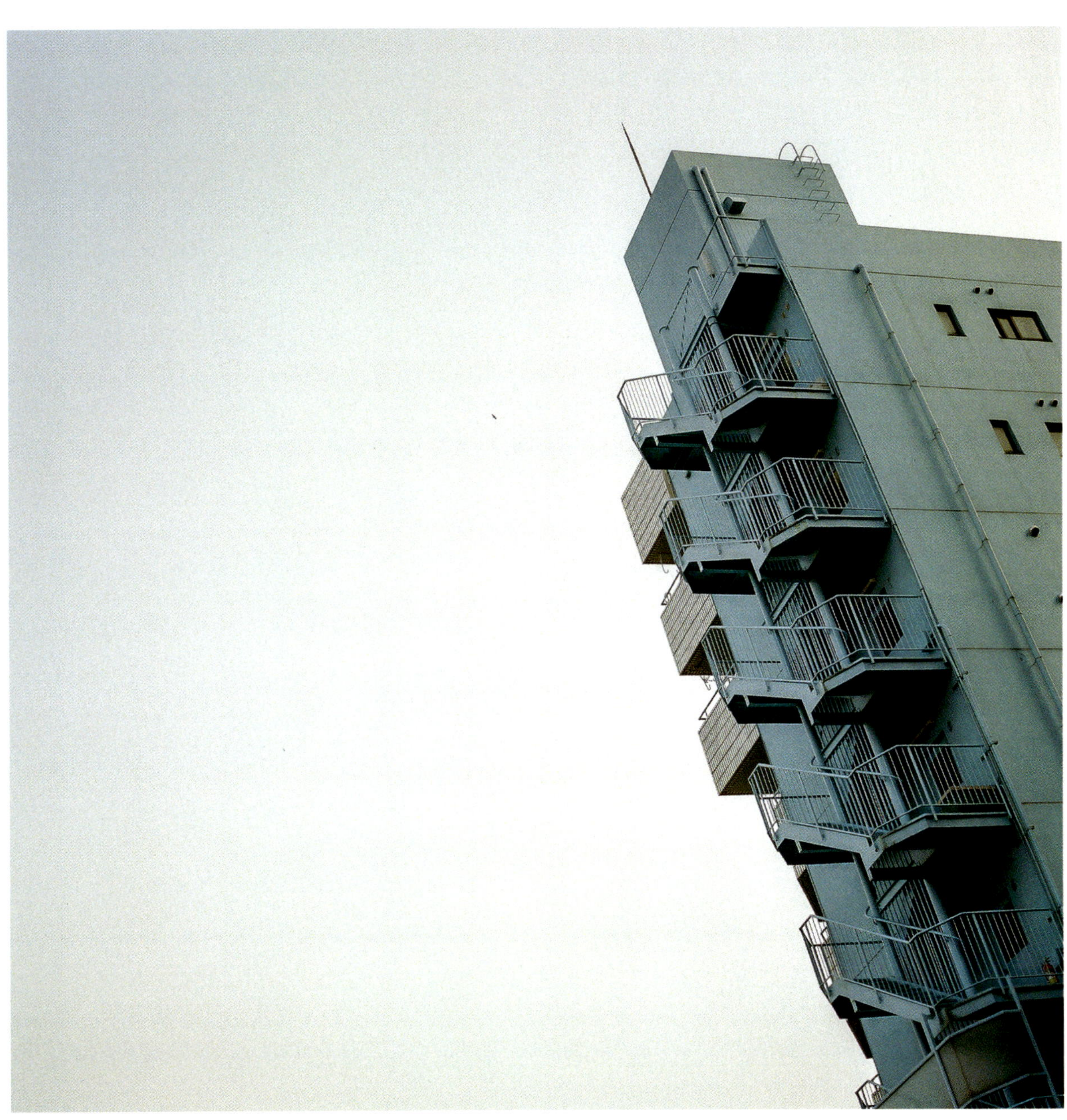

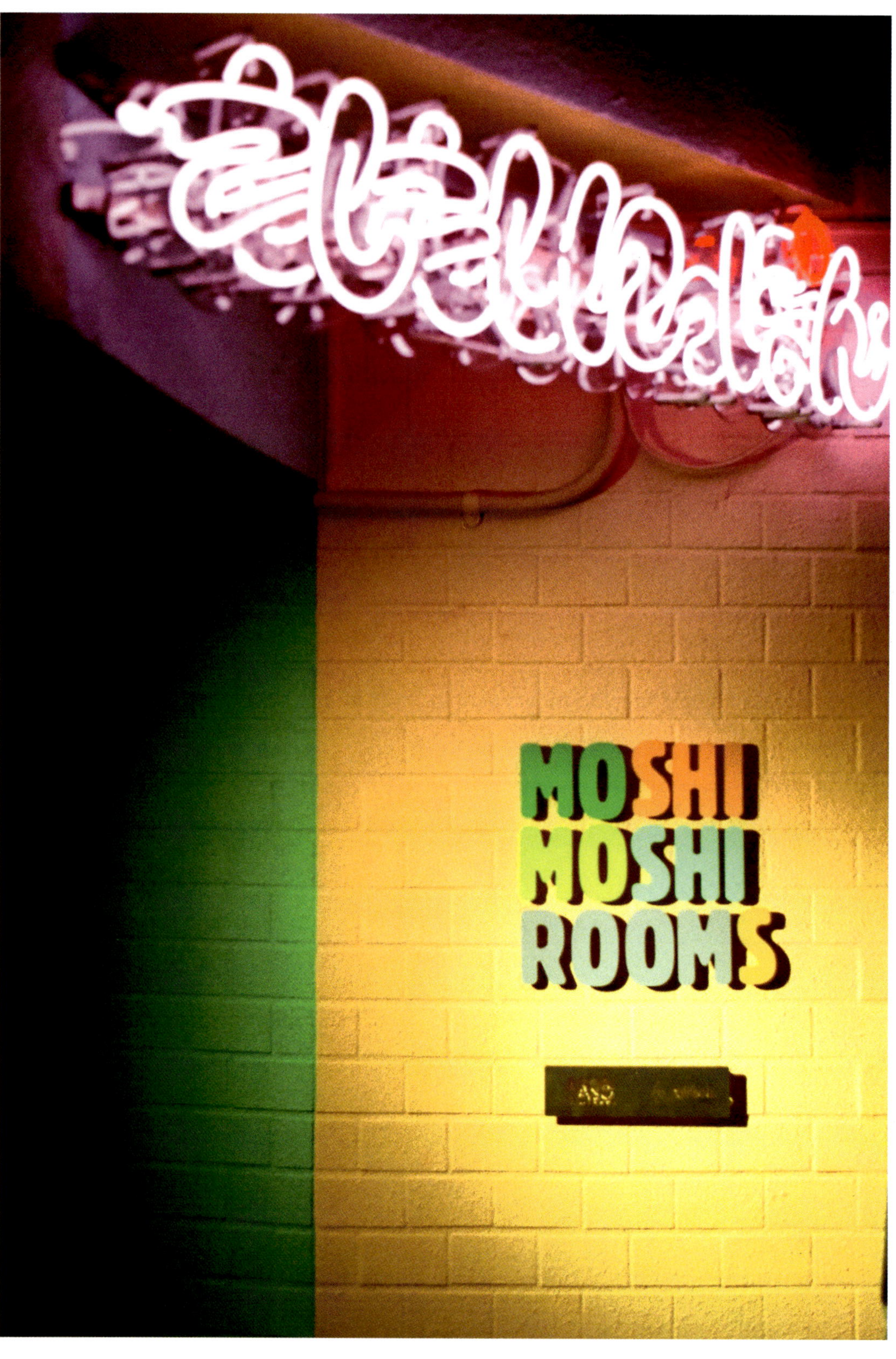
MOSHI
MOSHI
ROOMS

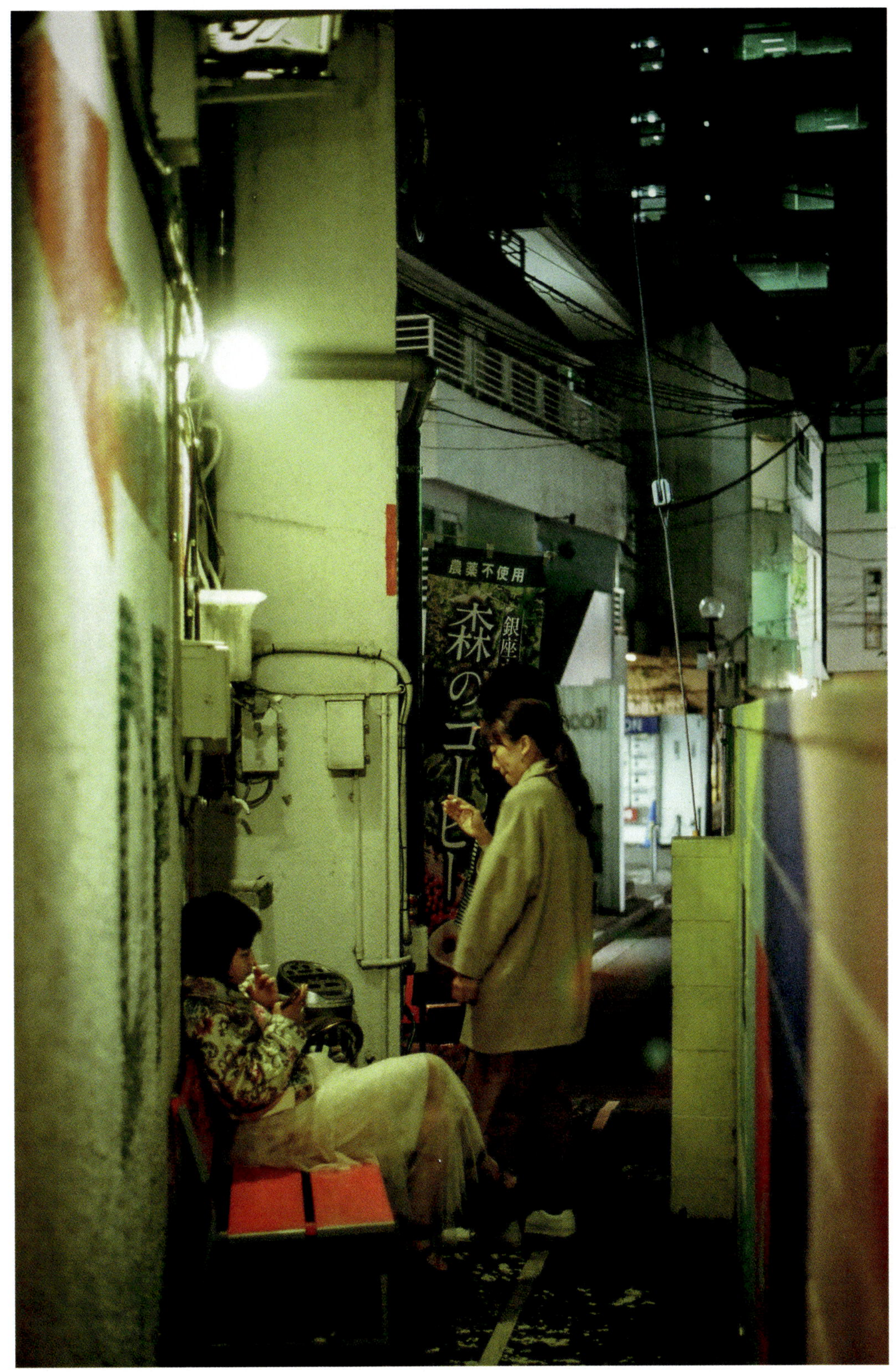

農薬不使用
銀座
森のコーヒー

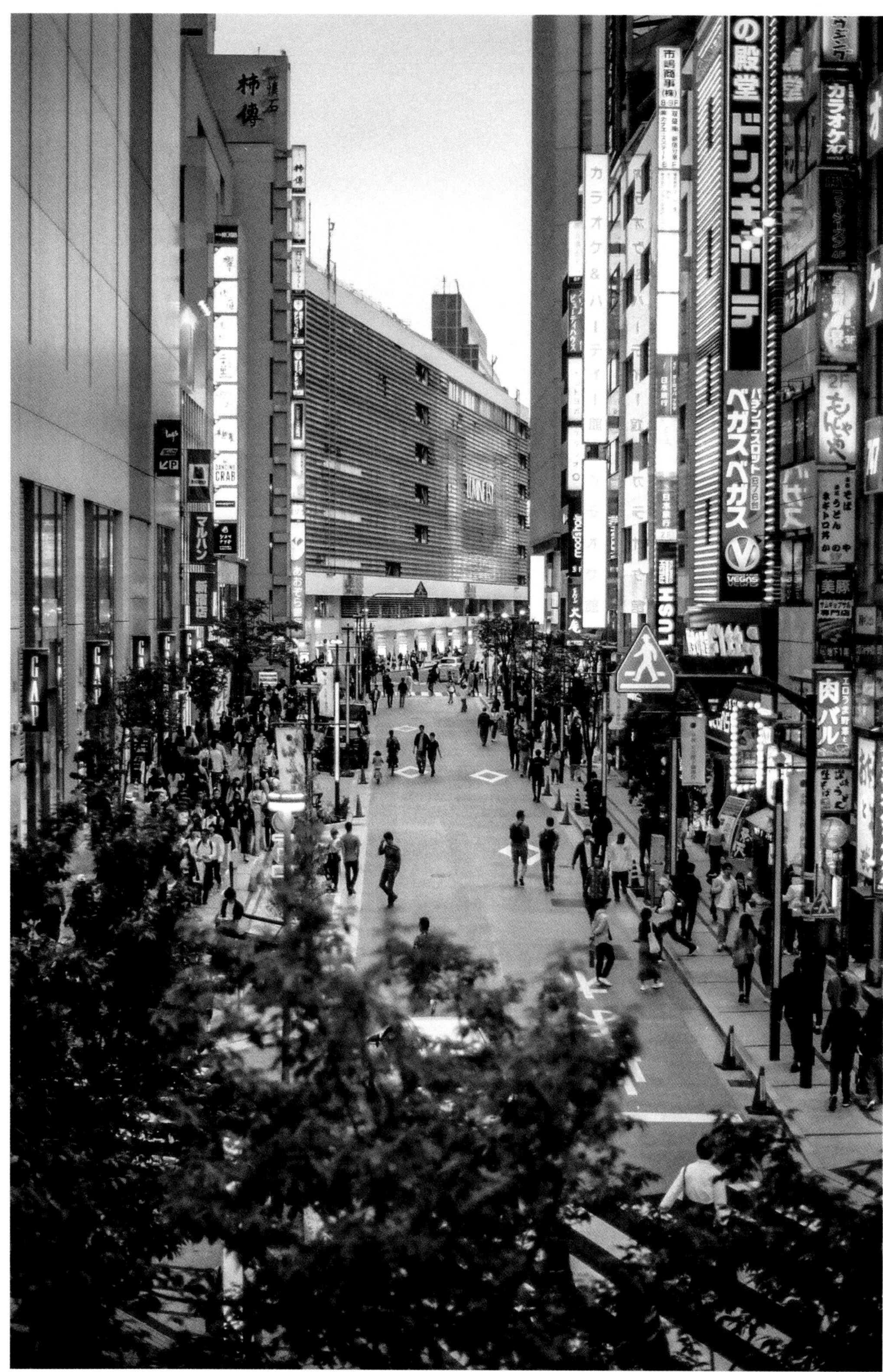

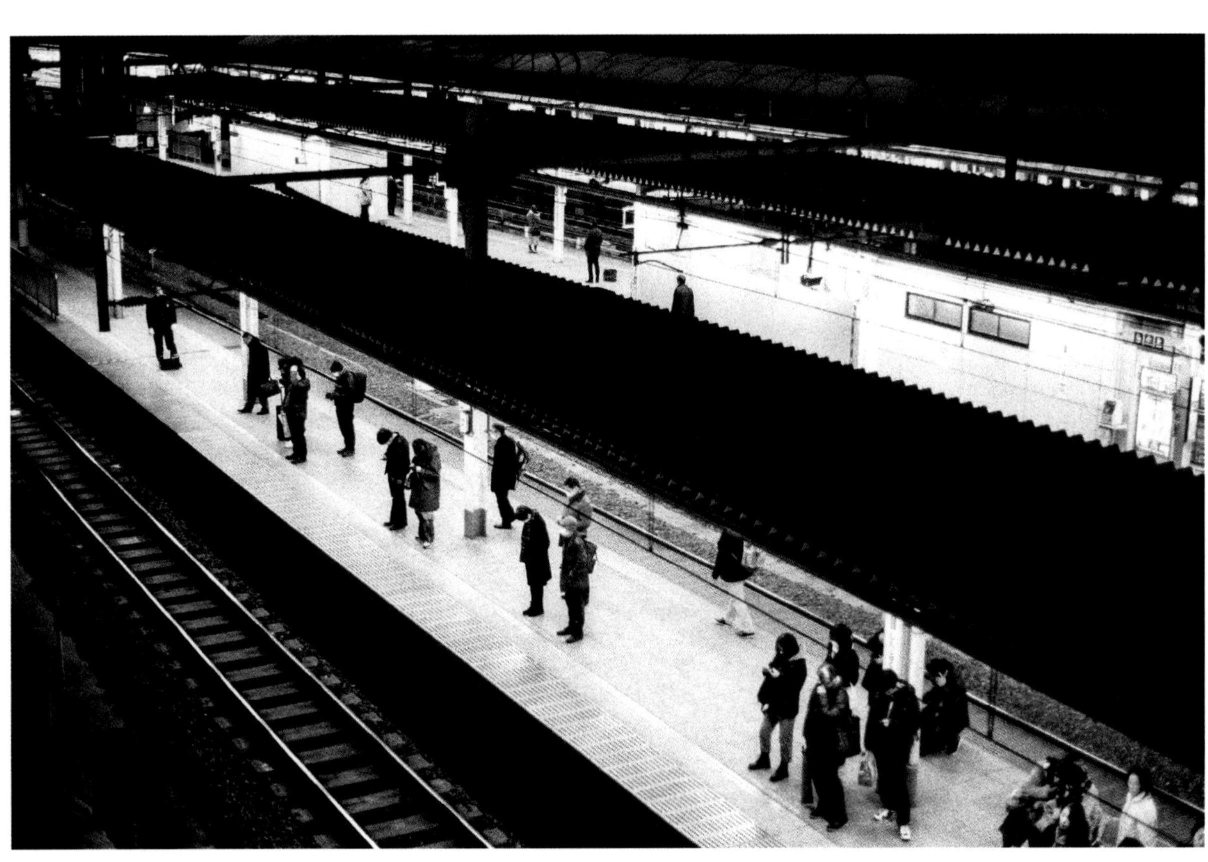

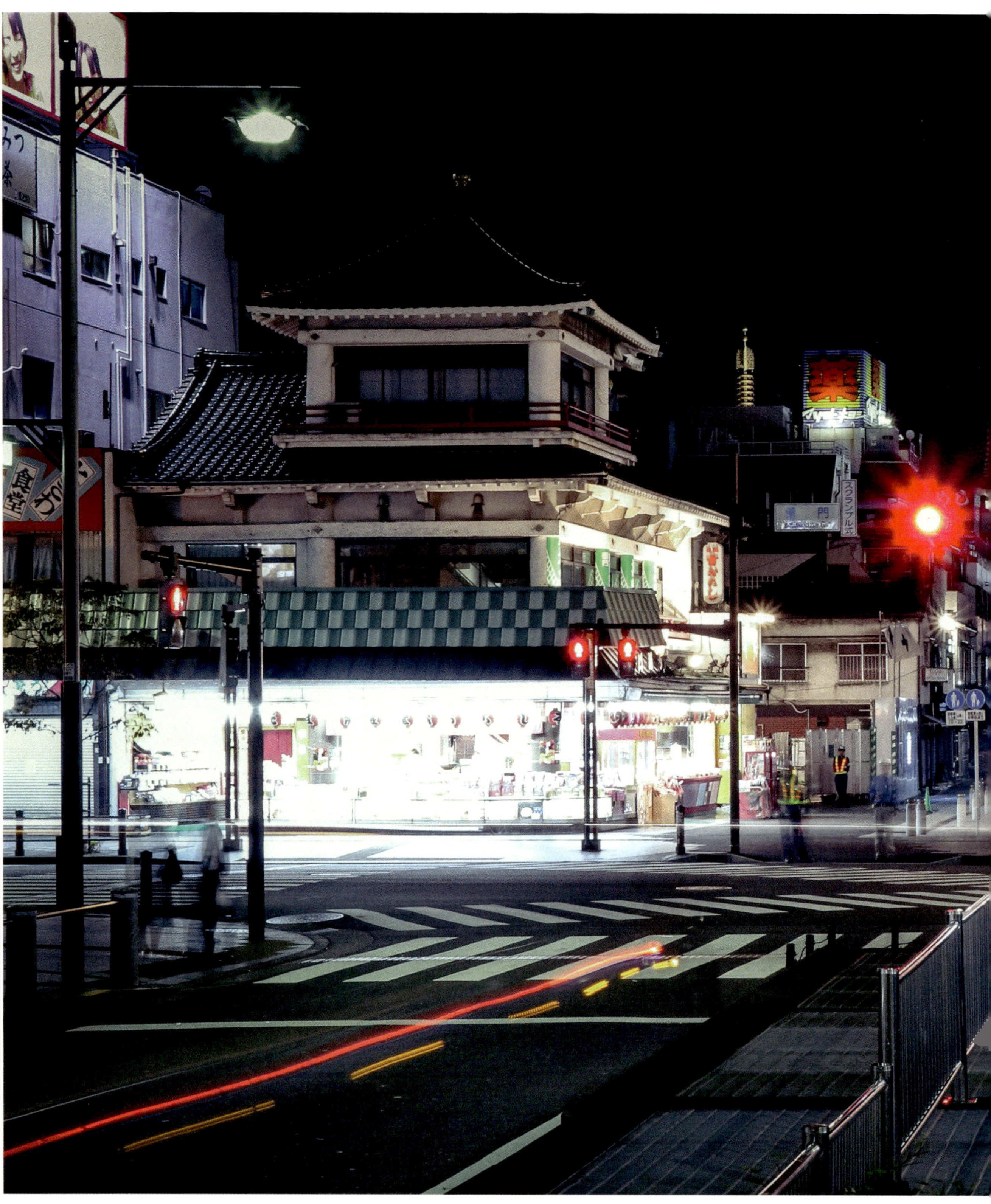

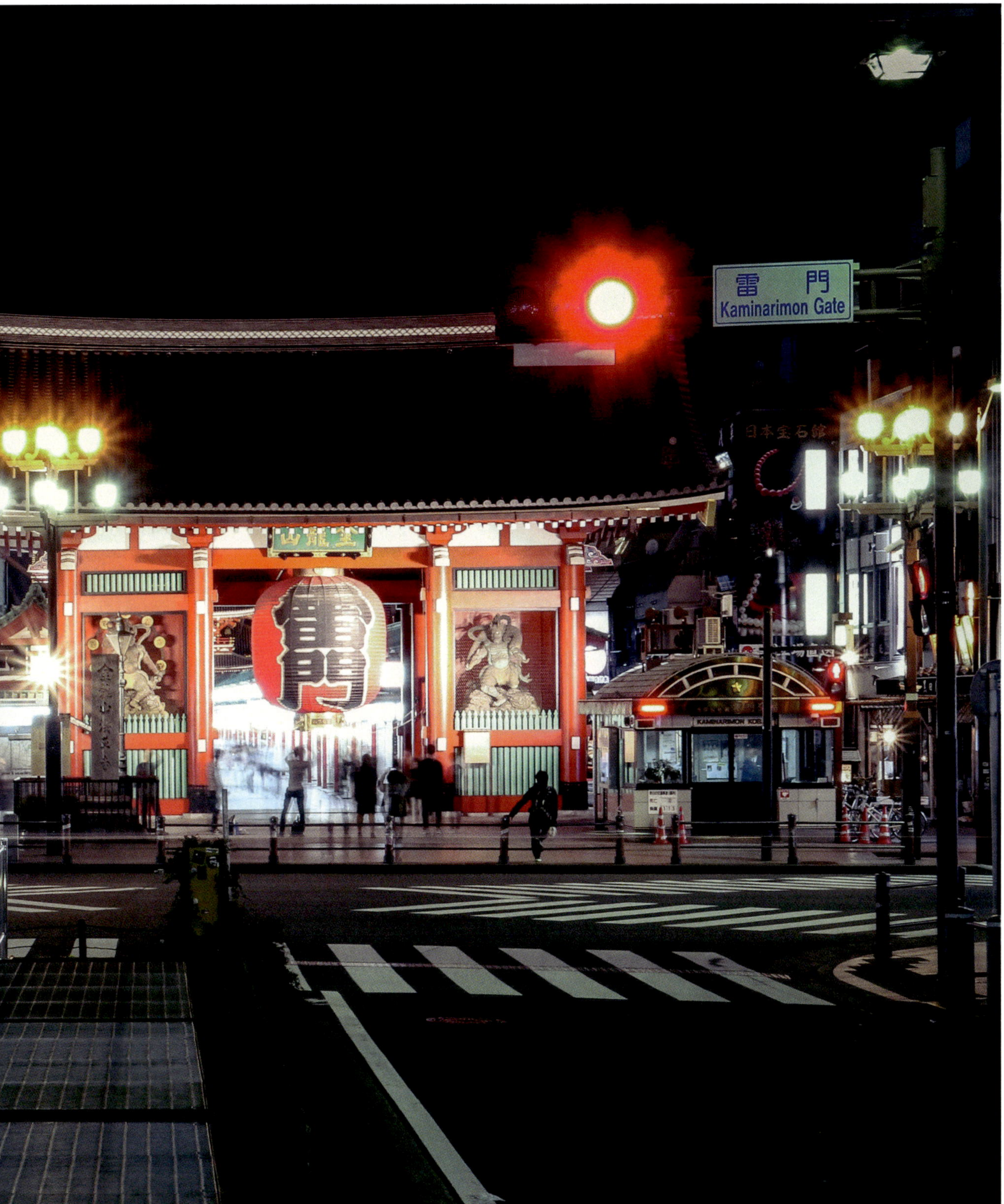

雷　門
Kaminarimon Gate
雷門
KAMINARIMON KOBAN

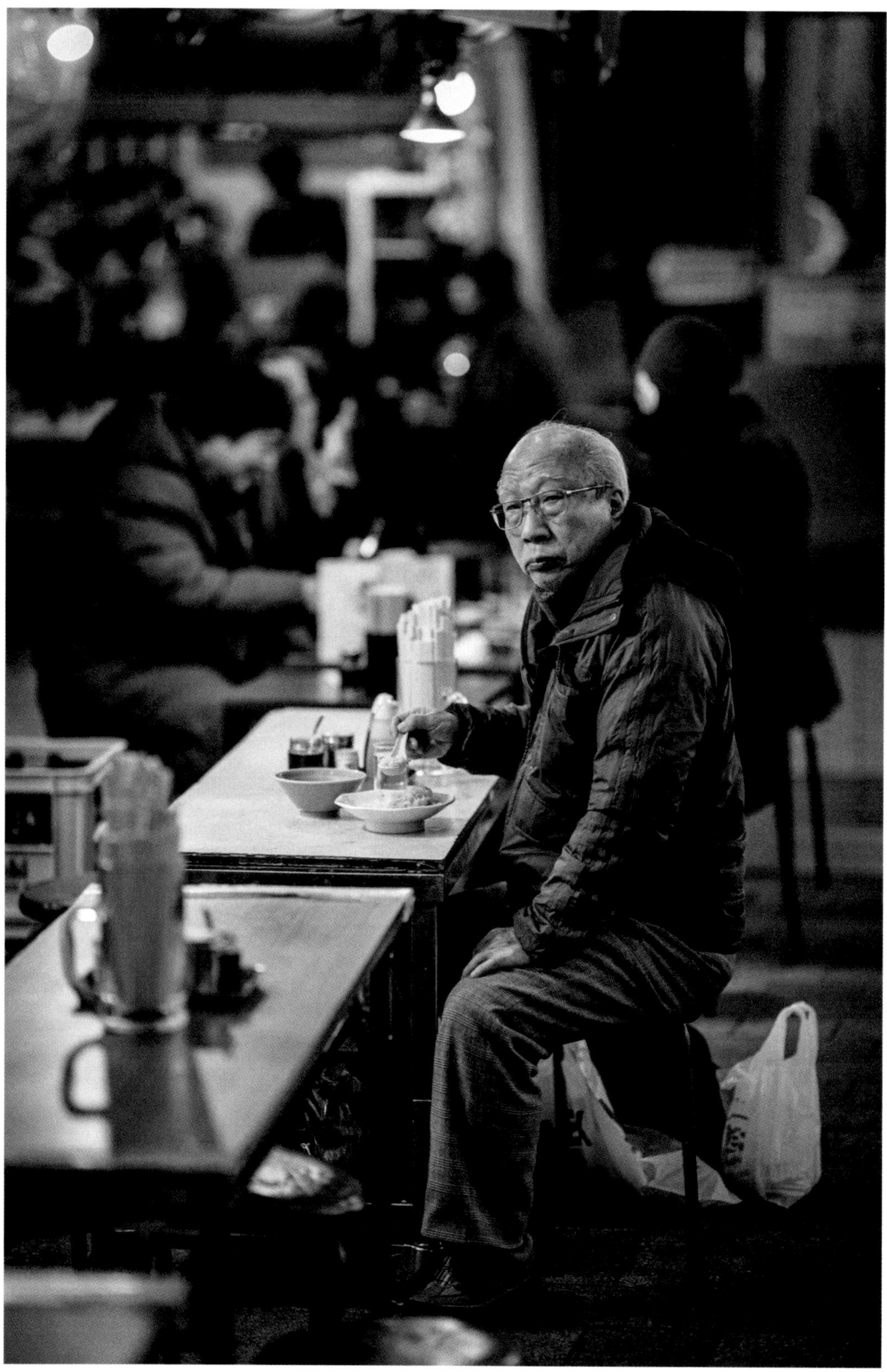

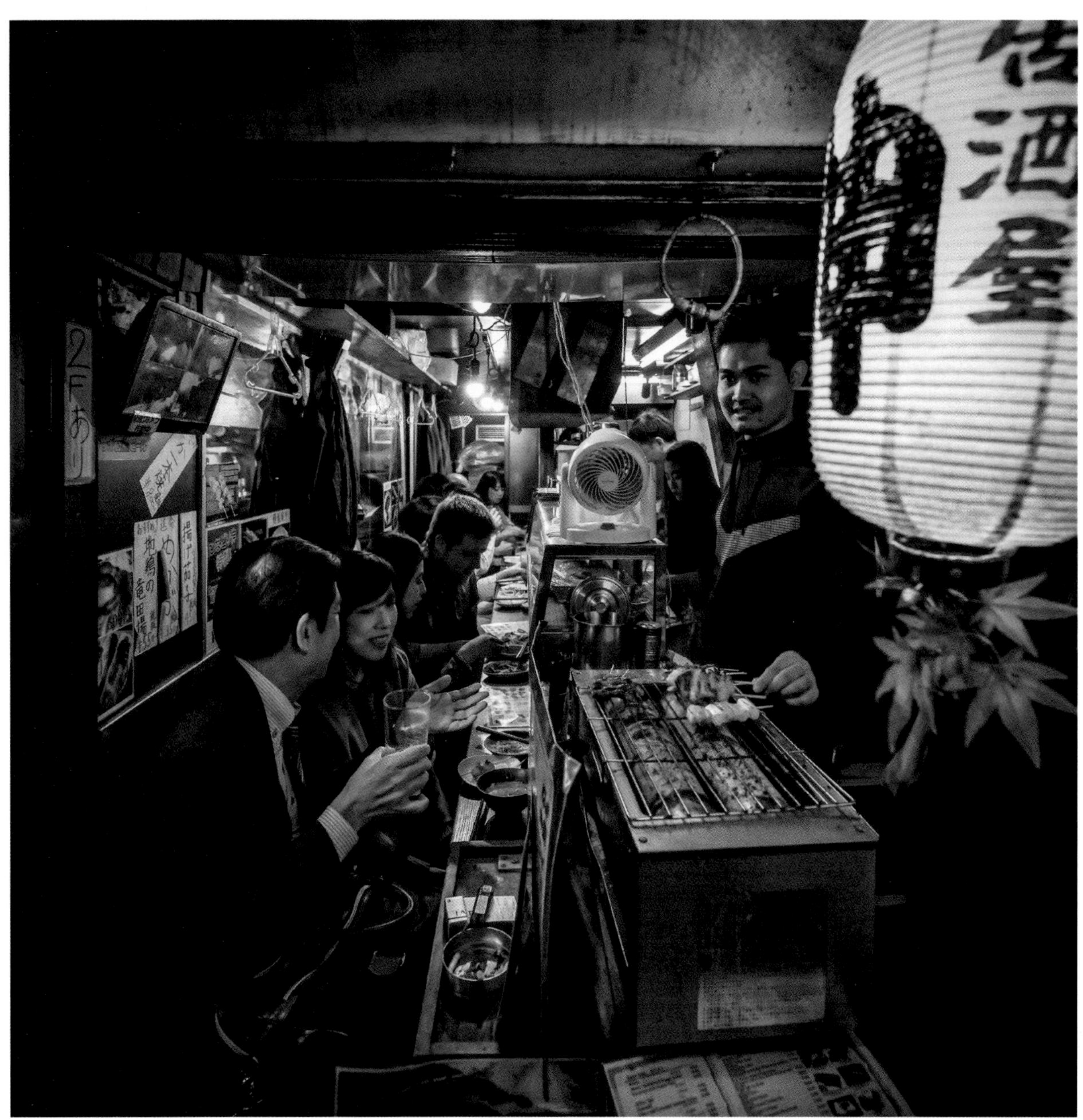

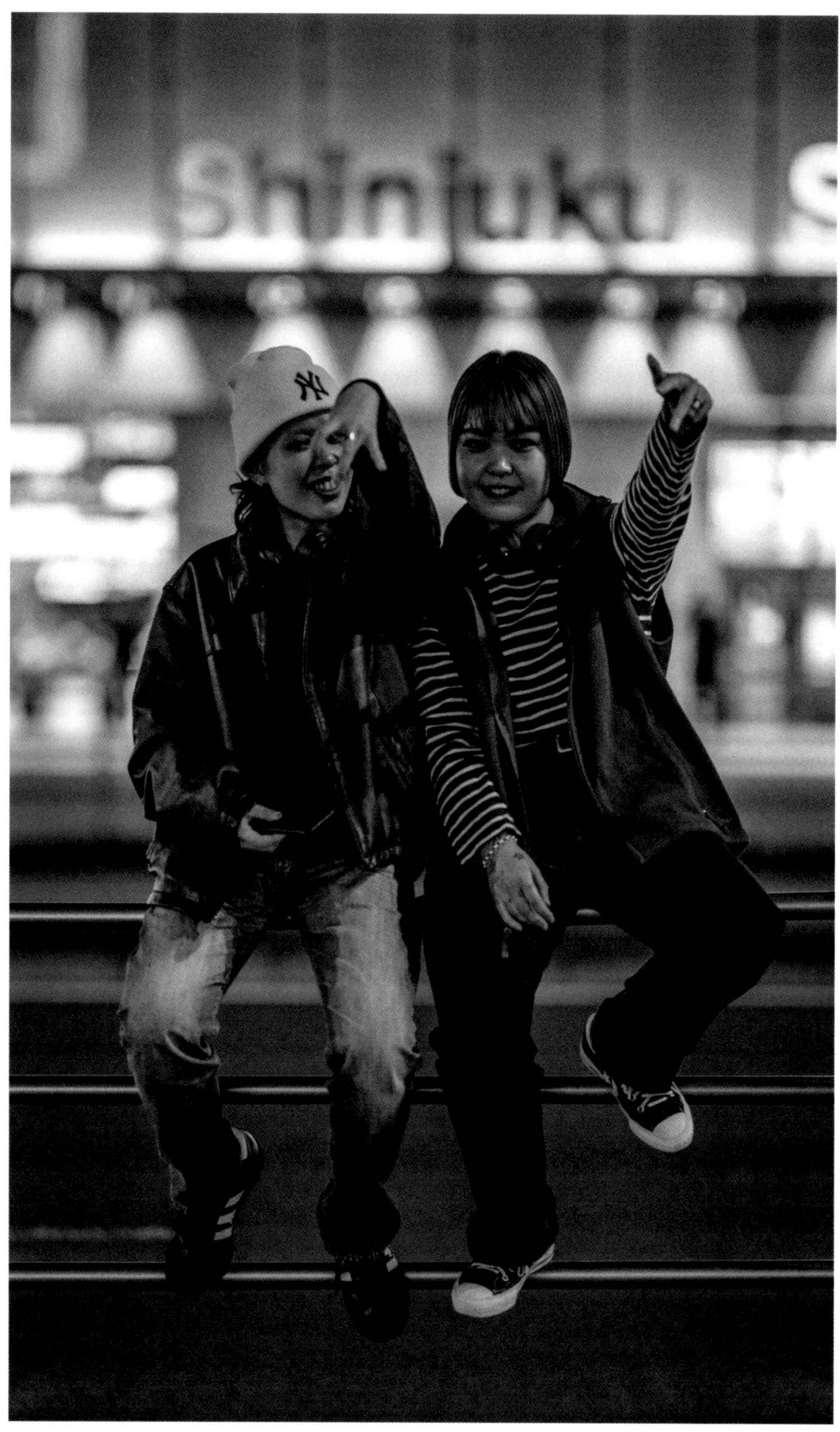
Shinjuku S
NY

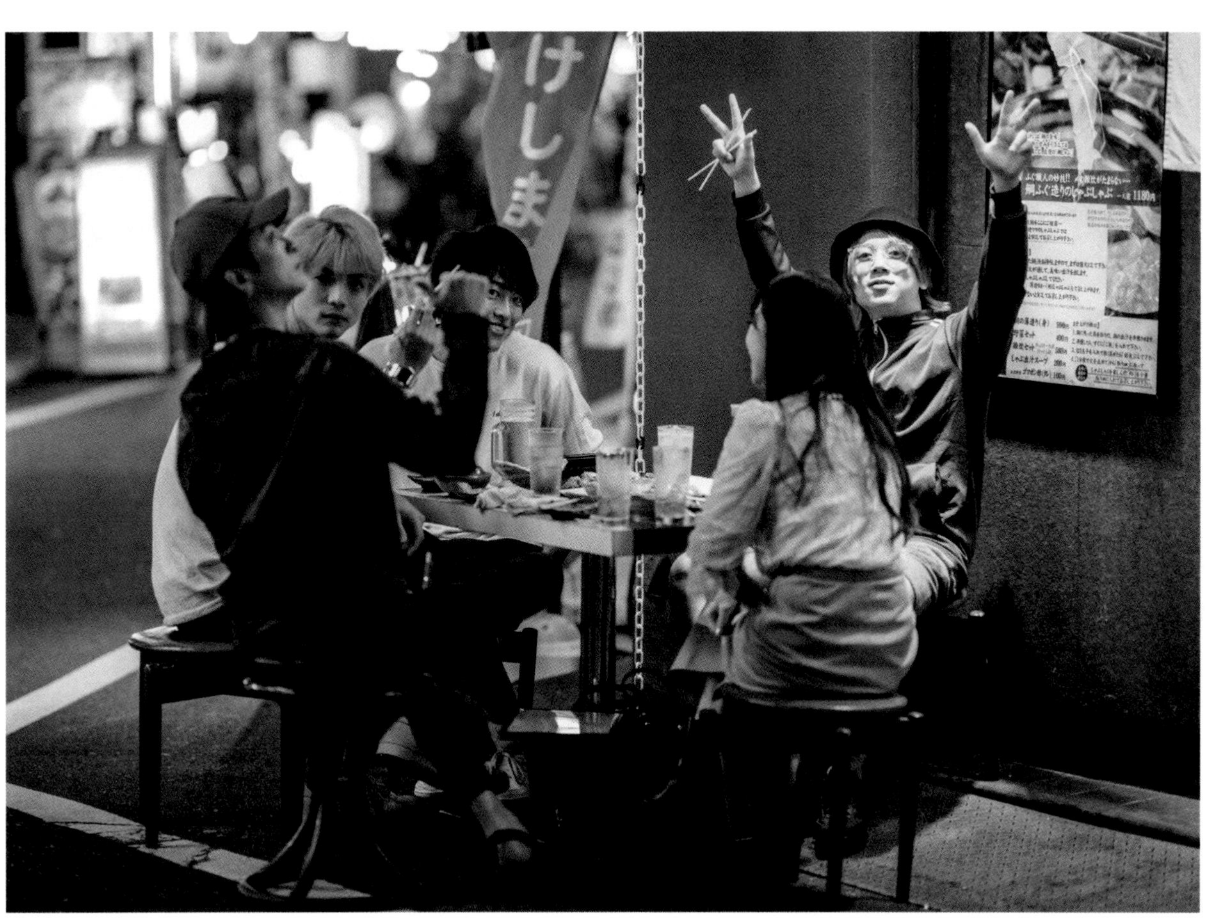

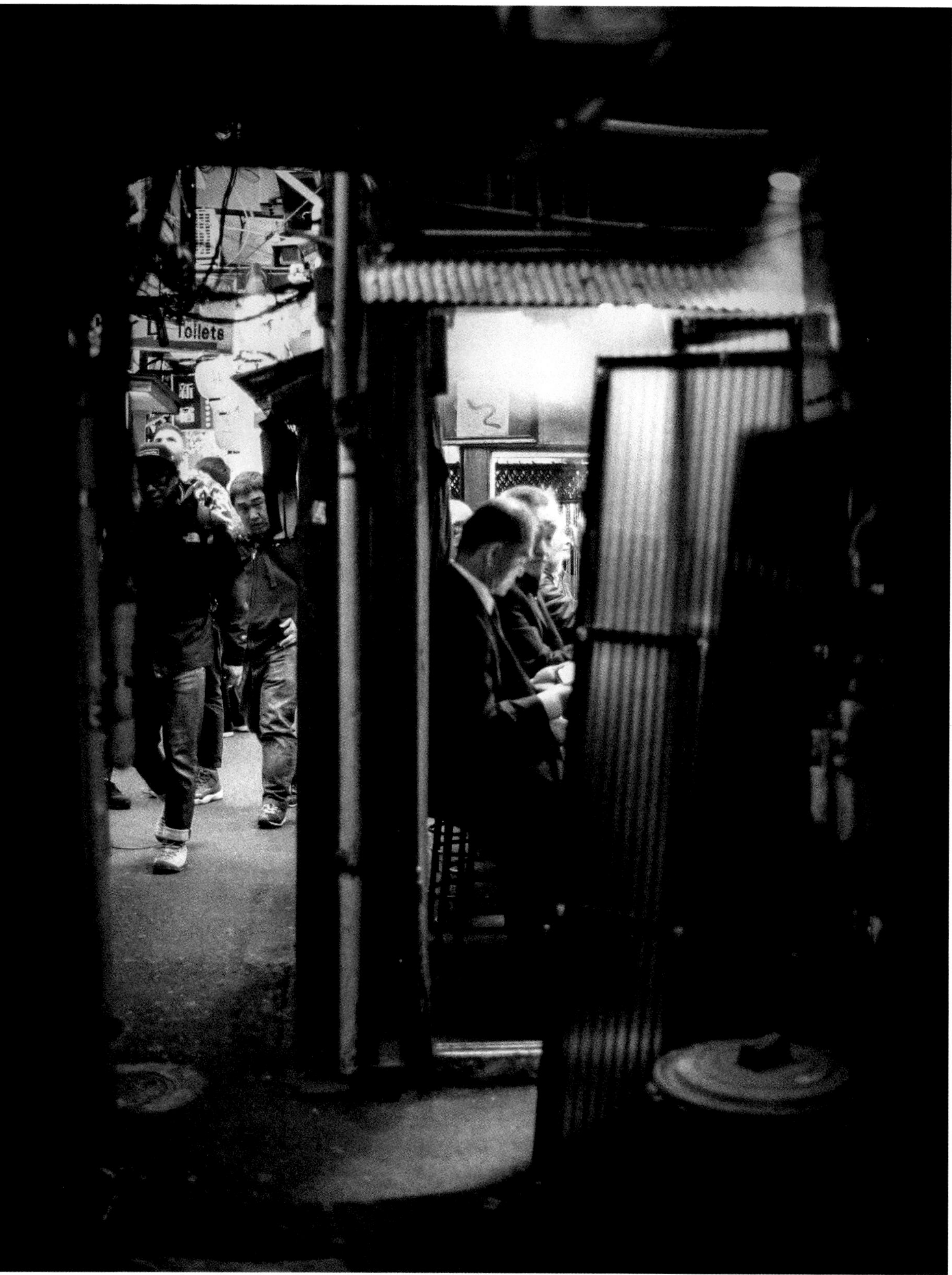
Toilets
新

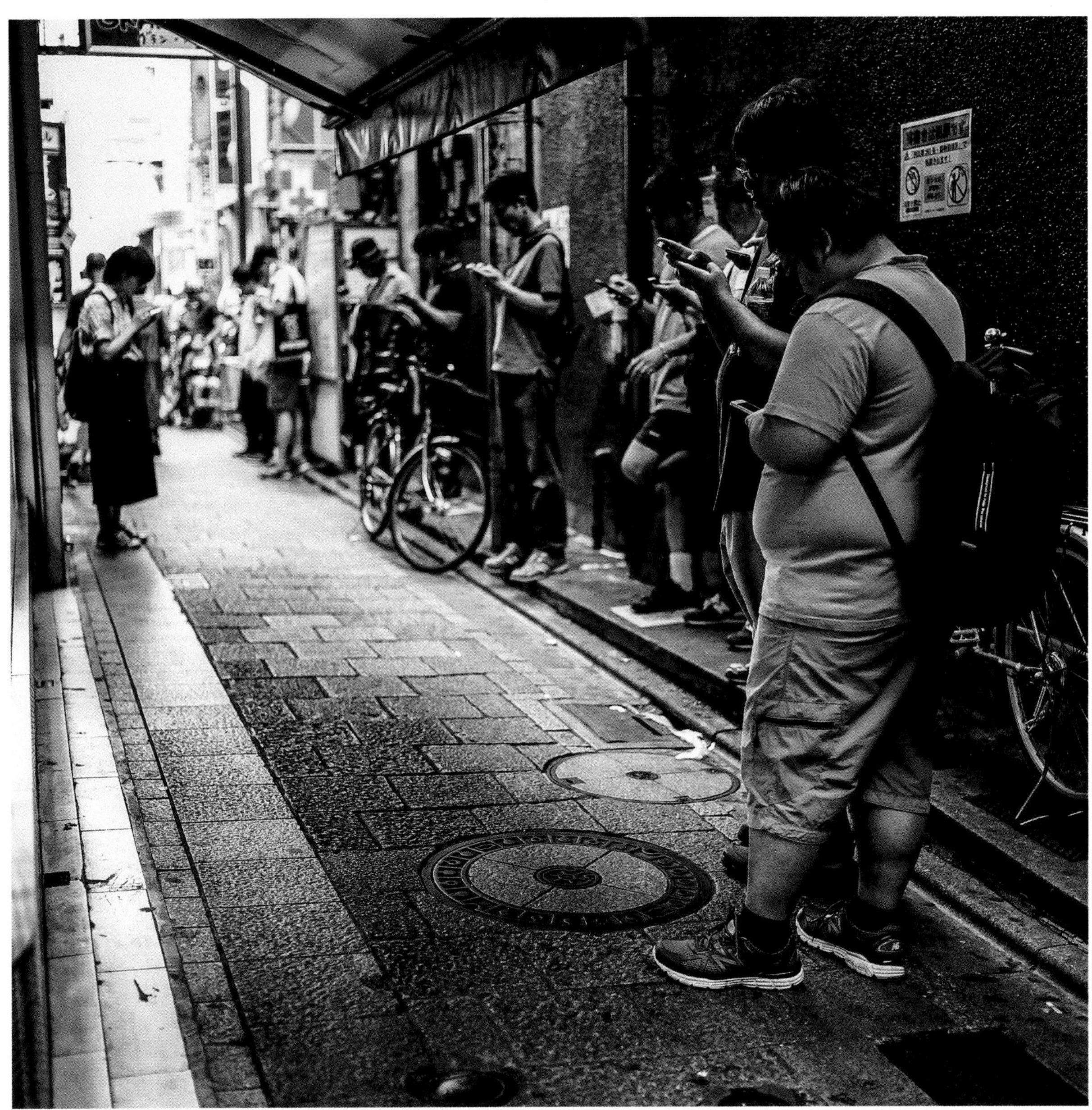

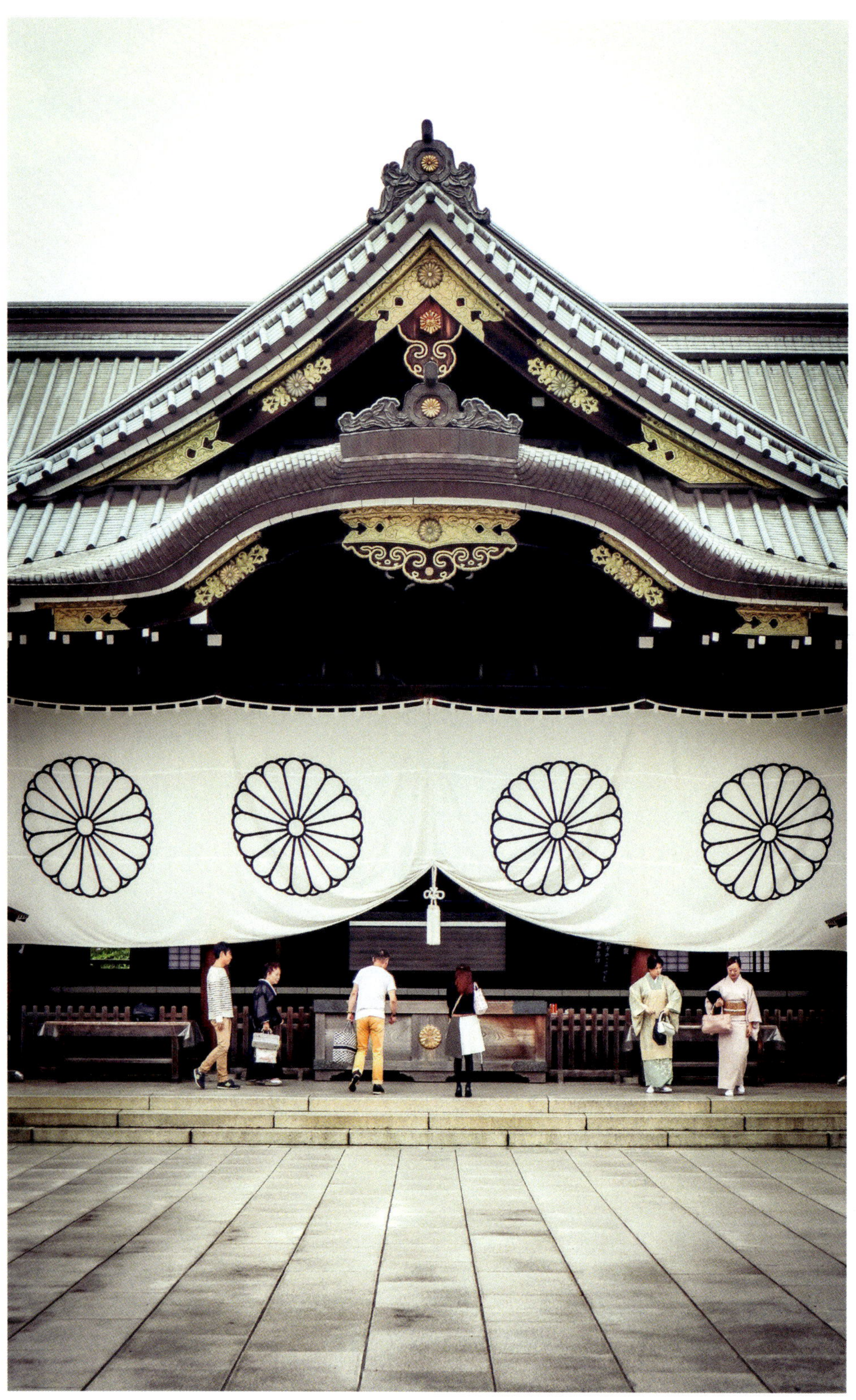

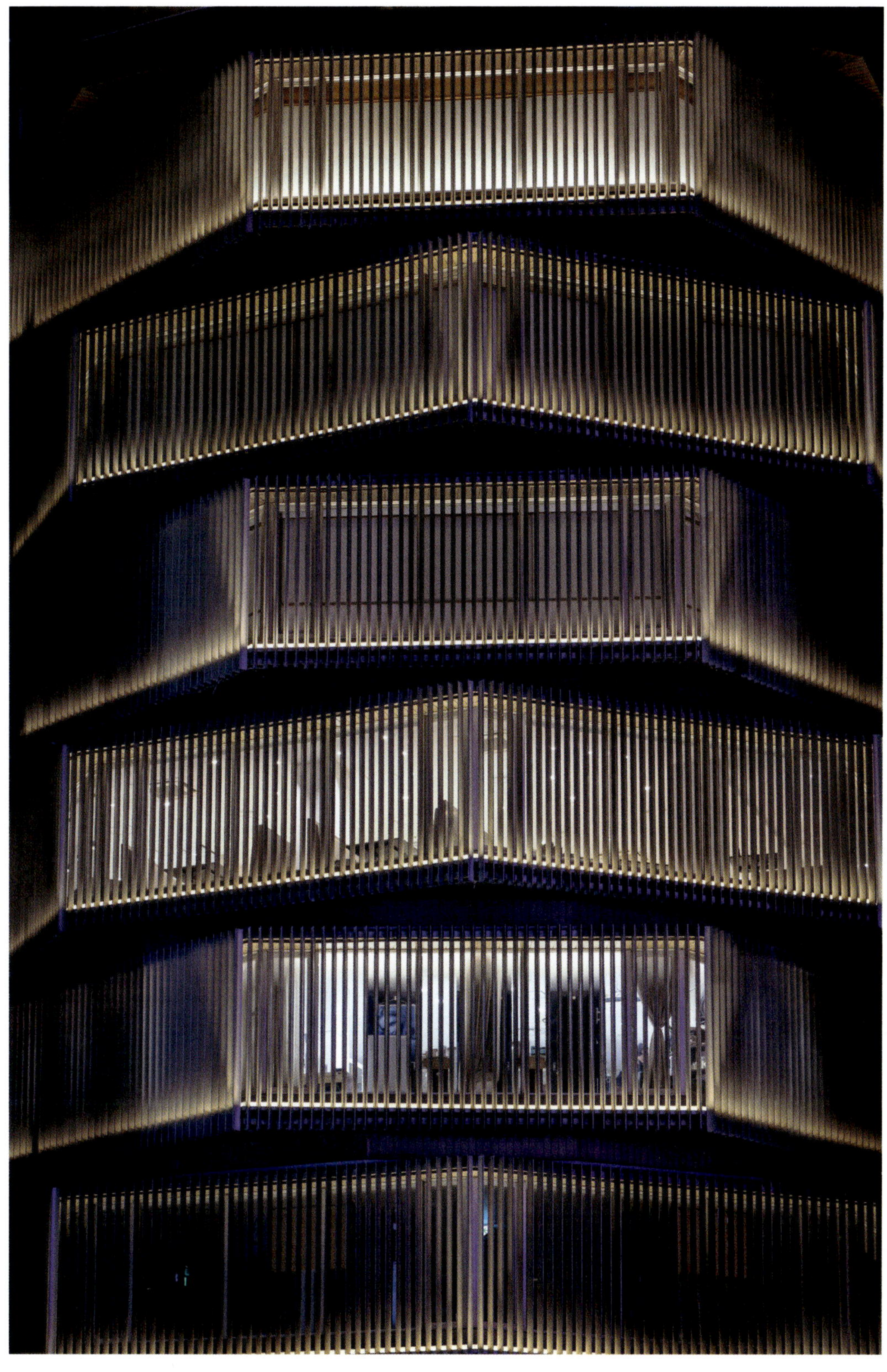

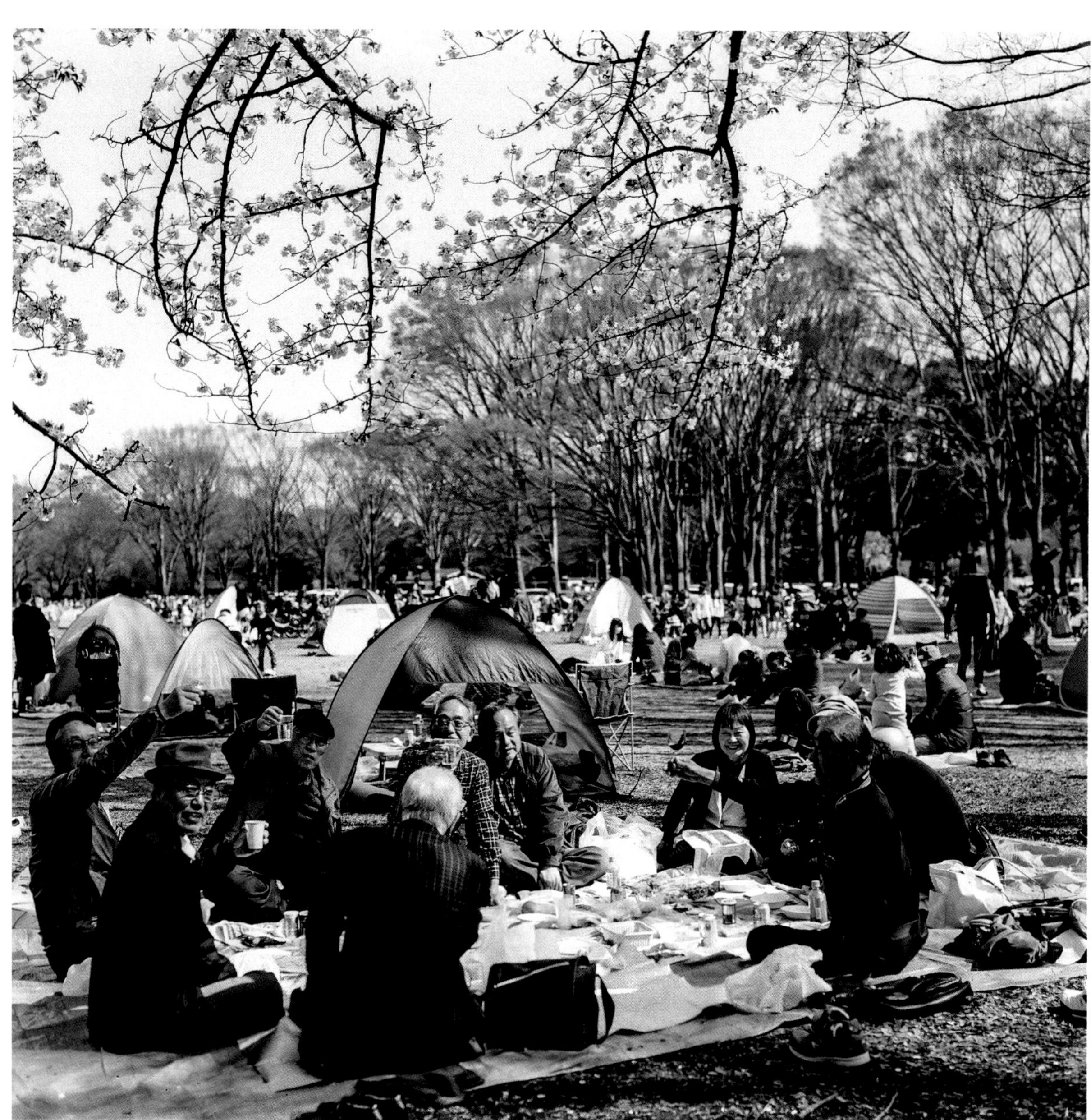

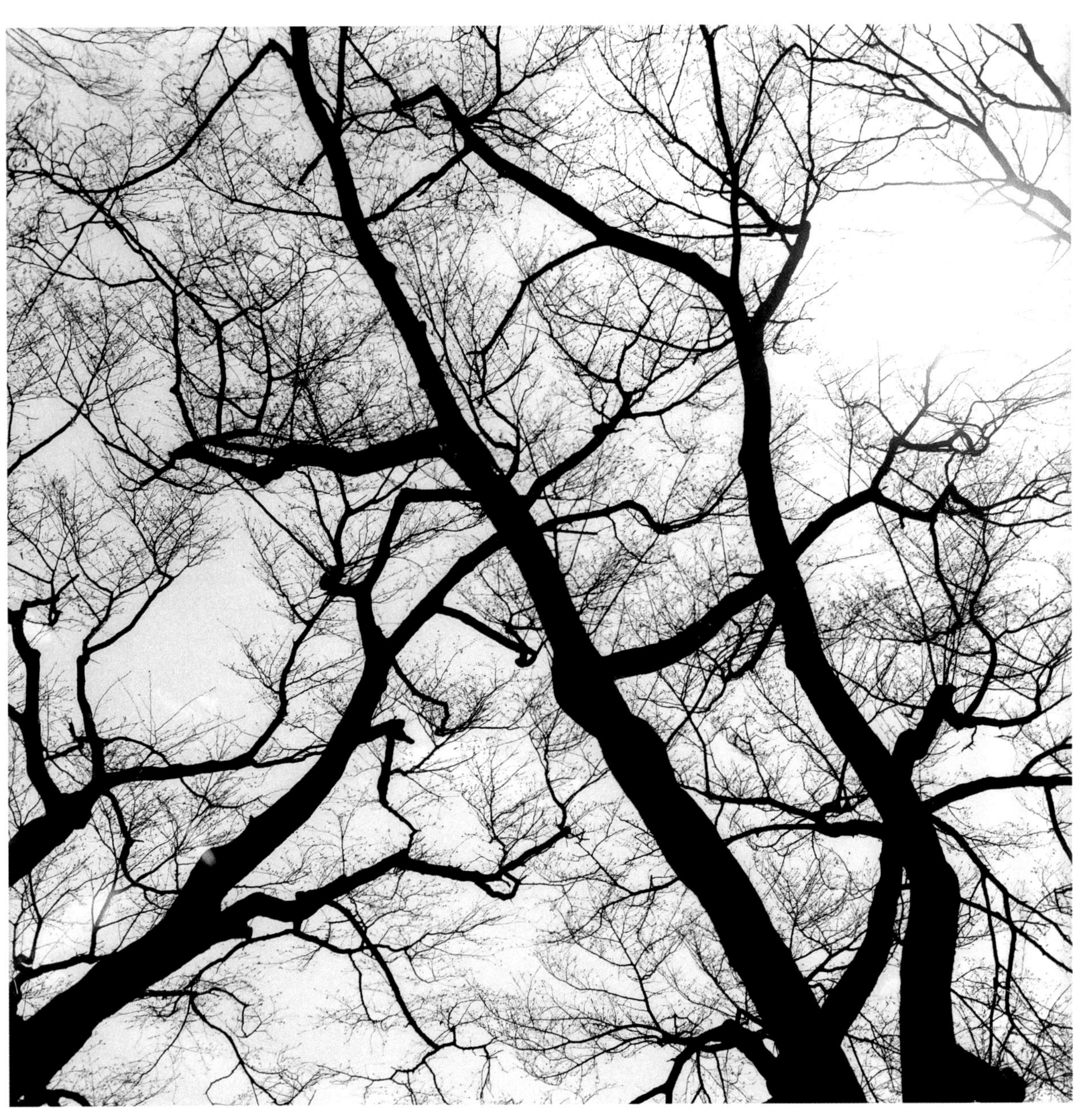

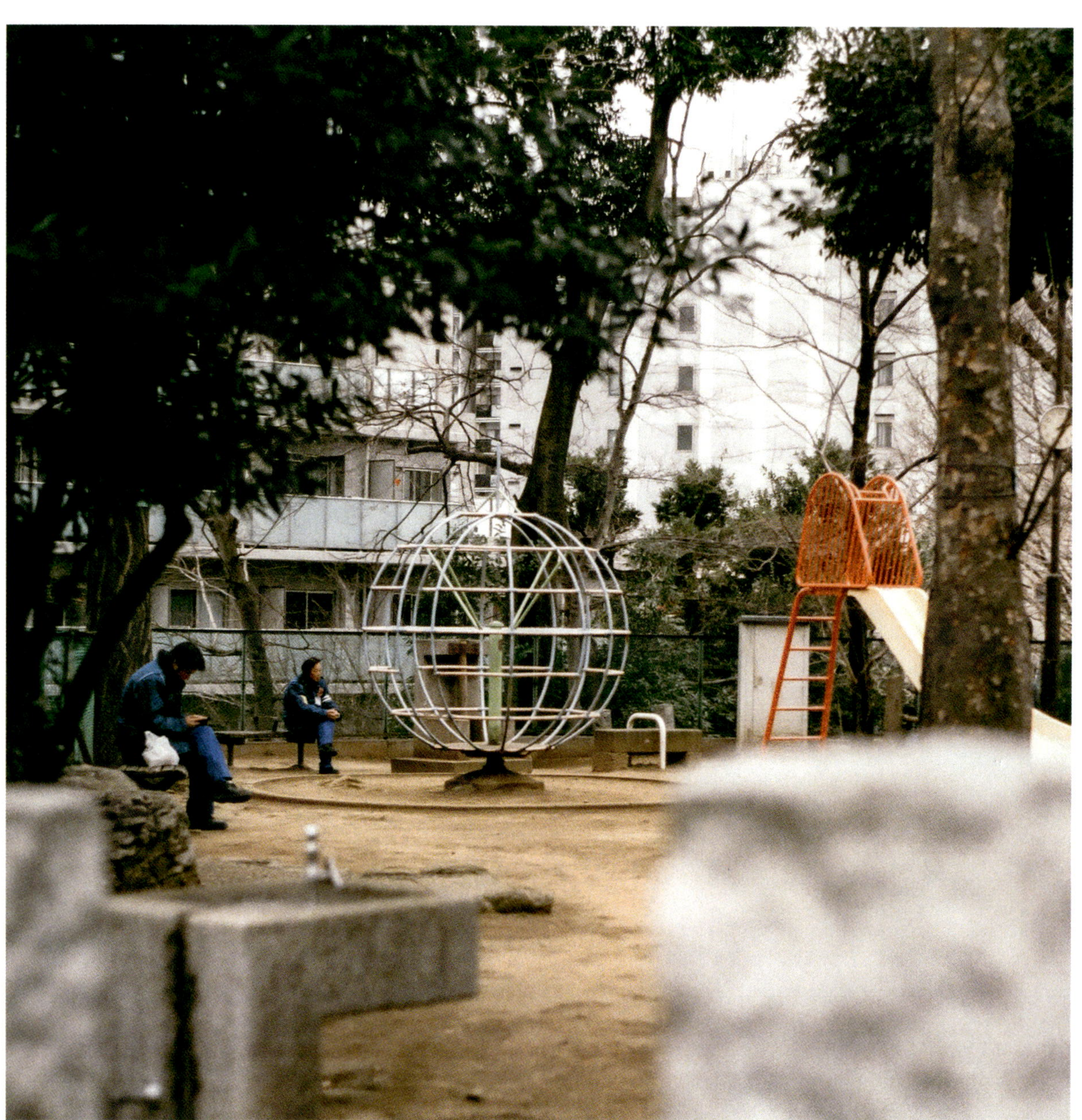

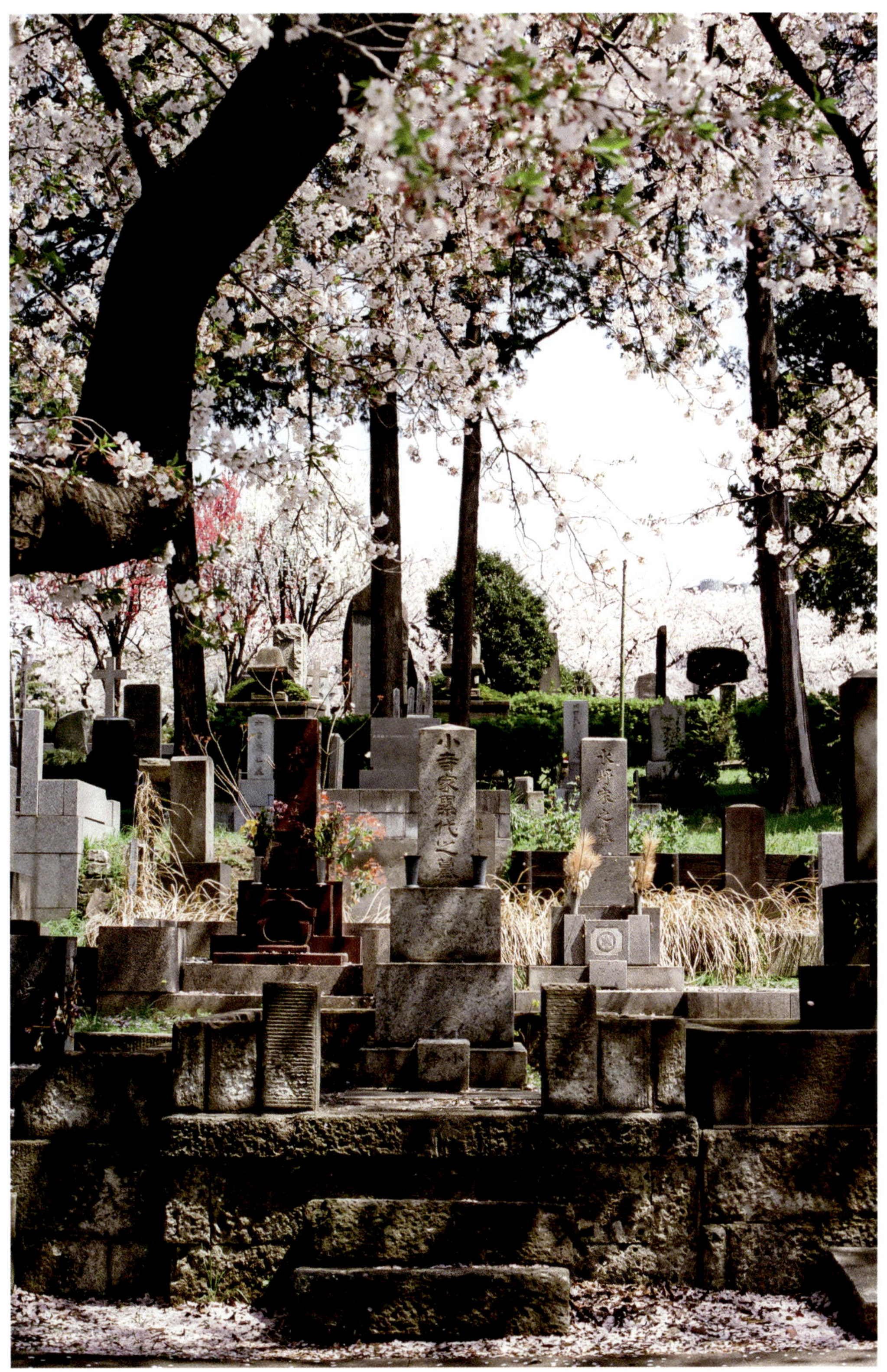

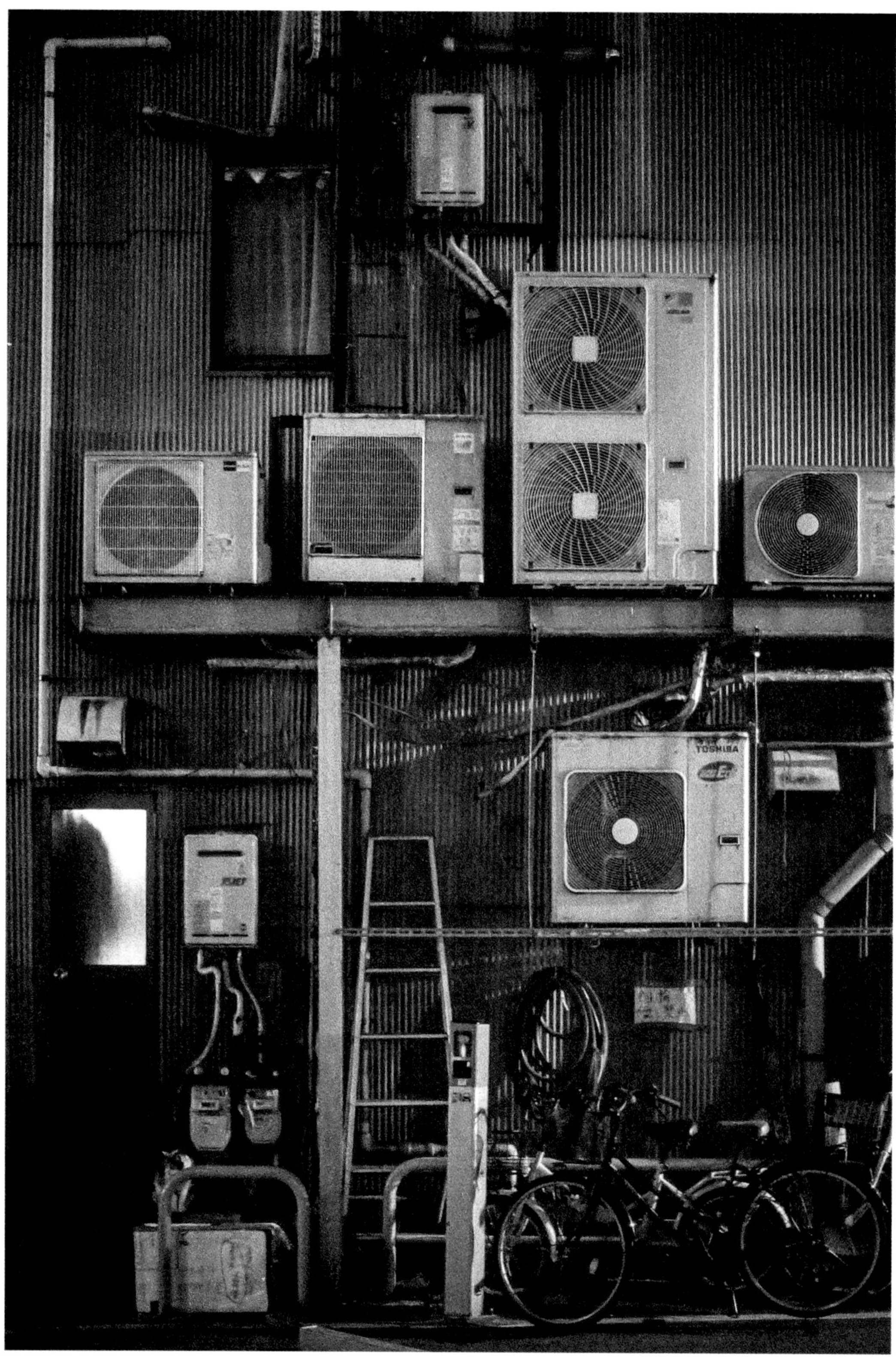

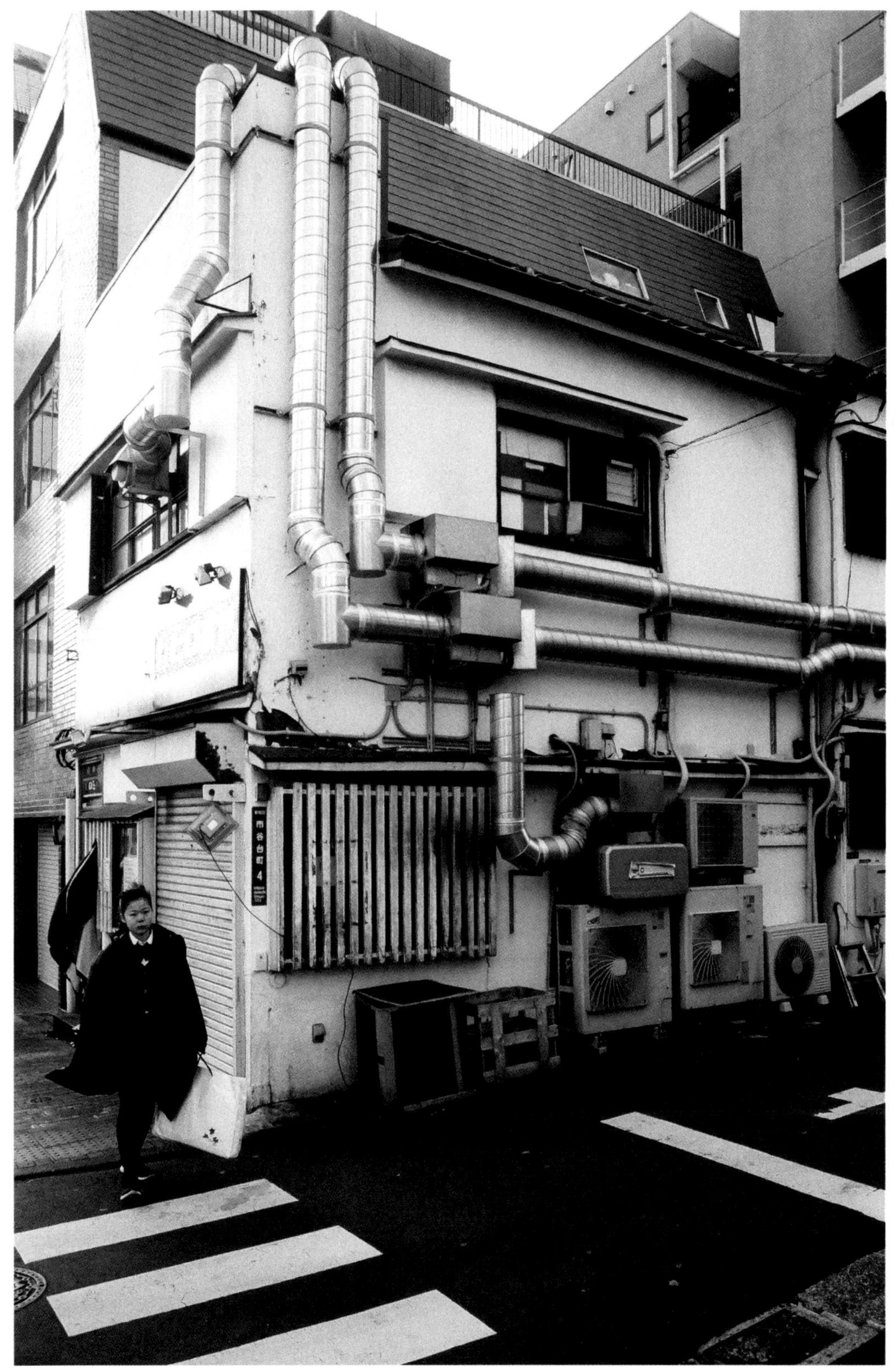

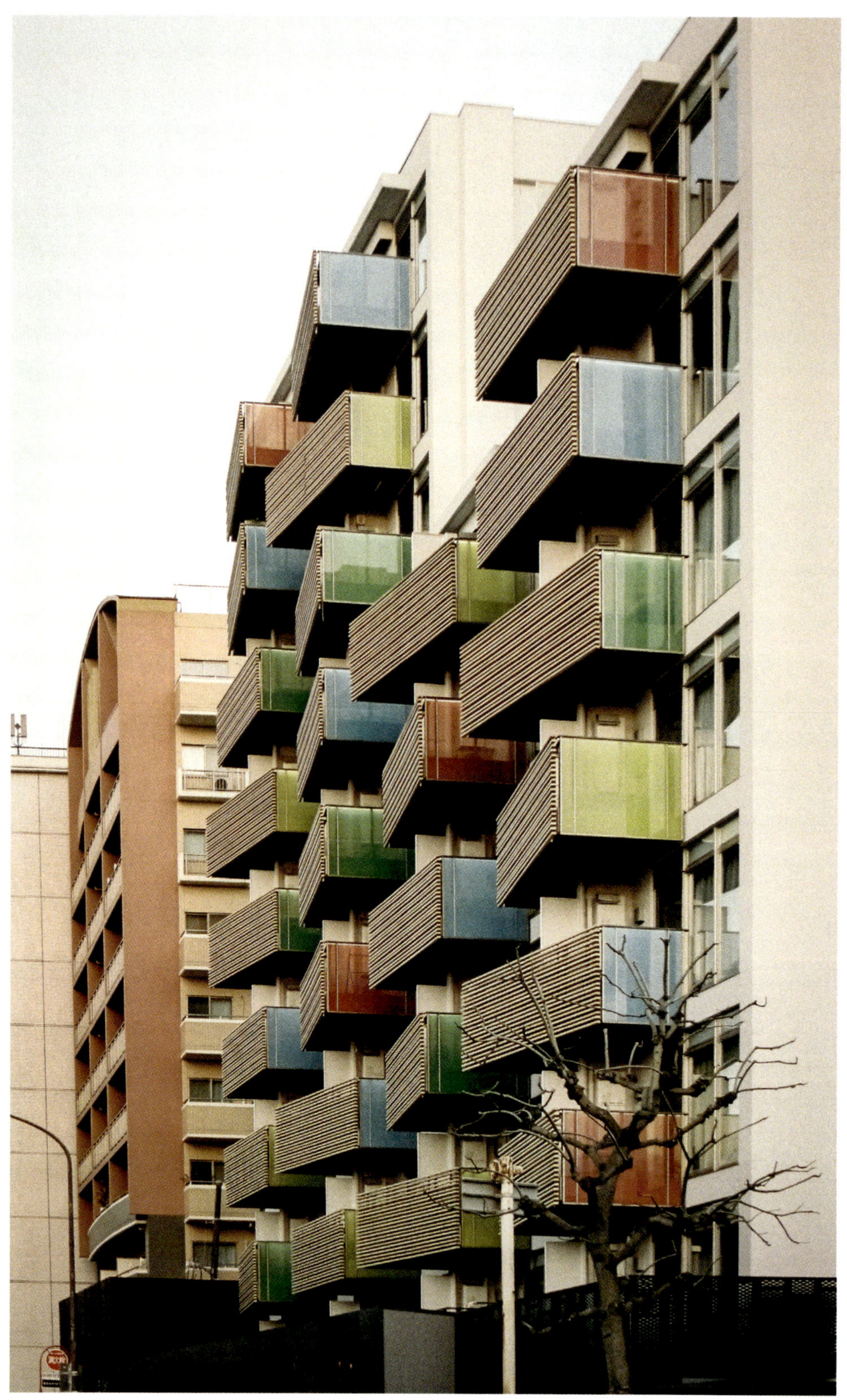

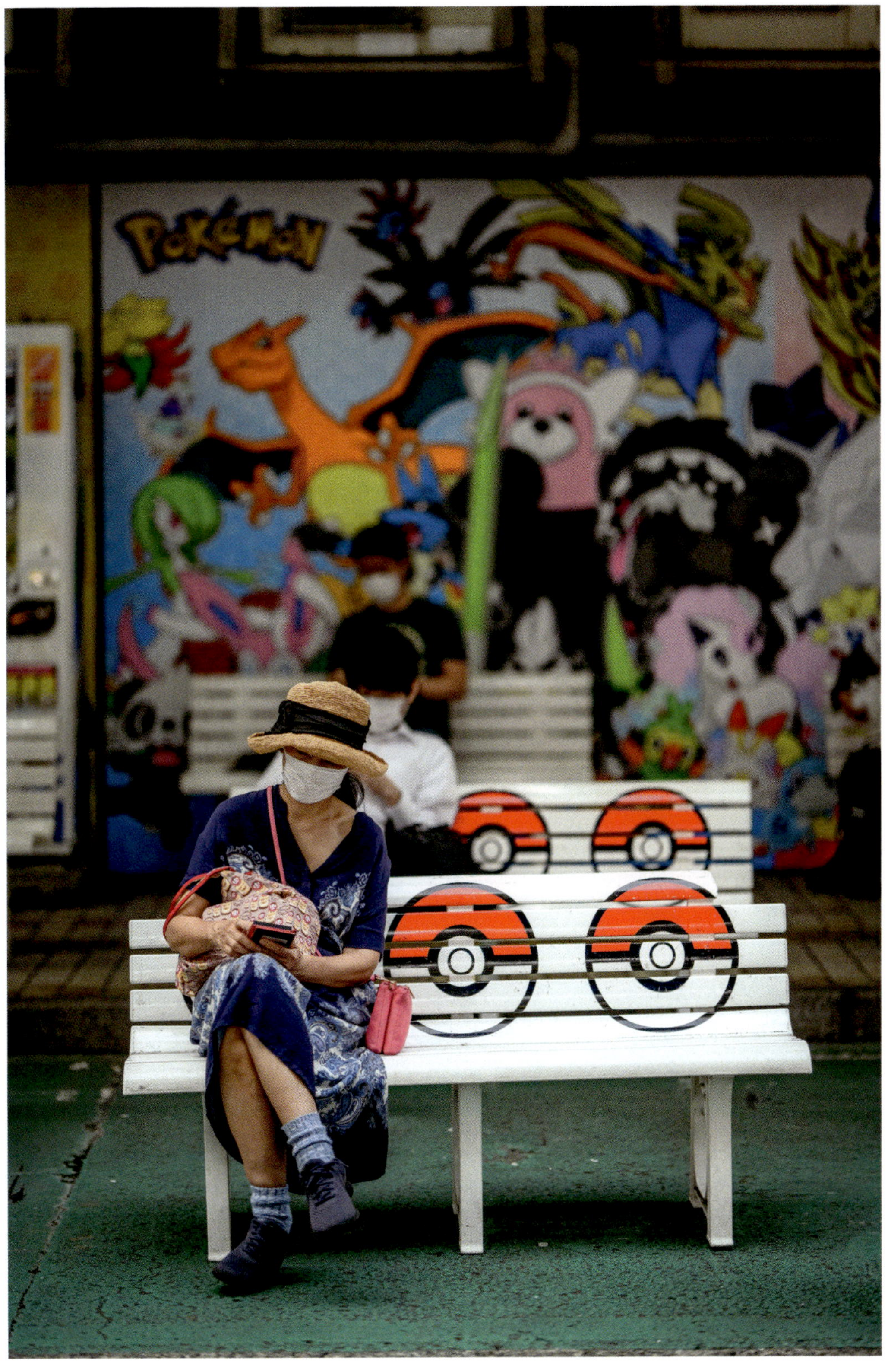

EPILOGUE

The door to my room opens, and Suzu chan enters. It's time for my evening medications, a ritual she has claimed as her own since turning three. My personal nurse now, she methodically opens the plastic box where I keep my pills, passing them to me one by one along with a glass of water. Sumire worries about this routine – afraid our young daughter might try to swallow these powerful medications herself. But I watch her every move, and we perform this ceremony in silence under the flickering light of my table lamp. To Suzu chan, these are simply for my 'headache'. How do you explain more to a three-year-old? Even Ryo, now seven, doesn't fully understand my illness, though he often questions how I can always have a headache. There's a knowing look in his eyes that suggests he senses there's more to it.

Suzu chan's care extends beyond dispensing medication. She likes to smooth the worry lines that form on my forehead during difficult moments. Her tiny fingers performing a facial massage prove more therapeutic than any prescription. During my deepest depressive episodes, when I can't even pull up my own blankets, she does it for me. Her instinctive nurturing surprises both Sumire and me.

I'd love to report that things are better lately – that the combination of medication and my photographic wanderings has permanently altered my condition. I wish I could say my little nurse's tender care works miracles. But recently, I experienced another sudden meltdown. The ghosts have returned, their voices a devastating chorus urging me toward suicide. These unanimous screams are nearly impossible to ignore. Severe panic attacks have resumed their daily visitations. Uncontrolled, unscheduled crying returns again and again.

The trigger for this meltdown isn't easily defined, though my recent promotion to Office Partner likely contributed. It finally happened – despite my initial doubts and lingering belief that I don't deserve the position. The advancement brought an immediate surge in both workload and overseas travel. I now juggle eight projects simultaneously, three of them particularly demanding. Though my team is excellent, we're understaffed. The toll on my stress levels is predictable.

Initially, the promotion triggered an adrenaline rush. A hypomanic phase punctuated my days, during which I impulsively discarded a month's worth of medication, convinced I no longer needed it. I threw myself completely into work. This period was brief – a shooting star that quickly burned out, followed by a week of depression so profound it confined me to bed. I had to return to my psychiatrist, shamefaced, to replace the medication I'd thrown away. He seemed alarmed by my account but remained reassuring, adjusting my medication cocktail once again. He reintroduced tranquillisers and strong sleeping pills that he hadn't prescribed for some time. Sumire bristles at these particular medications – they transform me into a zombie, especially during mornings when the children need attention. Before any road trips, she insists I skip them so I'm alert behind the wheel.

It's remarkable how this emotional tide, this ebb and flow of symptoms, can erode even the strongest foundation – Sumire herself. I'm beginning to notice cracks in her resilience. It's not that she's stopped loving me or wanting to help; rather, there's an exhaustion setting in. Despite my efforts to improve, the illness inevitably resurfaces, forcing us back to square one, or nearly so. It's impossible not to surrender to despondency in such circumstances.

I understand her desperate need to decompress with friends during my brief periods of improvement. Social life has become a distant memory for me – when I'm marginally better, I'm either catching my breath or caring for the children while Sumire takes her turn to escape.

Our growing distance is exacerbated by sleeping in separate rooms since the children arrived. I deeply miss our bedtime conversations – those moments when we'd watch television series together, either discussing them afterwards or simply drifting off to sleep mid-episode. Now our communication has withered to the bare essentials: good morning, good night, and the minimum coordination of morning tasks. When I return late, I find myself exchanging more words with the children than with her. I'm terrified of becoming a stranger to Sumire.

It would be easy to lay all the blame at work's door, though obviously the reality is more complex. Yet I see few career alternatives in Japan. The number of international architectural firms where I could work without speaking Japanese is limited, and none would offer the working conditions and role I currently hold. Moving abroad might be an option, but for Sumire, that's unthinkable while the children are young. I feel trapped in a cage of my own making.

My business trips have become another source of tension. Sumire shoulders the full weight of childcare alone during these absences, and in return, she requires time for herself – outings with friends to decompress and lighten her stress load. It's difficult to make her understand that my late nights aren't spent socialising; these trips aren't holidays but work. Perhaps she does understand but needs her own release valves regardless. Once again, I empathise with her position, yet find myself unable to resolve this impasse.

I can't even remember my last proper photographic outing. Last summer, in an inexplicable impulse, I posted an advertisement online offering my services as a model photographer, showcasing some of my work. Perhaps it was curiosity about a different photographic path, or simply an attempt to earn extra income. The response was overwhelming – professional models mixed with aspiring ones. Initially, the novelty intrigued me. It was so different from my usual work that it carried a certain appeal. But the interest quickly faded. I made excuses – not entirely false ones – about illness preventing me from completing assignments. The experience ended there, followed by a complete void. The sheer volume of office work has eliminated evening outings entirely. On those rare occasions when I manage to return home early, I naturally dedicate the time to family. My photo-therapy has been reduced to nothing.

I promised myself to dedicate at least one evening each month to photography, but even this modest goal remains unfulfilled. There are too many exceptions, too many trips, too many demanding workdays. I've tried to combine business travel with photography, but the schedules are relentless – packed with events from dawn to dusk. Though I always carry a camera, I inevitably collapse into bed each night, knowing another early start awaits.

Depression, of course, shows no respect for timing. It strikes when least convenient – during crucial client presentations, for instance, when you must perform at your peak. The effort required to present work professionally while maintaining a facade of happiness is exhausting. It's even worse when travelling with the boss. In those moments, you're truly alone. There's no family to return to at the hotel, and the episodes of crying become more frequent.

I visited Italy recently, combining projects in Croatia and Slovenia with conferences in Serbia where I represented the office. I managed two days in Venice to see my closest relatives – parents, siblings, a few cousins and aunts. The brevity of the visit meant once again neglecting friends.

In Italy, I'm cocooned in care. My parents, aware of my condition and workload, ensure I don't need to lift a finger at home and can sleep as much as possible. This nurturing helps immensely, though it's only sustainable short-term. I leave feeling regenerated, better able to face the long journey home – which typically proves more stressful than the outbound flight. The timing explains this: European-bound flights are overnight, while returns to Japan depart early morning and arrive early morning, creating an endless day without sleep, despite the comfort of business class.

My family members constantly seek reassurance about my wellbeing. "You look and sound so well, don't you?" they say repeatedly. I'm phobic about appearing the perpetual victim of my ailments, so I give them what they want. I force myself to reassure them even when I'm fighting back tears. I blame my red eyes on airplane air and jet lag. They seem to accept this.

The ghosts returned on my flight home. Perhaps it was sleep deprivation, or the pain of leaving my parents – whatever the cause, as I approached my seat, I saw an elderly gentleman occupying it. Later, I realised he was purely imaginary. I had to force myself to sit 'through' this apparition. Once seated, he materialised on the screen before me, hurling insults, making me feel worthless. Without my anti-hallucination medication or the comfort of my camera, panic overwhelmed me and I dissolved into tears. Calming down took ages. The flight attendant noticed my distress but couldn't fathom its source. I mumbled something about a headache, though she remained unconvinced. I couldn't

touch food or drink for the entire flight. I arrived exhausted, facing a full day ahead – morning arrivals are brutal. Sumire had long-standing plans with friends, so I knew I'd need to collect the children and care for them until late. In my state, it felt impossible, yet I steeled myself. Despite everything, the thought of seeing the children after three weeks in Europe lifted my spirits.

Sumire has finally relented about hiring a babysitter. Initially, she rejected the idea of strangers caring for our children, but the mounting stress has changed her perspective. Though this help hasn't started yet, simply knowing it's planned offers relief.

After unloading my bags and taking a long, restorative shower, I went to collect the children from school. Ryo and Suzu's joy at seeing me triggered tears. Thinking I was unwell, they began crying too, creating a ten-minute cascade of shared emotion. I recovered enough to explain these were happy tears, and we shared a long, soothing embrace that comforted us all. We prepared dinner together – meat and red wine risotto, Ryo's favourite – then went to bed early. We played beneath the blankets, and I read them stories until they drifted off. Once they were asleep, my tears returned. I washed my face but couldn't stop crying until exhaustion finally claimed me. Sumire returned home very late – too late for even a simple 'Tadaima' (I'm home) and *Okaeri* (welcome back) exchange.

We saw each other the next morning, and everything resumed its normal rhythm, as though I'd never left. Sumire asked about my condition, and I admitted it wasn't good. She blamed my work schedule and pleaded with me to return home early each day – a promise I couldn't make.

Now we're preparing for a family trip to Italy. Our expectations couldn't be more different: Ryo and Suzu anticipate Christmas presents and lunch with their little cousins, Sumire looks forward to Christmas markets and shopping, whilst I simply yearn for sleep and rest. We shall see how it unfolds.

Despite everything, I count myself fortunate. Loneliness is a savage beast when you're bipolar or depressed. Though part of you craves solitude, complete isolation breeds paranoia. A family that loves you despite your illness seems rare. Rarer still is being understood and understanding your own illness. This happens for me in both Japan and Italy – making me doubly blessed.

I speak with my family in Italy almost daily via WhatsApp, catching them after their lunch as my evening winds down. My parents never discuss my illness with Sumire, and she prefers to avoid the subject with others. When we gather, conversation centres on positive things and the children.

I exist in limbo – perpetually balanced between the deepest abyss and a mountaintop with a spectacular view. This emotional rollercoaster remains part of my daily life. Sometimes I feel like an outside observer, like in *Being John Malkovich* – watching my own indescribable psychodrama unfold.

I can't look beyond tomorrow. Extended planning proves impossible; I must proceed by trial and error. A persistent undercurrent of dissatisfaction and negativity remains. My character often baffles others as I live on the brink, swinging between exaggerated euphoria and pessimism – an unstable, wavering balance.

My privileges – the closeness of family, their determination to understand me, the outlet of a solitary hobby,

and a skilled psychiatrist – have been crucial in containing this illness. Containment is the right word – like a sturdy barrel preventing its contents from exploding. All things considered, I couldn't have hoped for better circumstances.

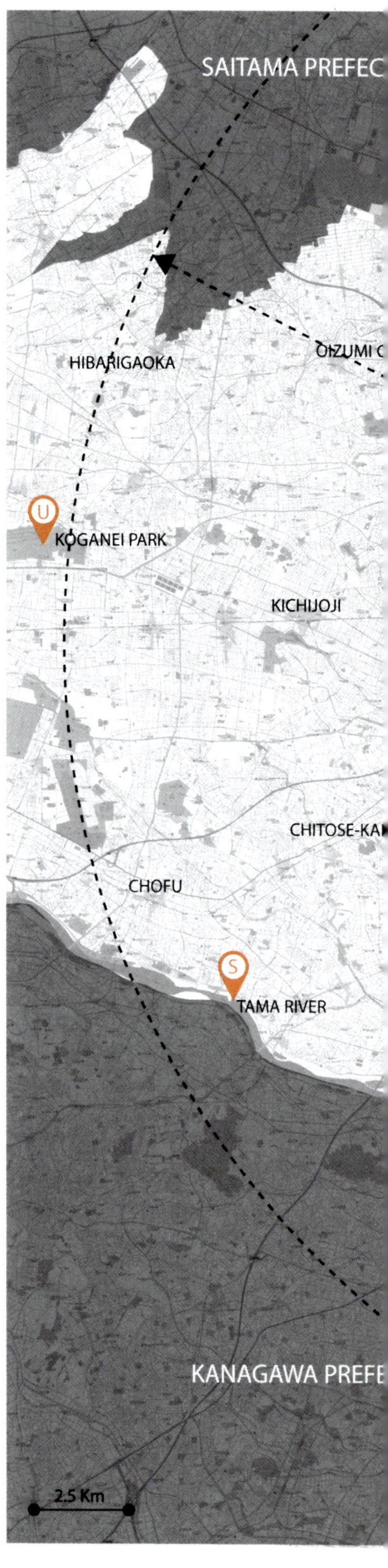

SAITAMA PREFEC
OIZUMI
HIBARIGAOKA
U
KOGANEI PARK
KICHIJOJI
CHITOSE-KA
CHOFU
S
TAMA RIVER
KANAGAWA PREFE
2.5 Km

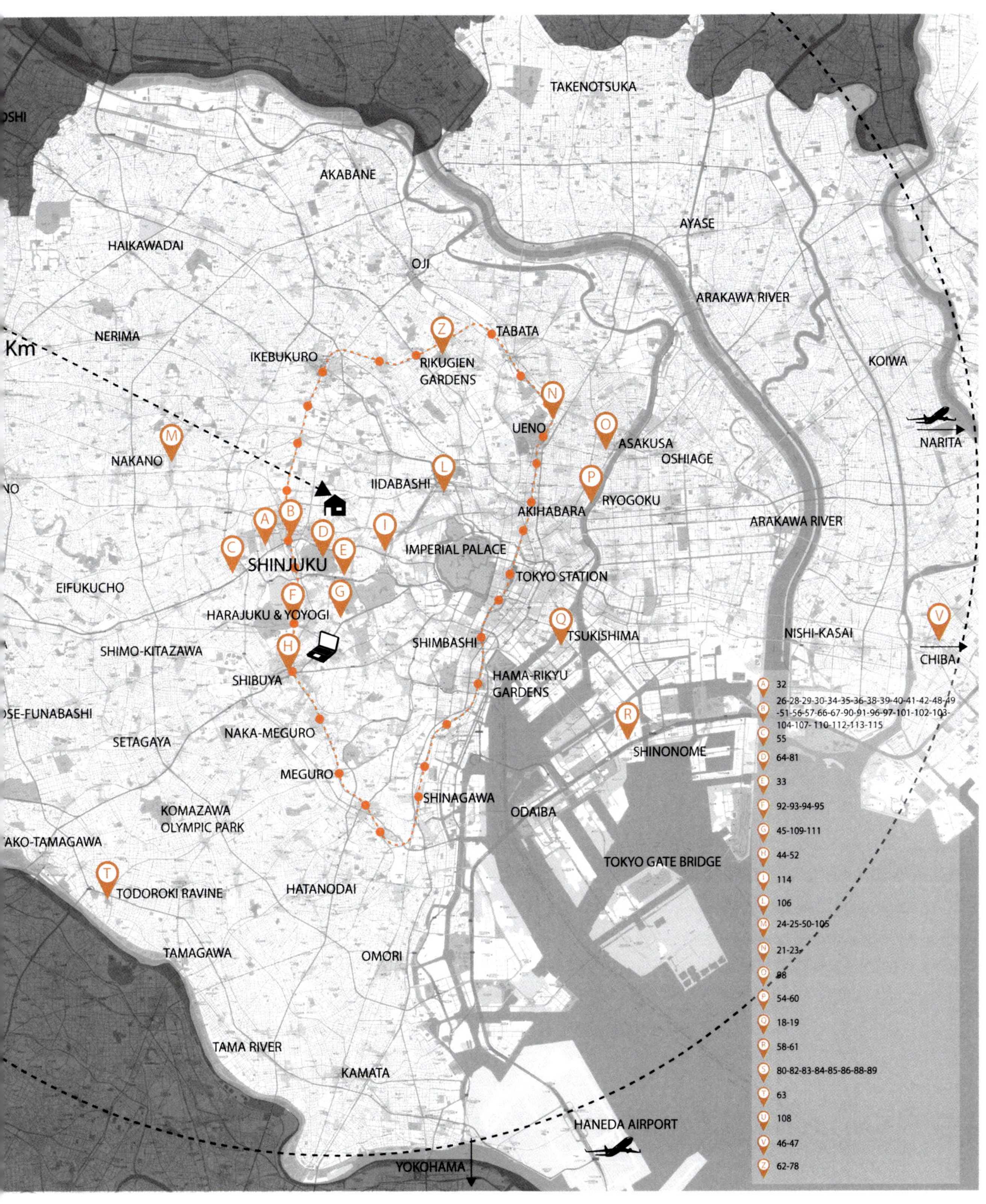
TAKENOTSUKA
OSHI
HAIKAWADAI
AKABANE
OJI
AYASE
ARAKAWA RIVER
NERIMA
Km
IKEBUKURO
TABATA
KOIWA
Z
RIKUGIEN GARDENS
N
NARITA
M
UENO
O
NAKANO
ASAKUSA
OSHIAGE
L
IIDABASHI
P
A B
RYOGOKU
D
AKIHABARA
ARAKAWA RIVER
C
E
I
SHINJUKU
IMPERIAL PALACE
EIFUKUCHO
F
G
TOKYO STATION
HARAJUKU & YOYOGI
V
H
NISHI-KASAI
SHIMO-KITAZAWA
SHIMBASHI
Q
CHIBA
TSUKISHIMA
SHIBUYA
SE-FUNABASHI
HAMA-RIKYU GARDENS
SETAGAYA
NAKA-MEGURO
R
KOMAZAWA OLYMPIC PARK
SHINONOME
AKO-TAMAGAWA
MEGURO
SHINAGAWA
ODAIBA
T
TODOROKI RAVINE
HATANODAI
TOKYO GATE BRIDGE
TAMAGAWA
OMORI
TAMA RIVER
KAMATA
HANEDA AIRPORT
YOKOHAMA
A   32
B   26-28-29-30-34-35-36-38-39-40-41-42-48-49
    -51-56-57-66-67-90-91-96-97-101-102-103-
    104-107- 110-112-113-115
C   55
D   64-81
E   33
F   92-93-94-95
G   45-109-111
H   44-52
I   114
L   106
M   24-25-50-105
N   21-23
O   98
P   54-60
Q   18-19
R   58-61
S   80-82-83-84-85-86-88-89
T   63
U   108
V   46-47
Z   62-78